ALSO BY BEVERLEY McLACHLIN

Full Disclosure

TRUTH
Be
TOLD

MY JOURNEY THROUGH LIFE
AND THE LAW

BEVERLEY
McLACHLIN

Published by Simon & Schuster

NEW YORK   LONDON   TORONTO   SYDNEY   NEW DELHI

SIMON &
SCHUSTER
CANADA

Simon & Schuster Canada
A Division of Simon & Schuster, Inc.
166 King Street East, Suite 300
Toronto, Ontario M5A 1J3

This Simon & Schuster Canada edition September 2019

SIMON & SCHUSTER CANADA and colophon are trademarks
of Simon & Schuster, Inc.

For information about special discounts for bulk purchases,
please contact Simon & Schuster Special Sales at 1-800-268-3216
or CustomerService@simonandschuster.ca.

Manufactured in the United States of America

10   9   8   7   6   5   4   3   2   1

Library and Archives Canada Cataloguing in Publication

Title: Truth be told : my journey through life and the law / by Beverley McLachlin.
Names: McLachlin, Beverley, 1943- author.
Identifiers: Canadiana (print) 20190107448 | Canadiana (ebook) 20190107464 |
    ISBN 9781982104962 (hardcover) | ISBN 9781982104986 (ebook)
Subjects: LCSH: McLachlin, Beverley, 1943- | LCSH: Canada. Supreme Court. |
    LCSH: Judges—Canada—Biography. | LCGFT: Autobiographies.
Classification: LCC KE8248.M36 A3 2019 | LCC KF345.Z9 M36 2019 kfmod |
    DDC 347.71/03534—dc23

ISBN 978-1-9821-0496-2
ISBN 978-1-9821-0498-6 (ebook)

For all those who brought me up and sustained me

CONTENTS

....

PART THREE THE JUDGE

PART FOUR THE CHIEF JUSTICE

Prologue

....

IN APRIL 1989, I was sworn in as a justice of the Supreme Court of Canada. Pundits hailed the appointment of a third woman to the court of nine as a remarkable advance for women's rights. I was less convinced. Male justices still outnumbered women by two to one. Most of the speakers at the swearing-in ceremony were men, and when I scanned the courtroom, I saw more male faces than female.

As I swore my oath of office in the august chamber of the court, I spared a thought for Emily Murphy, Henrietta Muir Edwards, Nellie McClung, Louise McKinney, and Irene Parlby—the so-called Famous Five. I had long admired and striven to live up to their legacy, and I knew that without them, this moment would not have happened. *Would they have been pleased to see a third woman named to the Supreme Court of Canada?* I wondered. *Yes*, I thought. *But they would also have been surprised that it took so long*. Seventy years had passed since they began fighting for women to be allowed to hold public office. Seventy years.

Many years after this momentous day, United States Supreme Court Justice Ruth Bader Ginsburg visited our court for the first time. As we sat talking after her tour, Justice Ginsburg fixed me with her dark eyes and, in her customary slow, deliberate manner, asked, "What is the history of women's legal rights in Canada?"

I considered a moment before answering. "It started with the Famous Five and the Persons Case."

It was 1919 in Edmonton, Alberta, a young community growing into a city. Edmonton was still frontier territory, filling up with people heading west from cities like Montreal and Toronto. Young men seeking wealth and adventure. Young women seeking husbands and sometimes more—an escape from the constraints of the settled East.

One of these women was Emily Murphy. The wife of an Anglican minister, mother to four children, and published author, Emily was determined to do whatever she could to help build her new community, and Edmonton urgently needed the rule of law. Emily had no legal experience, but she understood people and what went on in their lives, and she couldn't abide the practice of excluding women from courtrooms when the evidence was, in a (male) judge's view, "not fit for mixed company." She protested and lobbied—arguing that the government had an obligation to create a special court run by women for women—and finally, she secured an appointment as a city magistrate.

As she headed to court on her first day, I imagine Emily Murphy was buoyed by the fact that women like her were starting to make their way in the world, just as men did. Earlier that year, Alberta women, after decades of painful struggle, had finally won the right to vote. Headlines proclaimed that women were equal, with full political rights. But if Emily dreamed of a new age of equality, her hopes were soon to be dashed. As the story goes, she entered her little courtroom and the clerk called the case, but no one rose. After a few moments, the lawyer behind the defence table got to his feet. "I apprehend that my friend may have a preliminary motion to put before the court," he said, then sank back into his leather chair.

Emily looked inquiringly at counsel for the applicant.

"I find myself in a position of some difficulty," the man said. "It seems I am expected to address the court, but I find no court to address."

Emily shook her head. She had been duly sworn in the day before, to much hoopla. "Would you be so kind as to explain?"

"The matter is one of some delicacy, madam. But let me come to the point: only 'persons' are permitted to occupy positions of public office. Magistrate is a position of public office. A woman is not a 'person' under the law of Canada. You are a woman. Therefore, there is no magistrate in this room, no judge. I cannot proceed." He inclined his head. "If I may be so bold, madam, I suggest you retire so this court may be lawfully constituted before a proper judge."

We do not know the precise words spoken or actions taken on that day a century ago. Perhaps Emily was shocked to be told she had no right to sit as a judge—certainly she must have felt angry. What we do know is that she rejected the motion and went on to hear the case before her.

In the years that followed, other female magistrates in Alberta were challenged simply because they were women, and eventually the issue made its way to the Supreme Court of Alberta, which ruled that despite their gender, women were "persons" and hence capable of sitting as judges.

But the issue festered and rankled. Women could be judges in Alberta, but what about the rest of the country? And what about other public positions? Did women have the right to be members of Parliament or senators? The question would soon be answered. In 1922, Murphy herself was up for an appointment to the Senate.

Predictably, the government of Prime Minister Mackenzie King rejected her nomination on the grounds that Murphy was not a "person" capable of holding public office. Between 1917 and 1927, five different governments proposed women for Senate seats. The answer was always the same.

So once again, Emily Murphy took action. She invited Edwards, McClung, McKinney, and Parlby to her home. She proposed that the five of them draft a petition to the governor general, seeking a reference to the Supreme Court of Canada concerning the interpretation of the word "persons" in Section 24 of Canada's constitution, the *British North America Act*. The Famous Five, as they are now known, raised money, hired lawyers, and mounted a case to contest the established view that women were not "persons" and could not hold public office. Prime Minister King's government agreed. The Supreme Court of Canada did not. It was obliged—or felt itself obliged—to apply the law of the British Empire, which was that women were not "qualified" to hold public office.[1]

The Famous Five refused to accept defeat. They raised more money and hired a new lawyer to take their case to the final court of appeal—the Judicial Committee of the Privy Council in far-off London, England. To the surprise of everyone and the consternation of many, the women succeeded.

While newspaper editorials predicted the demise of civilized society, Viscount Sankey, writing for the Judicial Committee, stated that society had changed. More and more, women were occupying positions of public responsibility, he noted, and the time had come to recognize that women were indeed "persons" capable of holding public office. The constitution, he added, had "planted in Canada a living tree capable of growth and expansion within its natural limits."[2]

As I shared the story of the Persons Case with Justice Ginsburg and the other judges around the luncheon table, I reflected on how the case had changed Canadian law forever—not just in the rights it accorded women, but also in establishing that Canadian law was not frozen in time, but rather was capable of measured and principled evolution to keep pace with social change. It has been said that Canada came of age as a nation with its contribution to the ultimate victory of England and the Allies in the First World War. It can equally be said that Canada came of age as a legal and jurisprudential force, whose law would be studied and emulated elsewhere, with the Persons Case of 1929.

Sixty years after the Persons Case was decided, as I was sworn in as the third woman ever to sit on the Supreme Court of Canada, the path set by those early trailblazers was at the front of my mind. It was a moment of pride, tempered only by the thought of how many women in decades past had been denied the immense privilege of sitting on the country's highest court.

What took us so long? I thought. And then, *What is still holding us back?*

Thirty years later, I still ponder these questions. What follows is the story of one "person"—of her journey towards a world in which women and men are truly equal, where people of any gender, race, or background can aspire to the same goals.

PART ONE

....

THE STUDENT

Everyone has the following fundamental freedoms: (a) freedom of conscience and religion; (b) freedom of thought, belief, opinion and expression, including freedom of the press and other media of communication; (c) freedom of peaceful assembly; and (d) freedom of association.

—*Canadian Charter of Rights and Freedoms*, Section 2

CHAPTER ONE

An Ordinary Girl

PEOPLE ALWAYS ASK ME, "When did you decide to become a lawyer? A judge? The first woman chief justice of the Supreme Court of Canada?"

"Never," I reply. And it's true.

From a very early age, all I knew was that I wanted to do something that wasn't ordinary. Because for a small girl growing up in a remote prairie town in the 1940s, the ordinary was very ordinary indeed.

I came into the world overdue, plump, and at the cost of great suffering to my mother, as she repeatedly reminded me. The precise locale was a tall, many-roomed red-brick mansion-turned-hospital with white bay windows that stood at the top of a hill looking down on the little village of Pincher Creek, Alberta, huddled in the valley below. The building had once belonged to a family of Quebec merchants who had come to establish a new venture in the tiny town. The Catholic Church had long since acquired it, and when I was born, it was a hospital run by a covey of nuns who swished about in their black skirts and white wimples, clutching rosaries.

An ordinary baby in an ordinary town on an ordinary day. The only portent of an eventful future was the high wind, which, I am informed, swept down from the Rockies with particular force that day. My father had to park the car facing the wind so its doors wouldn't be torn off their hinges.

After a colicky start—something about rejecting my mother's milk, the first of my many rejections—I was put on a new diet and flourished. My parents, Ernest and Eleanora Gietz, took me from the hospital to my grandparents' home on the outskirts of town. But a new baby pressed walls and tempers, and soon my parents moved to a dusty farmhouse in the valley west of town. There I encountered the first landscape of my life: tall grass that waved on the banks of the nearby stream. Pincher Creek.

I was a biddable child, content with the world, but given to unexpected frolics that sent my parents into panics. My first clear memory—I must have been two—is of being fitted into a new dress and sunbonnet, all covered in tiny pink flowers. Slipping out the door, I made my way down the path to the creek. I bent to touch the water—how black it was, how strangely it moved in swirls and patterns—then found myself walking up the hill to the big road that led to town. I was nearly at the top when I heard my mother's cries behind me. She scooped me into her arms. Flailing, I waved the fist that clutched the dime I had stolen from the kitchen table. "I'm going to town to buy an ice cream cone," I wailed as she hauled me back to the house.

My father, who was on occasion given to exaggeration, boasted about my accomplishments. His stories remain in family lore, but no one fully believes them—how I talked at eight months, was toilet-trained before a year, and said "Rumpelstiltskin" (my father even claimed I could spell it, which cannot have been true) at two. Of this, I remember nothing.

The snatches of my early existence that I do remember are more prosaic. Two brothers, Irvin Leonard and Conrad Wayne, came along in short order, rending the quiet of the valley with their wails and putting an abrupt end to the parental doting and prating that my parents had once lavished on me.

Len, as he came to be known, was a sensitive child who railed against the world into which he'd emerged by crying all night and refusing to eat. With a sister in her terrible twos and a soon-to-arrive brother, he had to make do with shows of affection from my mother's younger sister, Doreen, and Grandma Gietz, who, as he grew older, would slip him dimes from her little leather purse. I recall feeling jealous that Grandma held Len on her knee longer than me—not that I really wanted to be on her knee, which was all fat and satin so shiny I might shoot off at any instant—but I came to understand that she sensed his unease in the world and was impelled to offer comfort. In time, Len adapted to the pains and injustices of life, covering them with a wicked and ribald sense of humour.

Conrad railed against existence in a different way. The third of three children in close succession, he, like Len, felt ignored and over-looked as our harried mother struggled to manage her increasingly burdened life. Even my father's custom of holding Conrad on his lap at mealtimes could not entirely reconcile my brother to the world, which he regarded as fundamentally unfair—particularly when I (always a hoarder) still had chocolate in my desk drawer at the end of the week, long after Conrad's had been devoured. On one occasion, that state of affairs undermined his toddling control to the point that he bit me on the leg.

Like most children, I didn't give much thought to my parents.

They were just there—my lively, talkative mother and my more taciturn father. Mom and Dad. Mom had charge of our day-to-day life: bathing us, dressing us, assigning chores like washing dishes or bringing in wood for the fire. Each Sunday, she tacked to the kitchen wall a chart on which she recorded our sins and omissions. The theory was that our sins would be counted on Saturdays, with a penny docked from our twenty-five-cent allowance for each one. But in the flurry of getting three kids out of the house, Mom usually forgot to check her sheet and would just sigh and hand out the quarters when we got to town.

Sunday was reserved for church and visiting relatives. But every other day of the week, Dad was away from dawn to dusk, working on the farms his parents had bought when they came to Pincher Creek from Poland in 1927 with five daughters and four sons. (Their eldest daughter, Alma, had married and remained in Poland until after the Second World War, and their eldest son, Edmund, was going to college and stayed behind to complete his studies.) Unlike most of his brothers, my father rejected high school in the new country and never went to university. Maybe (as a wicked cousin once whispered in my ear) he had "fallen on his head" as a kid; maybe he was a bit off in some difficult-to-define way. Or perhaps he was simply an iconoclast by nature. Whatever the cause, my father decided he didn't like school and could do better on his own. By day, he taught himself to ride, box, and play the trumpet. And by kerosene lamps in the evening, he embarked on a program of self-education. By the time he was twenty, he could read and write two languages, English and German, and converse in Polish and Russian. (Proud of his linguistic skill, he studied French much later in life, too.)

Passionately religious, Dad dreamed of becoming a minister. He took time away from the farm to go to bible school, where he won prizes for his oratorical skills and came home with a fine suit and an elegant Harris Tweed winter coat, determined to become a preacher. He returned from a clerical stint in southern Manitoba with a black Nash car (bestowed by my mother's wealthy uncle) that left the jalopies of Pincher Creek in the dust. But his dreams of being a churchman came to naught. Behind a façade of religious conformity, he harboured a deep distrust of organized religion that got in the way of church dogma and duties. Although he filled in as a lay preacher throughout his life, it was not to be his career. He returned home—a home strangely quiet. Brothers Ed, Bill, and Otto were off at university. Married sisters Alma, Martha, Adele, and Olga lived in distant towns. Selma had joined the army; Alice had gone south to pursue dreams of a fashion career; and Millie, who had been born in Canada, was off to art school. Alfred returned from a conscripted stint in the army moody and depressed. My father came home to help his aging parents run the family farms. The son who stayed behind.

When I was four, that first house in the valley of my earliest memories was replaced by a log house on a high foothills property acquired by the Gietz family as summer grazing land. The plan was that my father and his brother Fred would harvest the tall jack pine that clothed the hills. An old photo shows me, shortly after we moved in, improbably seated with my brothers at a tiny table in a sea of grass, Table Mountain looming behind us. I loved the ancient house, built of huge round logs with a porch stretching across its front; I loved the hill, which I could descend at the speed of light; I loved the sweetness of the mountain air and the dark velvet of the nights. Mom read us the story of Heidi, who found herself dropped in the Swiss Alps with only a hermit for company, and who came to relish the high clear air and mountain vistas. *Just like us*, I thought, as I ran through the grass in the summer or rolled in the snow in the winter. Our mountain retreat was the first of those special places that have touched me and become part of my soul.

One day, a man from Quebec came to help log the property. Dad and Uncle Fred marvelled at how trees seemed to melt at the touch of his "swede saw," as bow saws were called then (in those days, chainsaws were not common). Clearly, I concluded, French Canadians were a special lot. This inference was cemented when Frenchie, as we affectionately called him (those were different times), decided to carve a rocking horse for me from a huge piece of wood. Each evening for months, I watched him create its legs, its torso, its head and eyes and ears, before setting it on two carved wooden rockers. Finished at last, he righted the horse and placed me on it. I rocked and shrieked with glee.

I woke up the next morning to find everyone gathered around the horse. Tears sprang to my eyes when I saw why: a crack had widened across the horse's back, a deep, irreparable wound. I threw myself on the broken back and wept. "I rocked too hard," I cried. My first encounter with guilt—misplaced, in hindsight, as guilt often is.

My mountain idyll lasted less than two years. My restless father lost interest in the sawmill, and the time had come for me to go to school. A home closer to town was required. And so we moved into a two-storey house—my third—clad in grey asphalt siding, east of the town of Pincher Creek. The kitchen, dining room, and living room were on the first floor, and four bedrooms, one of which would become a bathroom if we ever got plumbing, were upstairs. I remember exactly the pattern of the wallpaper I was allowed to choose for my room—an arrangement of diamonds and roses. In the summer, we roamed the three acres of land with the neighbour children—there is not an inch I don't recall—and in the winter, we sat by the fire in the living room and read or played games.

It was a child's paradise of a different kind. No one paid us children much heed. The inexhaustible work of keeping bread on the table (my father's department) and keeping three young children fed and clothed (my mother's duty) consumed all available adult energy.

I recall, as a five-year-old, thinking about numbers. I found my mother frantically sweeping some mess off the kitchen floor.

"How long would it take to count to a hundred?" I asked.

She brushed me away.

I persisted. "Five minutes?" Brush, brush, brush. "Ten minutes?" Brush, brush, brush, brush. "An hour?"

"Yes," she said in exasperation and with a swish of the broom that shoved me out the door.

I must have looked disappointed—an hour in my child's mind was an enormous stretch of time. Mom paused in her sweeping. "You'll soon go to school," she said. "They'll teach you everything you need to know." Her face softened, and she launched into her own memories of her one-room prairie school. "I loved school," she said. "It was the best time of my life. But I had to leave before I finished . . ." Her voice trailed off. "The rest is history."

They'll teach you everything you need to know—the phrase preoccupied me. What did I, a girl, need to know? Not much, I thought, looking at my mother: how to cook, clean, shop, and look after the kids. But there was a wistfulness in those other words she spoke. I was too young to realize what my mother had given up just because she had made the choices expected of a girl. But the germ of a query fixed itself in my juvenile brain: Could there be more than what girls were expected to do? Other dreams? Other possibilities? I was too young to fully articulate the question, much less answer it. But it would never let me go.

....

CHAPTER TWO

Pincher Creek

PINCHER CREEK, A TOWN of two thousand souls, was the sun around which the lives of the local farmers and ranchers revolved, the source of all things exotic and enticing. As a young child, I yearned all week for Saturday afternoon, when my parents took us to town. Town: a marvellous metropolis filled with ice cream, my weekly chocolate bar, and Cracker Jack popcorn.

Pincher Creek's wonders continued to reveal themselves as I grew older. The hospital, where we raced when disaster struck—as when Conrad drank a can of kerosene—and were miraculously made whole. Shops with windows full of lovely dresses and watches and tooled leather saddles, to ogle if you could not buy. The Co-op, where at age twelve I stood mesmerized before the first television image I had ever seen. More churches than even the most self-respecting town required—Catholic, Anglican, United, Baptist, Mennonite, and more. Schools, both Catholic and Protestant, elementary and high. And the Pincher Creek Municipal Library, which loaned me two books a week to tide me over from Saturday to Saturday. A pool hall, a skating rink, and a curling rink. Beer parlours, viewed only from the outside and afar. A bawdy house, it was whispered, to which lonely cowboys could repair on Saturday nights. You never knew what marvels Pincher Creek would unveil.

In reality, the town of Pincher Creek was nothing more than a modest cluster of houses and businesses dotting a dusty main street that paralleled a small stream flowing from the Rocky Mountains, twenty-five miles to the west. Legend has it that someone lost a pair of pincers, or pliers, in the water of the creek when the RCMP was establishing a horse farm in the 1880s. The irate loser dubbed the creek Pincer Creek, which no one could pronounce. So it became Pincher Creek.

After the town's incorporation in 1906, the *Calgary Herald* published an editorial advising it to change its name immediately if it had any hope of respectability. As the *Herald*'s editorialists noted, "The diminutive character implied in the word 'creek' is sufficiently damaging without the 'Pincher' before it. Together they make as poor a name for a town as exists in Western Canada." Precedent dictated a change of name. "Rat Portage is glad it changed its name to Kenora," the newspaper declared, while "Regina was once Pile of Bones, a name which would have been sufficient to spoil its future." But being slightly off the groove never bothered Pincher Creekers.

The people who lived in and around Pincher Creek even before its incorporation were a diverse lot. The Piikani (formerly referred to as the Peigan), one of three nations of the Blackfoot Confederacy, had for centuries pitched their teepees on its banks and hunted its ravines. Scrounging in the creek's upstream canyon just west of town in the

1940s, a kid might unearth ancient arrowheads or—if really lucky, like my father once was—a beaten copper bracelet.

By the 1870s and 1880s, occasional settlers in covered wagons were crossing the stream, followed by whisky traders, the Mounties (to shut down the whisky traders), and the clergy. Father Lacombe, the famed friend of the Cree and Blackfoot, and a liaison between them and the settlers, came and stayed for a while in the 1880s. A few decades later, a Catholic school was established in Pincher Creek, along with a church and a convent. The Catholics were betting that the railway would pass through Crowsnest Pass and Pincher Creek, and that Pincher Creek would house the province's first university. They were woefully wrong, but remnants of their dreams remained.

Late in the nineteenth century, aristocratic Brits came to build ranches and play polo. Many of them were "remittance men," a term I absorbed as a child. These were wayward sons sent off to the colonies with an allowance, or remittance. Most returned to England to fight when the First World War erupted, but a few stayed behind. On our Saturday forays into town, Dad would point them out, old bearded men taking the sun on the front steps of the King Eddy Hotel. Sometimes we'd get a visit from a man named Noble Craig— a rugged, lively character, more raconteur than rancher. I pondered Noble's strange name and fantasized that he was the son of a remittance man whose mother thought the name appropriate.

In 1877, the government of Canada and the Plains First Nations— the Siksika (Blackfoot), Kainai (Blood), Piikani, Stoney-Nakoda, and Tsuut'ina (Sarcee)—signed Treaty 7, which created reserves of land for each First Nation and still left land open for settlement. The promise was that this agreement would allow the peaceful cohabitation of the First Nations and settlers and put a stop to ongoing skirmishes. The reality was a land surrendered in exchange for blankets, beads, and a future of residential schools and cultural deprivation.

In the early decades of the twentieth century, Pincher Creek was inundated by immigrants who settled the plains and valleys the Piikani people had once roamed freely. Brits and Scots were followed by French Canadians, Germans, Hutterites, and Mennonites. Some came for the beauty of this place where the plains meet the mountains. Some came for the good soil and sun. Some came just to get away. Many of them were wise, cultured, and rich in diverse experience—people who established libraries, put on plays, and thought poetry was something that anyone, including cowboys, could write. By the time I arrived in the 1940s, Pincher Creek had become a small crossroads of the world. It wasn't just my parents who raised me. The whole community—a heady mix of humankind—brought me up.

I WAS BORN IN Pincher Creek, but my family's story begins long before. If you ask me where I'm from, I'll say Pincher Creek. If you ask about my genes, I'll point vaguely east, in the direction of northern Europe and the Baltic Sea. Among that flood of early immigrants who formed part of the tapestry of Pincher Creek were my maternal and paternal grandparents, who brought with them their own unique old-world perspective.

According to genetic testing, I'm a mix of northern German, Scandinavian, and Russian, with a splash of Ashkenazi Jew thrown in—a heritage that reflects the flux of northern Europe as nations rose and fell and people emigrated in search of better lives. In the twentieth century, before Stalin and his allies drew an Iron Curtain between the East and the West, northern Europe was a place where cultures mingled and melded.

My mother's parents—Emma Weiss and Herman Kruschell—came with their parents to Canada from Germany in the early 1900s. Growing up, I heard family stories about the old country—tales of Dresden and a carpet factory, of Alsace-Lorraine and a great-great-grandmother who served as the village doctor (while her son built coffins for those who did not survive her ministrations). The Weiss and Kruschell families settled around Morden, Manitoba, close to the border with North Dakota, and that's where my grandparents, Herman and Emma, met and married. When they heard rumours of fertile land being given away in eastern Alberta, they moved to the hamlet of Compeer in pursuit of new opportunities.

I never met Grandmother Emma, but I came to know her through my mother, who, during lonely afternoons and evenings, would tell us how it was when she was young. She painted a vivid picture of Emma in her younger years—a gifted, independent woman who loved books and ideas, and mortified the local farmwives by gallivanting around in her motor vehicle instead of staying home and cooking like a proper wife should. And then, mysteriously, Emma became ill, weakening every year until she died at just forty-five.

"Why did she get sick?" I'd ask.

My mother would just shake her head. "Pernicious anemia in the end," she said. I was used to Mom using big words I didn't understand—she bandied them about with pride—but I must have frowned. "She was weak, thin, had to stay in bed more and more," Mom explained.

Many years later, when I was diagnosed with celiac disease, a genetically inherited intolerance to gluten that causes pernicious anemia, I understood why my grandmother had died so young. The cure was so simple—avoid gluten. But back then, no one knew.

After my grandmother's death, Grandpa Kruschell lived on in solitary grief. An ill-considered attempt to replace Emma with a new wife ended in separation, and he came to live with us (every farm or ranch had a little house where widowed grandparents or aunts and uncles could live). In a pattern that soon established itself in our young lives, he would stay a few months, then move on to somewhere else for a spell, then suddenly return. He was short and plump; deep lines etched his eyes and mouth beneath a broad forehead topped by white hair, receding at the temples. Not until I encountered Verdi's *Rigoletto* as an adult did I understand his character—infinite sadness disguised by a façade of jokes and good cheer.

When Grandpa Kruschell arrived, the house brightened. In younger, happier days in Compeer, he'd led a prairie band that played at all the local dances and fairs. "I was just a kid, saw a woman playing the trombone at a fair," he told me. "My, could she play. I decided that I would learn to play, too." Everyone in the family was expected to pitch in and join the band. A clarinet was needed, so my mother, still just a girl, learned to play. Only Emma was exempted from the family edict that everyone had to play something. That life was gone by the time I knew him, but Grandpa's passion for the trombone remained undimmed.

Each afternoon, I would hurry home from school and run to Grandpa Kruschell's little house to listen to his stories. Sooner rather than later, he would take out his beloved trombone and play for me—his eyes above puffed cheeks drawing my attention to a resonant bass note or a long mellow slide. My mother, ever the good Christian, persuaded him to stop drinking, smoking, and cursing, and got him to substitute hymns for his favourite marches and rags. But still he played. I would find him in his room in the late afternoon, transcribing notes from hymn books so he could perform them on trombone, just as he had transcribed his life to suit my mother's demands. He was genial and hated discord. He would pretend to agree with things even when he didn't and would put up with any amount of pomposity. All this and more he would accept, as long as he was allowed a few hours at the end of the day with his beloved trombone.

TO LISTEN TO MY mother, her girlhood had been a time of bliss. She excelled in school, played softball, revelled in family band concerts. One winter, Herman, Emma, and their children, Eleanora and Leonard (Doreen wasn't born yet), travelled by train to Vancouver and down the coast to California, a trip my mother talked about for the rest of her life. "The trees in Stanley Park," she would marvel. "So big, so beautiful. I was a prairie girl. I had never seen trees like that."

But then, as quickly as it had come, the good life was gone, swept away by the Great Depression of the 1930s. The once-rich prairie soil lay exhausted, and dry winds blew it into billowing clouds so dense that people lost their way. And when the winds were done, hordes of crickets descended to eat the stubble left behind. Proud landowners who could no longer afford fuel had to convert their cars into horse-drawn Bennett buggies (named for R.B. Bennett, the prime minister who presided over this misfortune); many lived off scraps scrounged from the back of railway cars from Ontario. There were no longer dances or country fairs. The band no longer played.

There was nowhere for my mother's family to go but west once again. Herman regrouped and bought a store in a rural community northwest of Edmonton called Tiger Lily, after the orange lilies that grew wild in the fields. He liked the store—the Kruschells had always been good at business—but life for my mother, then seventeen, was hard. Barely out of childhood, she was forced to quit school. Her duty was clear—help run the store, care for her brother and sister, and nurse her dying mother in the family apartment upstairs.

My father's family was as dour and contained as my mother's was fun-loving and social. My grandparents, Frederick and Caroline Gietz, were Germans who lived on lands lying between the Baltic Sea and the Hanseatic city of Toruń, Poland, not far from the Vistula River. Successive invasions by Swedish and Russian armies over the centuries might account for the dark lens that clouded their view of the world; one never knew who or what was coming next.

In 1927, Frederick and Caroline sold their land in Poland and came to Canada, nine children in tow, to settle in Pincher Creek. To their neighbours in Toruń, this seemed a strange decision. They had a good life there and had just built a fine new brick house for their growing family. Frederick, a staunch Lutheran, was respected for his piety and compassion. Why throw it all away for a struggling existence in a foreign land with a strange language?

Family lore suggests this decision was made for a number of reasons. Local ethnic tension was one. Poles and Germans and Jews had long jostled for physical and spiritual space in the lands to the south of the Baltic Sea, but now tensions were rising. A Jewish teacher came begging for shelter, and my grandparents found themselves housing him and his family in their front room.

Exacerbating the situation was the fear of war. During the First World War, the family had been compelled to billet German officers; now, as the Weimar Republic flailed and tensions between Germany and Russia grew, they feared worse was to come.

The final factor inducing the move was the spirit of adventure my grandparents shared. As a young man, Frederick had travelled to America, where he worked in Chicago. Independently—it's not clear they knew each other at the time—Caroline had travelled to New York, where she worked in a posh household as a lady's maid.

In 1927, with tensions rising and the winds of war once more stirring, my grandparents' memories of a freer world came back. I imagine them looking at each other and saying, "Good. Let's sell the property while we can and move to America, where we will have peace and our children will have a future."

So they did. How they ended up in Canada rather than the United States is a mystery. In fact, I learned they got Canadian papers in Warsaw. How they ended up in a tiny town in the southwest corner of Alberta is an even bigger mystery. All I know is that they did. They bought a farm on the edge of town with a house overlooking the creek, and settled in with their children. My father, Ernest, was thirteen.

Life in their new community was not easy. My grandmother struggled to learn Canadian ways, with some success, but my grandfather became increasingly reclusive. And while they were not rejected, no one went out of their way to welcome them, either. They found refuge in the local Mennonite community among people who spoke German and shared their evangelical beliefs.

My Gietz grandparents had the misfortune to arrive in Pincher Creek just as ethnic tensions in Canada were increasing in the run-up to the Second World War; these tensions would stoke hostility towards foreigners and send thousands of Japanese, Italians, Germans, and Ukrainians to internment camps. Not that the town was a stranger to prejudice. Like many western Canadian towns, deep ethnic tensions simmered beneath a façade of polite tolerance. The first British colonizers of the late nineteenth century had dreamed of creating a new Britain on the plains. They wore spats and top hats and battled each other in Sunday polo matches, followed by tea and sandwiches (and whisky for the men after the ladies retired). The ordinary Brits and Scots who followed may have lacked their predecessors' aristocratic refinements, but they were staunch supporters of the empire. Loyalty to the empire persisted even in the 1950s, when I was growing up. I knew the men of the town met each evening at the Legion Hall, while the women served afternoon tea at meetings of the Imperial Order of the Daughters of the Empire—better known as the IODE.

By the early decades of the twentieth century, the dream of a new Britain ran up against an influx of strange people from eastern Europe. In a bid to settle western Canada, the federal government launched a massive advertising campaign in continental Europe, offering large plots of land for a dollar. Farmers and peasants from Ukraine, Germany, and other nations responded en masse. The plains filled up with people who wore babushkas and spoke indecipherable—to British ears—languages. Resentment against the newcomers grew among British settlers, who saw their vision of Canada jeopardized. In Saskatchewan, people flocked to rallies denouncing the new waves of immigrants. The Ku Klux Klan, sniffing fertile ground, sallied north across the border to stir things up.

There were no rallies in Pincher Creek, no visits from the Klan. But you couldn't grow up there without sensing the tensions between members of the old British establishment and those who had come after. No one discussed it, but it was there. As a child, I felt it. No one ever mocked my German last name, Gietz, but when an invitation to sing at an IODE concert was inexplicably withdrawn, I suspected prejudice. In my heart, I longed for an Anglo name like Smith or Jones or McTavish.

Once, walking home from school, a friend with a Mennonite name suddenly declared, "I hate being German. I feel second class." I couldn't bring myself to say I shared her feeling—to say the words would somehow betray my family, betray myself—but I felt her pain.

It was the same for Grandma Gietz. As events raced towards the Second World War, the simmering tension became overt. Some in the Anglo community regarded the new German family on the outskirts of town with suspicion. Who were they? What were they fleeing? Why had they come? The suspicion culminated in an unauthorized RCMP search of my grandparents' house, an event that the family ever after referred to euphemistically as "the day the RCMP visited Grandma." My grandmother politely invited the officers in. They searched the main floor and found nothing. They clomped upstairs to the bedrooms. Again, nothing. Finally, in the attic, they discovered a trunk filled with family memorabilia and my grandmother's most precious papers. They opened it. This time they found something— my grandmother's scrapbook of the British royal family. Determined to learn the ways of her new country, she had been buying the *Toronto Star Weekly* every Saturday and assiduously clipping photos of Canada's king and queen and Princesses Elizabeth and Margaret. The officers left empty-handed. No one remembers if they apologized.

The incident cast a shadow over my early years. We were German; we were different. And yet, we looked the same and did the same things. I studied my far-flung family members on their periodic visits home to Pincher Creek and saw how they blended seamlessly into the mainstream matrix. My uncles went to university and my aunts wore stylish dresses and fine leather pumps, even on Sunday picnic outings to Waterton Park. Yet the shadow tagged me everywhere I went. I could not shake it. Young as I was, I understood what it meant to be the same yet different, to be equal yet on probation.

In the end, my grandparents' decision to come to Canada turned out to be wise. During the Second World War, Soviet troops overran the property they had sold in Poland. Had they remained, they would have lost everything, including, quite possibly, their lives. Caroline and Frederick never fully adjusted to life in Canada, but their children and grandchildren—including me and my brothers—would thrive in its embrace. And as I grew older, the shadow of my family history receded.

··

CHAPTER THREE

An Education

JUST BEFORE MY SIXTH birthday, my mother found me in the living room of our grey asphalt house. Often she was distracted, running from this crisis to that family disaster, but this time, I saw the focus in her blue eyes. She meant business.

"Tomorrow you're going to school," she said. "You need to know how to write your name." She sat me down and made me practise, over and over, all nineteen letters—B-E-V-E-R-L-E-Y M-A-R-I-A-N G-I-E-T-Z—until I had them down pat.

I learned a lot in that, my first academic lesson. How to hold the pencil between my thumb and index finger. How to make the letters of the alphabet. The difference between lowercase and uppercase and why it matters—or doesn't (I was a skeptic even at the age of five). How you could draw the shapes sloppily, so the letters fell off their lines and grew thick and indecipherable, or do it neatly, so they looked good and could be easily read. And the big take-away, one that fascinates me to this day: how a pencil can create shapes that magically acquire meaning and allow you to talk to other people.

I approached my first day of grade one in a state of high anticipation mixed with trepidation. I had asked many questions about the world as I negotiated the transition from babyhood to childhood. Why were flowers the way they were? Why did my father read the Bible every day, and what was going on in his head when he did? How did numbers work? And, of course, my burning query: How long would it take to count to one hundred? Now, at last, all my questions would be answered.

On the appointed day, my mother dressed me in a new gingham frock, helped me buckle my patent leather shoes over white socks, and combed my dark hair into a tidy pageboy do. Then she drove me to the school. It seemed enormous to me. A two-storey edifice lined with long-paned windows, it loomed like a yellow colossus as my mother pulled me from the car and marched me to the entrance. As the double doors swung shut behind us, the warm scent of oiled wooden floors floated up. Everywhere, strange kids and their mothers rushed about, all intent on the same task—to find the place where they belonged.

My grade one teacher was Mrs. Hinman, a thin woman with a narrow white face and bright red hair. She could not have been more than forty, but to me she seemed very old. Every teacher, I soon learned, had a reputation, and Mrs. Hinman's was that she was strict.

I quickly became friends with a little blonde girl named Gail Davis, who sat behind me in our classroom. We would race through our exercises to see who could complete them first, which required me to turn around to check where she was on the page. One day, Mrs. Hinman observed this and concluded I was copying. She marched me to the front of the room, read the indictment to the class, found me guilty, and ordered me to put out my hand for punishment. Six whacks with a steel-edged ruler. As my classmates looked on, I stood before my teacher and took the blows—no crying, no protest, outwardly calm, inwardly dying of mortification and shame. Punishment duly rendered and endured, I slunk back to my place in misery. Suddenly racing through lessons with Gail wasn't fun anymore. Suddenly the joy with which I had picked up my pencil had vanished. I had had my first taste of justice—or more accurately, injustice.

It never occurred to me to be angry with Mrs. Hinman or to complain to my parents. They would just ask why I got into trouble and probably punish me again. Better to say nothing, I rationalized. I was learning a vital lesson—the world wasn't always fair.

Mrs. Hinman and the teachers who followed her in subsequent years did what they were paid to do. They maintained discipline in the schoolroom. They taught us to read, write, and do arithmetic. They did not expect much of me, Len, or Conrad, and made no attempt to get to know us as individuals or find out what we were capable of.

We found our enrichment outside class. Play taught us to respect rules and get along. We played simple sports like softball and skating, as well as made-up games in the backyard—in our cowboy town, we would stage mock stampedes in which we were wild horses coming out of chute number two. Our "chute" was the backyard outhouse. Once, in my eagerness to get off to a flying start, I cracked my collarbone on the stick designed to hold the door back that some boy had left sticking out.

In 1953, when I was ten and a half, my sister, Judi, was born, to much joy in the household. I loved to help Mother bathe her and loved to wheel her in her big black buggy. The perfection of her tiny feet and hands enthralled me. On nice days, Mom would leave the buggy on the front porch so Judi could sleep in the fresh air. On a quiet afternoon, while Mom lay napping and I was supposed to be in charge, the air was suddenly split by the wails of Conrad, age five. He had decided to take Judi for a ride, in the course of which he tipped the buggy and spilled her onto the ground. I ran to pick up the silent bundle of her wrapped body, certain that she was dead. Conrad stood over her, howling. Our world went black—we had failed our duty of care and killed our sister. And then she let out a yowl. I hugged her to my chest and breathed a silent prayer of thanks. Mom came running; Judi was brushed off, returned to her buggy, and wheeled back onto the porch, where she quickly fell asleep again. I did not leave her side for the rest of the day.

Much as I adored my new sister, she was too little to play. For that, I was stuck with my brothers and their buddies, which meant that most of the kids in the backyard were boys. It was an era of misogyny, and quite often the boys (never Len and Conrad—they knew better) would remind me I was just a girl and tell me I couldn't play. When I insisted on joining in, they tried to stop me. In vain.

On one occasion, a boy named Billy Smith, annoyed that I had insisted on my turn on our newly acquired bike—a second-hand black contraption that we were all obliged to share—stuck his leg in my path. In my panic, it never occurred to me to swerve or fall to the side. I watched with horror as the wheels of the bike rolled over Billy's leg. I brought the bike to a stop, dismounted, and returned to the scene of the crime, where Billy was moaning and nursing his leg. He limped to his feet and muttered a curse, saving me the need to apologize, even if I had wanted to.

To my astonishment, the accidental act of riding over Billy Smith's leg cemented my reputation among the neighbourhood kids for steely resolve. "Don't mess with her," my brothers would tell their friends, and their friends would tell their friends. And that was that. After a while, even I started to believe it. Maybe I was tough, as the boys seemed to think. Or maybe, on some subliminal level, I didn't respond well even then to being told I couldn't participate. One thing was sure: I was learning how I operated. If you tried to stop me, I would go around you—or over you, if necessary—and then, with luck, simply carry on.

If childhood sport taught me to deal with exclusion, the Pincher Creek Municipal Library saved me from premature intellectual death. It was my only enrichment program—and what a program it was. The local matrons—Mrs. Boyden, Mrs. Telford, Mrs. Allison, and more—had at some point decided that Pincher Creek needed a book collection. I don't know how they managed it, but they persuaded the town to found and (modestly) fund the library. A few thousand books were acquired, catalogued, and shelved in a large room on the second floor of the town hall. There was no money left over for wages, but each Wednesday at noon and every Saturday afternoon, one of the matrons would unlock the door and take a seat behind a big oak desk to await the local custom. Sometimes business was brisk—ladies in hats jostling with cowboys for space at shelves that housed Western novels (Zane Grey was a favourite) or historical fiction (popular takes on everything from King Henry VIII's queens to the Napoleonic Wars). Other days, I was free to roam the shelves unimpeded by adult competition.

Every Saturday, I rushed through lunch to get to the library so that I could check out the two books that members were allowed each week. The cost of membership was fifty cents a year—two weeks' allowance but worth it. Between us, Len and I had four books, and we usually got through all of them before the week was out. I worked my way through the Bobbsey Twins, Nancy Drew, the Hardy Boys, and every Anne of Green Gables book Lucy Maud Montgomery ever wrote. I started at age eight, and by my tenth birthday, I had read the library's entire children's selection.

There was nothing to do, I decided, but start on the grown-up options. Timorously at first, then with increasing hunger, I pulled the volumes down from their shelves. No slim juvenile tomes were these.

They were fat books with fine print and thousands of words—big words, little words, words at whose meanings I could only guess. I discovered delights beyond belief. Historical novels, mystery novels, Westerns galore—all were grist for my mental mill. I explored the ancient civilizations of Egypt, Greece, and Rome. I lived, for hours at a time, with medieval ladies and knights.

The matrons behind the desk watched warily as my fingers roamed the high shelves. Sometimes they greeted my weekly choices with a raised eyebrow and pursed lips. They would rub the stamp in the ink pad with unnecessary vigour before bringing it down with a defiant thump on the sheet glued to the inside back cover. But they never told me to put a book back.

The Pincher Creek Municipal Library saved my life. Or so it seems to me now. Would I have survived without it? Probably. Would I have grown up to be the person I am without it? Most certainly not. In the pages of those books, I learned new ways of writing and thinking and feeling and being. And I discovered new worlds far away from my provincial little town in the foothills of southern Alberta.

Occasionally, though, new worlds came right to our doorstep. Someone of renown would pass through town en route to a back-packing trip with nature conservationist and guide Andy Russell, or a famous musician might be drawn to a nearby ranch. When I was fourteen or so, the great Sir Ernest MacMillan, an eminent composer and conductor known as "Canada's only musical knight," came to visit the Lynch-Stauntons, an old ranching family with roots in Quebec. Locals arranged a musical soiree in a dance hall. Sir Ernest, the consummate entertainer, told stories, pounded out a few classics on an out-of-tune piano, and led the audience in singing rollicking folk songs while a slender woman in black (undoubtedly from the big city of Toronto) looked on with benign amusement. I never spoke to Sir Ernest or the elegant woman in black, but I went away in wonder.

Truth be told, I had been looking for glimpses of other worlds long before my chance encounter with Sir Ernest MacMillan. At the age of seven, I developed a crush on Princess Elizabeth. At the age of nine, with my idol now preparing to be crowned the Queen of England in a great June ceremony in Westminster, my crush morphed into full-blown infatuation. Every Saturday, I scoured the *Star Weekly* for stories and colour photos of the young and beautiful queen and her royal acolytes, just as my grandmother had done years before. After reading every word and poring over every photo, I would take myself to the kitchen table to cut out the pictures and paste them in scrapbooks—one on her childhood, another on her wedding to the dashing Prince Philip, and yet another on her ascension to the throne and coronation. Beside each photo, I provided a carefully printed label explaining what the photo represented.

I was a kid who liked horses and games, who had never been to a big city, who'd never seen a politician, much less a queen, yet I was smitten with a young monarch half a world away. I cannot say why. Perhaps I inherited my grandmother's fondness for the royal family. Perhaps I was dazzled by a glamorous world I could barely conceive. Perhaps, in some way, I was besotted by the image of a woman, at once beautiful and eminently serious, doing important work. For whatever reason, my infatuation with all things royal dominated my days and dreams for an entire year. Eventually, my love affair with the queen faded as new passions and concerns emerged. But I never completely relinquished it.

In Pincher Creek, I had no preschool, no kindergarten, no enrichment programs. My parents, my brothers, my classmates, my library, the glossy weekend pages of the *Star Weekly*—these were my extracurricular teachers. They helped me understand the world I inhabited and introduced me to other worlds far beyond my comprehension. They taught me about myself, both my weaknesses and my strengths.

If I ran the world, every child would start school at age three, as

French children do, and every one would be provided with whatever it takes to allow her to follow her particular passion. Children would grow up healthier and better socialized, incipient problems would be caught when they can be more easily corrected, and anti-social behaviour later in life would be reduced, a great saving of productive lives and costs to society. But education comes in many forms. I got lucky.

ONE EVENING WHEN I was ten, I returned home to find my mother in tears. I knew this was the day of parent-teacher interviews and I feared the worst. I loved school and did well. Still, you never knew what the teacher would tell your mom when she came for the annual conference.

"What's wrong?" I asked.

My mother wiped her eyes. "You're all right. It's your brothers."

Between sobs, she revealed that Len was unable to comprehend long division and Conrad spent most afternoons standing in the corner of his grade one class for disruptive behaviour. My mother, an enthusiastic student who had always led the class in her prairie schoolrooms, could not understand why they weren't excelling.

"Mom," I said, "they'll be fine. They're actually pretty smart." I knew this to be true because they consistently trounced me at checkers and outwitted me at scoring the biggest cookies after school. But my words didn't seem to comfort her, and I didn't know what else to say.

In fact, my sisterly premonition was right. Despite not appearing to care overmuch—perhaps a reaction to coming after a "brainy" sister—my brothers earned respectable passes as they proceeded through elementary and high school. Instead of going straight to the big university in Edmonton, as I would do, they did their first two years of post-secondary education at Lethbridge Junior College. It was there, Len told me later, that he learned to apply himself, study, and get good grades. Twenty years after the teacher rendered her painful verdicts about my brothers at that parent-teacher interview, Conrad, the apparent rebel, was deep in science studies and had become a committed Christian and the soul of rectitude. And Len was finishing a degree in math and physics and had been accepted into medical school at the University of Alberta.

"Do you remember that grade three teacher who said you would never master long division?" I asked Len when I heard his good news about medical school.

He laughed. "They wanted me to go through the whole drill, all the silly steps—divide this into that, remainder, carry over. I couldn't see why I had to do that when I had the answer in my head. So I refused."

Israeli prime minister Shimon Peres once ruminated on the social practice of making wired teenage boys sit behind desks all day. Torture, he argued, might not be the best way to get kids to learn—perhaps we should consider putting boys nine and up to work and let them learn from that. On a more modest level, Len's experience made me ask why every student should be forced to do long division (or art or music or English) in precisely the same way as every other—the way the rules say it should be done. Or even more radically, why kids shouldn't be assigned real-life activities as part of their learning processes.

I thought of our early teachers—conscientious, overburdened, struggling to succeed without teachers' assistants or days off for enrichment and relief. "They did their best," I said to Len. "And all things said, it was pretty good."

"What was in the water?" people ask when they look at the number of luminaries produced by the little town of Pincher Creek—among them, four chief justices; world-famous naturalist Andy Russell and his son Charlie; Ruth Collins-Nakai, a president of the

Canadian Medical Association; and renowned theoretical physicist Gordon Semenoff. My personal view is that it didn't have anything to do with the water, although the cold glacier flow we imbibed wasn't bad. It was a combination of three things: first, a community that exposed us to books, learning, music, and art; second, time to play, explore, and daydream (in other words, benign parental neglect); and third, responsibility and work.

From an early age, we had chores, as did all kids in Pincher Creek. Bringing in firewood, washing and drying the dishes, sweeping the floor after every meal, helping outdoors on the farm. We worked our way up through the hierarchy of homely tasks—often complaining, but also taking pride in our advancement and fortitude, and in the prospect of new adventures. I recently discovered a letter that my mother, age eleven, wrote to her cousin Erna. The joy in her childish voice shines through. "Daddy says I can go out with him and help haul grain this year. I can't wait." She wasn't alone. A generation later, the kids I grew up with were, like my mother, looking forward to spring so they could help haul the hay or take part in the cattle roundup.

Work was an integral part of our life. Even after the ubiquitous child labour of Victorian times was rightly outlawed, it persisted on farms and ranches. During my childhood, kids were sometimes forced to work too hard or too much, to skip school for harvest or spring planting, or to labour at tedious tasks for unending hours. And occasionally, farm accidents did occur. I was spared the worst of it because my mother needed me in the house, but my brothers spent their summer holidays working at the sawmill my parents ran on the ranch. "I hated the work," Len remarked, looking back. Then he smiled. "I hated it so much that I decided to get an education."

In Robert Frost's poem "Two Tramps in Mud Time," the poet cedes the spring wood chopping—which he was eagerly awaiting—to two passing tramps who need the work more than he. He then reflects on the nature of work and the need to find work that you love:

But yield who will to their separation,
My object in living is to unite
My avocation and my vocation
As my two eyes make one in sight.

Work educated us, not only about how to do the job at hand but also about what we might accomplish with our lives. Work taught me to accept that I could not always do what I wanted to do. It also taught me to organize—the better you organized a task, the sooner it was done—and to improve my performance. I learned that no matter how much you are loved, there is no free ride—everyone is important, and everyone must contribute to the family enterprise. I learned that given enough practice, I could achieve modest competency in certain things. I learned that I could be useful. I learned that I mattered, at least in the small scheme of things. Most important, I learned that what counts in life is finding work that will sustain you and bring you joy.

....

CHAPTER FOUR

Rich in Difference

D IFFERENCE IS EASY FOR the people on top. It's not always easy for those below. If Canada was a mosaic, as the schoolbooks I studied proclaimed, then my family was a shabby tile hidden in the corner. We were part of the picture, but barely. No colour, no lustre, definitely a grade inferior. We had a strange foreign name. We had a strange religion proclaiming you were either saved or going to hell—ideas that didn't appeal to me, and that most people I knew thought were crazy.

And we were poor, in a peculiar sense that only I seemed to feel.

The easy prosperity that came to my educated aunts and uncles as the province moved from an agricultural to an oil-based economy passed our family by. My father was the odd child out. He never went to school, never attended university. He failed as a minister and found himself condemned to a lifetime of scrabbling a living from the land in whatever way he could—working on oil rigs, farming, ranching, running a sawmill. He never thought to blame anyone else for this situation, although he railed against the government's "tight money" policy when it prevented him from taking up a perceived opportunity. In those days, there were no remedial schemes. "Rely on yourself, work hard, and always be honest—if things don't work out, it's nobody's fault but your own," Dad would lecture us at night.

What does it mean to be poor? For some people, being poor is not having a roof over their heads or enough to eat. For others, it's not having a car. For still others, it's not having enough money to buy books or art. For me, being poor was a constant state of anxiety. We always had a roof over our heads. We always had good food—what with gardens and chickens and cows, as well as the elk my father brought home each hunting season. We always had clothing. Sure, we mostly wore jeans, but my brothers had their little Sunday suits, and Judi and I wore pretty dresses when the occasion called for them. My mother, who cared about appearances, made sure we were well dressed. She followed the fashions of the 1950s and liked sewing. She whipped up clothes my friends begged to borrow—tight-waisted dresses and wraparound skirts. But despite having everything I needed, I felt poor.

It wasn't for lack of things, nor was it for feeling that others had more; they did, but we had as much as most and more than many. It was the what-ifs that made me feel poor, the constant threat hovering in the wings that our world would suddenly come tumbling down, taking our lives with it. I absorbed my parents' worried whispers at night when they thought we kids weren't listening: How would they meet the next bank payment? Where would the money to pay the hired men come from? How would they scrape together enough to fix the truck? Cattle prices were down, demand for lumber was off, the economy was tanking and taking them—us—down.

"We'll manage," my parents would say, and somehow, with

everyone's efforts, we always did. I didn't mind the work, but I hated that word: "manage." To manage is to eke by. To manage is to live in constant anxiety. To manage is to forfeit freedom. In a word, to manage is to be poor. Without consciously articulating it, I formed a conviction deep within my child's mind: I wanted a life where I would not be compelled to manage.

While money worries sometimes made me feel poor, I grew up feeling rich in other ways. When I was eleven, my parents bought a thousand acres in the high foothills twenty-five miles southwest of Pincher Creek, across the canyon from the family property where I had lived as a toddler. The price was right—no one wanted an inaccessible piece of land so far from civilization, even if it was beautiful.

For my father, it was the landscape of dreams. But for my mother, a sociable woman with many friends, it was unutterably lonely. The domestic arrangements were humble. Once again, we lived in a log house. There was no electricity; we had kerosene lamps. There was no plumbing; we had an outhouse. At night, we listened to packrats running between the walls and the log exterior.

Still, I thought the ranch was the most beautiful place I had ever seen. Crammed between my parents in the front seat of a pickup truck, I followed every turn of the rudimentary road as it wound through miles of high foothills. Just when I despaired of ever arriving anywhere, when I feared we were lost forever, we rounded the bend of a cliff, and there it was—a scene that took my breath away. Before me stretched a long meadow of waving grass. To the east, spruce-clad slopes stretched gently upwards. And when I caught my breath and turned west, I surveyed forested hills rising to a perfect ring of mountains, crags of white and icy blue.

Growing up on the ranch indelibly imprinted on my soul the importance of beauty in life. Each time I looked down the meadow towards the mountains or galloped my horse home to the barn, I felt rich. Life might be hard, life might be tedious, life might be an unending round of work and worry, but as long as I could look down the meadow towards the mountains, life was good. Wherever I have lived, I have sought out beautiful places—our Vancouver house on the fringe of Pacific Rim Park, my gardened house near the cliffs of the Ottawa River, my cottage on Lac Brogan in the Gatineau Valley of Quebec. Magically, my world brightens in these landscapes and I see my way through problems. Suddenly, I feel blessed.

IT WAS ON THE ranch, my fourth home, that I learned first-hand about living and working with people who came from different backgrounds and different ways of life—the experience we now describe with the ubiquitous word "diversity."

To run the sawmill and the ranch, we needed help, and so a constant stream of people—some with families, some alone—passed through our lives. Some came to visit; some came to work. Some left quickly; others stayed so long they became family. All sorts found refuge in our house: Americans, Canadians, church friends, townspeople, hired men from Ontario, romantic young men looking for adventure in the not-so-wild West, idealists (male and occasionally female) drawn by the beauty of the place, Indigenous peoples from the nearby Piikani reserve or the more distant prairies. In the summer, they pitched their tents and baked bannock and brewed tea over open fires. I hovered at the flap door of their dwellings and waited for a taste.

My mother, condemned to live in a remote hinterland, was enormously empathetic. People sought her out, making their way up the long and winding road through the hills and around the cliff, where only six inches lay between the outer rim of a car's tires and oblivion. They risked life and limb to take tea and visit. My mother talked, but mostly she listened.

Occasionally, our visitors would give us advance notice. After some years on the ranch, we acquired a telephone—a wooden box on the wall with an earpiece on a string and a horn for your voice. It was a party line with a different ring—so many longs and shorts—for each ranch. Everyone "rubbernecked" on everyone else, and the line was seldom free. More often than not, people just arrived. "A car's coming around the bend," one of my siblings would say, peering out the living room's picture window, and the house would fall to a fury of sweeping and dusting and plumping of cushions.

Food was central to these occasions. There was no question of a person's visiting without being asked to share tea or a meal. Sometimes visitors would bring something—Cousin Walter from Lethbridge always arrived with a gallon jug of root beer, which I learned to love—but more often they came empty-handed. Early in the visit, Mom would suss out its duration.

"Are you staying for supper?" she would ask.

Almost always, an insincere "We really shouldn't" turned into a "Sure, why not?"

Mom would briefly retire to the kitchen to see what she had on hand. "Here's what we'll do, Bevy," she'd say to me, and rattle off an impromptu menu du jour.

Preparing all the things she'd decided on was no small feat. Food for company did not need to be fancy, but it had to be varied and good and run to at least two courses—meat or poultry accompanied by a variety of side dishes, condiments, and salads, followed by dessert (cake or pie) and coffee with cookies and candies, should anyone still have room. Both my mother and my father were excellent cooks, and I inherited their love of food. From the moment I baked my first potato, I was hooked on the chemistry of transforming raw materials into tasty bits and the art of presenting them in the most enticing fashion possible.

Mom had a unique capacity to enter into the life of whomever she was with until she became their surrogate self, absorbing their passions, disappointments, and sorrows. I see her now, seated as she listened to the newcomer to town, hands tucked in her frilled apron, oblivious to the dishes stacked in the sink behind her. Sometimes, pressed by impending household chaos, she worked as she listened, circulating with a mixing bowl in hand among guests in the living room, beating cake batter while she inclined to this person or that.

All sorts of people came to visit on summer Sundays. City cousins who talked about traffic and streetcars and insisted on endangering their lives by riding our high-spirited horses, even though we advised them to stick to the Mule, a lazy grey horse we kept just for this purpose. Businessmen from town, American oil-patch bosses, neighbouring ranchers and farmers, Piikani selling horses, Hutterites buying lumber—all these and more passed through our front door and stayed awhile. I watched and listened, drawn in by the diversity of humankind.

Of course, I knew people came in different colours, sizes, and ways of being long before I arrived at the ranch. Books had revealed the lives of those in foreign climes—slave owners in the American South, aristocrats in England, "colonials" in Southeast Asia, children in India, China, and Africa. And closer to home, I also encountered people who were "different," or more accurately, were treated as different.

The Piikani reserve was twelve miles from town. The Piikani came to town to buy supplies and came to the ranch to work and buy lumber. Yet they lived separate lives. I wondered why. Why didn't the Piikani children go to school with us or come to our church? Dad told me they couldn't vote and weren't allowed to buy liquor or to enter the bar of the King Eddy Hotel. I didn't understand why.

At some point in the 1950s, the town erected a small building to serve as a public washroom, gents on one side, women on the other. I remember my mother leading me up the steps to the women's. I looked at the sign near the door.

"Why does it say that, Mom? Why does it say 'No Indians'?"

My mother opened the door and pushed me in without reply, but I could tell by the shake of her head that she didn't approve.

Not long after my question, my parents took us to the reserve for a church service. It was held in a two-room log house. There was very little furniture—a stove, a table, some chairs, and a couple of beds—and the floors were swept bare. I remember thinking how uncluttered it was, how clean. After prayers, our hostess, a dignified older woman with a thick braid of grey hair down her back, served us tea. I thought about the public washroom, wondered how it could be that this gracious woman was forbidden to use it.

Hutterites were also different, I learned. Like the Piikani, they mostly kept to themselves, living on two farming colonies near Pincher Creek. They also dressed differently. No child in Pincher Creek could grow up without encountering black-clothed men and women in long dresses and kerchiefs in the streets.

The Hutterites were highly successful farmers. They lived simply and saved most of the money they made. People complained that they didn't pay their fair share of taxes (given the communal nature of their business), and that they were buying up too much land. At one point, the resentment led to a movement to ask the provincial government to limit the Hutterites' ability to acquire new lands. I remember my father ranting about the wrong-headedness of this. And then he put on his ten-gallon hat and drove twenty-five miles to a community meeting called to promote these limits. No doubt he did not endear himself to the local ranchers. But he made his statement: "This is a free society. Everyone is equal. Exclusion and discrimination are unacceptable." The restrictions on the Hutterite acquisition of lands were never implemented.

Some of the discrimination I saw, like that of the Piikani and the Hutterites, was overt. Other inequities were more subtle. On the main street of Pincher Creek sat a Chinese restaurant called—improbably in our village of two thousand souls—the City Café. In those days, before McDonald's or Burger King, it was the only place in town to get a meal. I don't remember the name of the man who provided this essential service, but his broad face, crinkled by a smile as we entered, is indelibly etched in my memory.

The booths of his restaurant were always full for lunch and dinner. There was a jukebox at each table where you could call up a country tune for a dime, and a scale in the front entrance where, at age thirteen, I weighed myself and learned I was 113 pounds, including coat and boots.

It was only later, in university, that I learned the man's history. In the 1880s, Chinese labourers came to Canada to work on the construction of the Canadian Pacific Railway. It was hard, dangerous work: digging tunnels, placing explosives deep in the mountains, and running for their lives before they blew up. Many men were injured, and many died. After the railway was completed, the Chinese labourers settled down in restaurants and laundry businesses across the country and established commercial and residential enclaves in all of the major cities of Canada.

There was a catch, though—one to which most Canadians who stroll to Chinatown for dim sum on a weekend morning are oblivious. Although those Chinese men were welcomed as railway labourers and tolerated as servants and business owners thereafter, public opinion favoured a white, Euro-centric Canada. People of Chinese origin did not fit this vision. The solution? In 1885, the federal government enacted a law imposing a head tax on Chinese family members who wanted to come to Canada.[1] Some men managed to scrape up the money for the tax and bring their wives. But many could not. Families were divided.

Pincher Creek was no different from many small towns across the rest of Canada. The town thought of itself as white and mostly Anglo-Saxon. Almost everyone in the schools was white; almost everyone in the shops was white. Everyone who mattered, it seemed, was white. Yet the reality was different. Beneath its homogeneous white surface, Pincher Creek was a diverse, multicultural town. The diversity was there, patent and real. People just chose to ignore it.

My parents didn't preach the modern message of inclusion, but they lived it. They treated each person as a human being, worthy of dignity. There was room for anyone and everyone at their table. They taught me—not by what they said, but by the way they lived their lives—that it was wrong to exclude people because they were different. Many children are less fortunate than I was. They grow up in a world of "us" versus "them," in homes where conversation is casually peppered with racist innuendo and the air is darkened by laments that "those people" are responsible for life's ills. Racism and discrimination are carried forward, generation by generation.

I never saw the man who owned the City Café with a wife, never met his children in my school. Maybe he didn't have a family. Maybe he never managed the money for the head tax. Or maybe he just gave up and stopped trying. In my young mind, I envisioned hundreds of Chinese men running their restaurants, laundries, or shops in small towns all across the country. I thought about how no one bothered with them, how no one cared. Long, barren lives in a strange land, without family, without love. Alone. Easy to imagine. Hard to live.

·····························

CHAPTER FIVE

Home on the Ranch

Life on the ranch was enthralling and rich. But it was also tough, I discovered. The initial euphoria of my first summer there faded as the autumn winds changed to winter blasts and the snow rose around our little house. Barely twelve, I found my world slowly closing in.

"What was it like to live without plumbing and electricity?" people often ask.

"Difficult," I say. And then I remind myself that people have lived without these things for most of human history.

As toddlers, we didn't puddle in the bath every night, nor did we shower every morning. My mother gave each of us a daily sponge bath from a basin in the kitchen sink. We washed our hands and faces before each meal and usually after. If our feet got dirty from playing in the dust, we washed them. On Saturday night, we were totally immersed in a round tub of galvanized steel filled with water heated in the reservoir of the wood-burning cookstove. On Sunday, we appeared in church, shoes polished, faces gleaming, hair shining.

In the first summer, I hadn't cared about plumbing or power. There were horses to ride and mountains to climb. I roamed the hills, learning the names of the wildflowers that painted them pink and purple and creamy white. For a while, I even forgot about the library and my books. In those glorious first months on the ranch, I didn't think much about what would happen when summer drew to a close.

And then, September was suddenly upon us. "What will we do for school?" I asked my parents, a panicked feeling in the pit of my stomach. I loved school, and preparing for the first day of class had always been an exciting time—new teachers, new friends, new books. Now the long winter months loomed like a void.

"You'll take correspondence," my parents said. They added for good measure, "Lots of kids on remote ranches take correspondence."

Instead of going to school in town, Mom explained, we would learn by correspondence with teachers in the Department of Education in a far-off place called Edmonton. We would work every day. Once a week, we would bundle our work into a package and mail it to Edmonton. Then, later each week, we would pick up the previous week's corrected exercises at the Pincher Creek post office.

"It will be fine," Mom assured us. She noted that her cousin Dr. Berthold Figur was in charge of the entire provincial correspondence division and would personally make sure we got everything we needed. Her words comforted me. Maybe it would work out.

In mid-September, our packets arrived, one for me and one for each of my brothers (Judi was still too little for school). At the top of the pile was a letter from my new teacher. "Dear Beverley," it began.

"Welcome to Correspondence School. I hope you will enjoy it and learn a lot."

I got to work immediately. I took out each book—math, social studies, reading, science—and laid it on the kitchen table, placing the relevant exercise book beside it. My eyes lit up at what I found buried in the bottom of my box: a library curriculum. "Just tell us what books you might like to read," my teacher wrote, "and we'll send them to you."

"I told you Berthold would look after us," said my mother, scanning the list avidly. "I'll read them when you're done."

"I think I'll ask them for George Sand," I said, running my finger down the list.

Mother frowned.

"She's a woman, Mom."

"With a name like George?"

"Yeah. Women can't use girls' names when they write. Has to be a man's name."

My mother looked dubious. "Lucy Maud Montgomery didn't have a problem." She, like me, had adored Anne Shirley as a girl and devoured every volume of her saga.

"The world is changing," I said with the condescension only a girl of twelve can muster. "In case you haven't noticed."

"If you say so." She paused, then whispered, "When I was your age, I dreamed of being a writer."

It had been a long time since I'd looked at my mother, really looked. She was just there, like all moms were, part of the furniture, as she had been since my earliest memories—black-haired, pretty, vivacious. Now my eyes widened at what I saw. She was only thirty-four, but her hair was streaked with white and her face was pale and hollow. There was a sallowness to her skin—she was always paying visits to the doctor for her anemia. The cousin she had played games with as a young girl was now a doctor running a significant chunk of the world from a big office in Edmonton, while she was here, wan with work, exhausted with kids, stuck in ill health and the prospect of an isolated winter. Would it someday be the same for me?

Each morning after the breakfast dishes were cleared, Len, Conrad, and I got our lessons out, spread them on the kitchen table, and got to work. We breezed through each day's lessons in a matter of hours. *Is that all there is to school?* I wondered.

When the first snows came, blocking the roads and making horseback riding impossible, the answer came—that was *not* all there was to school. School was about lessons and learning, sure, but it was also about games at recess, conclaves over lunch, gossip sessions with friends, and speculations on the love lives of teachers. It was about getting there and getting home, dressing up and dressing down, a hundred rituals that had given structure to my days and life. Without them, a sense of loneliness descended on me like the grey onset of a December blizzard.

I buried my growing anxiety in work. I might not have my friends, I thought, but I still had questions to consider and answers to formulate. I still had the comfort of numbers and words and ideas. I raced through my correspondence lessons with renewed passion. Every week, I sent two big brown envelopes to Edmonton, instead of the required one. And then, in early December, reality hit.

"You're on lesson twenty-nine," Mom said, frowning.

"Yeah? So what?"

"There are only thirty-two lessons. You'll be done by Christmas."

"So?"

"So what will you do then?"

I stared at her. I had no answer.

The winter deepened. With each snowfall, the whiteness outside mounted until it reached beyond the sills of the windows and threatened to bury the house in darkness. My father dug paths, deep like tunnels, from the front door to the bunkhouses, where the hired men stayed, and the other outbuildings. Every few hours, I scurried through chasms to the outhouse, walls of white on every side. There was beauty: the sun on the white expanse of the meadow and the crags of the mountains beyond still took my breath away. But the days grew short and darkness came quickly, smothering us in desolation.

Christmas had always been a time of joy and excitement for me: concerts, visits, gifts, special food, and, above all, family around us like an embrace—Grandpa Kruschell, Uncle Len, Aunt Doreen, and a dozen others who found their way to our hearth each year. That year, though, no one came—the snow was too deep and the roads too precarious for any sane visitor to risk.

"We need a tree," I said to Mom five days before Christmas.

"Of course. There are a thousand trees around. We'll go out and cut one," she replied, but without enthusiasm. An irrational fear clutched at me: perhaps we would not have Christmas at all this year.

We did have Christmas, and we did have a tree. Gifts appeared beneath it and a sumptuous feast was mounted on the appointed day. We sang carols, and little Judi's eyes shone at the wonder of tinsel and toys. My spirits briefly lifted.

But as winter progressed, a gnawing angst returned. I didn't have a word for it then, but now I do: isolation. My parents, my siblings, and me, confined in a small house, hour after hour, day after day, week after week. No place to play, no place to go. No friends. No teachers. After each storm, my father and one of the hired men would clear the road and we would drive into town, but no school bus braved the winding paths to our remote ranch. We were alone, cut off from the world outside.

What was happening to me was bigger than isolation, more complicated than loneliness. I felt myself growing inward and away, watching events from a distance even as I participated in them. Was I angry, afraid? Now I know I must have been. But then, even as I felt these things, I buried them inside me. My mind, perhaps fed on too many books, began to question the religious beliefs I had once taken as sacred. More guilt, burying my spirit as surely as the heavy banks of snow were burying our house. I hated the thoughts I had and hated myself for having them. I shared none of this with anyone.

A place in John Bunyan's *Pilgrim's Progress*, the 1678 allegory about a Christian's journey, haunted me: the Slough of Despond. The figure of the pilgrim in my illustrated version—a frail man with a huge load on his back as he struggled to stand upright in the marshes that dragged him down—dominated my darkening dreams. Like Bunyan's pilgrim, I could not rid myself of my load, or navigate the morass I had fallen into; unlike his pilgrim, I had no assurance I would make my way through the slough to firmer ground on the other side.

Some days were good, however. So long as the daylight crept over the snowbanks through the top of the windows, I kept busy. I learned to bake cakes and cookies. On a whim, I taught myself to knit and produced heavy sweaters of passing quality for my father and my little sister.

On good days, when a chinook arrived and melted the snow on the high slopes, I would saddle a horse and go for a ride, racing down the meadow and pulling up on a high hill to view the snow-capped mountains. For that hour or two, I felt free and dared to dream of a different world. Then I would turn back, unsaddle the horse, and return to the log house whose walls crushed in on me.

On good days, I read books. Now that I had finished grade seven and no longer had access to the correspondence school library, I was back to my old reading routine. Saturday was shopping day, and we all went into town. I would make my way up the wooden stairs to the Pincher Creek Municipal Library to take out my weekly allotment of two books.

Some days were bad. I did my chores but little more. I vacillated between lashing out at my mother and agonizing over minor sins. I hated the hired men, who sometimes looked at my budding body in ways I did not like.

Every evening, my father lit the gas lamp and placed it in the middle of the kitchen table. It rested like an anchor in the centre of the room. We gathered around it, my father sharpening his chainsaw, my mother crocheting a cushion cover, me immersed in my library selection of the week. For a few hours, my books took me to strange and distant worlds. I would sit at the table and imbibe the stories, oblivious to my sparring brothers, my toddling sister, the walls of rude wood and snow that pressed down on me.

At ten o'clock—sometimes earlier—Dad would announce that he was turning the light out. I would shut my book and reluctantly drag myself back to the real world. If Dad wasn't too tired, he would read a chapter from the Bible and say a prayer. I would squeeze my eyes shut and pretend to go along, not admitting the doubts that gnawed at me. Darkness would descend, the inky hollow of blackness. No streetlights, no passing cars. Alone on my narrow bed, I struggled to keep the demons at bay. For demons there were. My Slough of Despond had deepened into grim thoughts that tore at my mind. Where they came from or why they beset me, I did not know. Just that they came.

Like all country folk, we had guns—long rifles, loaded and stashed in a convenient corner against the possibility of a marauding bear. Even in the dark, I knew exactly where they were and exactly what to do. What I wanted to do. What I could do. Slip across the room while my parents slept. Take the .30-03 from the corner. Put the barrel in my mouth. Pull the trigger.

I never crossed the room, never put the barrel in my mouth or pulled the trigger. Deep down, I wanted to live. While those thoughts plagued me, telling me I must end it, I lay rigid, gripping the bed rails to restrain myself. At some point, exhausted, I would fall asleep, only to wake in the early morning hours knowing that tonight, again, it would be the same. Or maybe not. Maybe this time, I would give in. Repeating these acts of will was the hardest thing I have ever done.

Eventually, the days grew longer; the snow began to melt. Gradually the dark thoughts grew weaker, until they ceased to come at all. I woke up one morning and realized I had passed through my time of trial and found firmer ground on the other side. Still, I was not about to tempt fate.

"In the fall, I will go to school," I told Mom.

It was not a request. It was a statement. Neither she nor my father argued. Somehow they sensed the utter seriousness of my purpose.

Decades later, as a young lawyer, I was retained by an Indigenous family grieving the loss of their teenage child to suicide. The boy had been taken into police custody on a minor offence. In the morning, he was found dead, hanging from a noose of neatly knotted shoelaces. The jailers claimed they had no idea he was suicidal, and hence had not taken the boy's laces away from him. I wondered what had been in the young man's mind, what thoughts had tormented him. His road had been more difficult than mine—I hadn't suffered the evils of intergenerational trauma or discrimination—but I thought about how easy it is to miss the signs of anguish in a young person.

These days, the suicide of an Indigenous youth might provoke a news story, or perhaps an inquiry. But not then. For the first of many times in my legal life, I was overcome by a sense of impotent, hopeless frustration. I could not bring the boy back. Nor could I obtain redress for his lost life.

I understood. I had been there. Almost.

I WENT BACK TO school in Pincher Creek for grade eight with high hopes, but left in a miasma of restless discontent. To stay in school, I had to find somewhere to board during the week. For ten months,

I shuttled through a series of indifferent homes until I landed in the kindly house of Aunt Tina and Uncle Fred, my father's brother. They had their own children, but their welcome was unquestioning.

"We have a room upstairs for you," said Aunt Tina.

"A change is as good as a rest," Uncle Fred assured me.

I understood the meaning of family—people who take you in, no questions asked.

The constant moving had crushed any notion I had that people might like me, or that I was good at anything. The girl I'd thought was my best friend left me for a daintier, prettier girl who took pleasure in abusing and insulting me. I took a stab at accordion lessons—my mother played the accordion and lent me hers—but the teacher deemed my talent limited and ended them. I tried to play basketball, but spent most of the games on the bench. I felt clumsy and uncomfortable in my body. There was no place for a girl like me in the world.

Despite my insecurities, the demons that had plagued me at night at the ranch had retreated. I felt strong. Whatever happened, I could—I would—handle it. Life could be tough, but whatever it brought, I would get through it.

I slid through the school year in a haze of academic indifference. Having longed achingly the year before for real school, I now convinced myself that correspondence and books had already taught me everything the teachers were trying to convey. Apart from a brief passion for Napoleon and his lightning conquest of Europe, I have no recollection of what I learned in grade eight. And so it didn't come as a surprise to hear that my teachers entertained a low opinion of my future prospects.

Our school had no counsellor and no career guidance program. But all grade eight students were given a series of tests designed to suss out what they might be good at. When the test results came back, the homeroom teacher took me aside to explain them and offer advice. I perched myself on the edge of a chair she had placed beside her desk. She pulled a sheet from the pile before her and studied it, then peered at me over her half-moon glasses.

"I don't know what to tell you," she said.

I sat silent.

"Well," the teacher said, holding my test results under her right palm, "you have an extremely high reading-retention score. But that won't do you much good." She paused. "As a girl, you know."

She ran her finger down the lines of print. "You also have the lowest alertness score I've ever seen." She shook her head in a flurry of tight grey curls, searching for a piece of useful advice. "One thing I can tell you: you must never be a waitress or a telephone operator."

She pushed my paper aside and pulled the next one from the pile. "That is all. Please ask Jimmy to come up."

At the end of the school year, I packed up my few books and went home for the summer. The wildflowers that graced the hills were lovely as never before, and my parents wanted to build a new house on a west-facing slope—a house with plumbing and electricity. Since no one else seemed to be doing it, I designed the house, drawing the lines for the walls and windows on graph paper. I sketched out a soaring open-beamed ceiling over picture windows that would look over the meadow to the mountains. I had no idea what I was doing, but that didn't stop me.

My father looked at it, nodded, and said, "We'll build it."

"Okay!" I said, and I felt the inkling of a fresh start.

CHAPTER SIX

Lady Jane Grey

IN THE FALL OF 1957, my anticipation of the start of a school year was heightened. This would be my first year of high school—Matthew Halton High School, a sprawling new edifice named for the CBC radio journalist who had grown up in Pincher Creek and gone on to international renown reporting on the Second World War. The subjects in high school would be more difficult, and thus more interesting. And it was serious. At the end of the year, every grade nine student was required to sit departmental exams. No fudging, no sliding through on teachers' good graces. Someone in a distant city would mark the exams that would determine whether I passed or sank into oblivion.

This time, where I would live was not in doubt. I would board at the Dorm—a residence that the Pincher Creek School Board operated to house students like me whose families lived on ranches or farms too remote for school bus service. My brothers would continue with correspondence lessons at home until they, too, reached grade nine.

The Dorm sat like an aging dowager on a hillside three blocks west of the school. The good bones she prided herself on in her youth had grown fragile, and her once-graceful façade was sagging. Still, a remnant of her former elegance remained. A glass vestibule led to a central hall that ran the length of the house to the kitchen. To the right lay the former dining room and the salon, now fused into a long-tabled dining hall for the students. To the left were the bedroom and sitting room of the matron—a formidable woman named Mrs. Hegel whose tiny husband sat behind the sitting room door and painted Western scenes of mountain goats and horses while his wife took control (sort of) of thirty-six unruly teenagers.

A wide staircase led to the second floor, where a suite of bedrooms housed the twenty-odd girls. The back staircase led to the boys' bedrooms on the attic floor. The passage connecting the girls' floor to the boys' was boarded up—reminding us each time we passed that the other sex was on the opposite side, so near yet infinitely far.

The Dorm was self-sustaining. Under the eagle eye of Mrs. Hegel, we residents did the cleaning and kitchen prep work. Each week brought a new assigned task and a time for doing it. Sweeping the dining room, setting the long table, serving and clearing the food—these were the girls' tasks. The boys got the heavier jobs, like peeling buckets of potatoes each morning, doing the dishes, polishing the windows, and mopping the kitchen floor. We grumbled at the work and called Mrs. Hegel names behind her back, but we never really minded. I marvelled at what a handful of rebellious teenagers could accomplish when efficiently organized and instructed. The power of working together: a lesson I never forgot.

I had never been in a house so large, and yet never had I felt more constrained. I shared a large bunk-lined bedroom with five other girls. Competition for everything—lower bunks, first crack at the sink, first dibs on the toilet—was fierce. A small but aggressive girl appointed herself den leader. In need of someone to humiliate, she chose me. Shy and timid, I bore her assaults and insults in miserable silence. My self-confidence, already battered, ebbed even lower. Bullying, we call it today. Back then, I couldn't find the word.

On weekends at home, the aggression I had suppressed all week boiled up, and I railed against my mother. I had a sharp tongue and an innate feel for sarcasm. My mother, bewildered, suffered. My father remonstrated: "Don't be so hard on Mom. This needs to stop." He was right, and I decided to mend my ways.

Why did I fall into berating my mother, even though I loved her dearly and knew she loved me? Because, steeped in religious tropes, she continually admonished me not to wear lipstick and told me that playing cards and dancing were the road to hell? Because she harped that I should marry a "good Christian boy"? Because she nagged me about the dangers of becoming fat and told me to diet? Because I abhorred how she had ceded her personal independence and dreams to the edict that wives must submit to their husbands? Because I shrank from her conformity and innocent credulity? Because I was a confused, angry, and rebellious teenager? All of the above.

By contemporary standards, my rebellions were minor. I didn't wear lipstick or play cards. And if some sweaty-handed youth coaxed me to the dance floor at a school event—a rare occurrence—I shuffled about guiltily, too scared to enjoy myself. I worked at home on weekends, and I applied myself diligently to my schoolwork, coming through the dreaded grade nine departmental exams with good grades. I sang in the school choir and starred in its plays and concerts. I went to church on Sundays and yearned for the religious certainty of my parents. The Bible said many are called but few are chosen. I was one of those not chosen, and was condemned, by disposition or fate or maybe God, to wonder why.

From the outside, I was the model adolescent. Inside, I was a mess of mixed emotions. Like most teens, I struggled to fit in, to belong, to slide into the adult world so seamlessly that no one would notice the transition. Yet the child inside was still struggling to catch up. I should have figured this out, but I had become good at hiding my own truths.

IN MY TWELFTH YEAR of school, the board extended its bus runs westward, and our ranch was at last within range of the school. My final year was a good one. Perhaps my teachers had grown a lot smarter over the summer. Or perhaps I had. Mr. Semenoff, the math teacher (and father to Gordon, the future theoretical physicist). Mr. Daley, a former engineer turned science teacher. Mrs. Boyden, who lived in a farmhouse in the valley and understood books and Shakespeare's plays. Our fearsome principal, Cy Richards, who I realized only years later was mortal. Suddenly, what they were saying made sense. Suddenly, I was having interesting after-school conversations with them. Suddenly, I was enjoying French and history and English literature. Suddenly, chemistry and biology and understanding the underpinnings of the world seemed essential endeavours. I read, as I had from childhood, everything and anything I could find in the library. I tried my hand at poetry. I found the beginnings of some small sense of competence.

Emerging from my chrysalis of middle-school misery, I tentatively reached out and made friends. Girlfriends to pal around with and visit on the weekends. I grew particularly close to Diana Jack (now Reid). A farm girl like me, she preferred helping her dad in the fields to pottering in the kitchen. Red-haired and freckled, she was a gifted musician who played the piano for all the student musical events. Our music teacher, Mrs. Farrow, who imagined her students more capable than they were, would hand Diana the score for

Handel's "Hallelujah" chorus or *The Pirates of Penzance* and expect her to master it overnight. In Diana's case, Mrs. Farrow's confidence was not misplaced—it took her no longer than a week to master even the most complex score.

Diana and I were both sensible girls. While we didn't mind boys—Diana already had a steady boyfriend, and romance was blossoming for me with a good Christian boy who was studying to be a teacher and came down to the ranch on weekends—we weren't given to giggling about the opposite sex or having deep discussions about different shades of lipstick. After gaining her credentials as a teacher, Diana married and remained on the farm. My path took me a different direction. But I still feel a sense of closeness when I think of her, my first best friend.

I made another good friend, too—Peter Yellow Horn. In my last year of school, students from the nearby Piikani reserve came to Matthew Halton High for the first time. Until then, Indigenous kids had received what little education they got from residential schools or day schools on the reserve, though I was unaware of this at the time.

I walked into class on the first day, looked across the aisle, and saw Peter—tall and broad-shouldered, with a wide pockmarked face, dark eyes, and a craggy nose—and his friend George Crowshoe. I had never had an Indigenous classmate. Now, suddenly, I had two.

"Hi," I said awkwardly.

"Hello," Peter replied gravely.

Little did I know then, but that first hello was the start of friendship. Although still a teenager, Peter possessed great dignity. He was deep and intellectual and loved irony. We talked about many things—school, family, and, of course, our futures. In his presence, I grew calm. Diana and I gravitated to him.

"I'm going to be a lawyer," Peter told me one day. He didn't need to say why. By then, I knew that he was devoted to his people and their future. That would be his life. As a lawyer, he would be able to help them achieve a better future.

Peter and George were embraced by the entire class. They got good grades. Their watercolours evoking the prairie where they grew up made my attempts look puerile. They excelled at basketball, *the* school sport in southern Alberta. Peter even used to claim, only half-jokingly, that he planned to set foot on Mars after he became a lawyer. They made our class and our school richer and better. *Where have they been all this time?* I wondered.

THE WARM WEATHER CAME, and with it, the push for our end-of-year, province-wide departmental exams. As in years past, it came down to just me and my exam paper; my work throughout the year, good or bad, counted for nothing. Whether I went to university or got a scholarship—in a word, everything—depended on the marks I made in my booklet during the three-hour exam period.

Mr. Daley, my science teacher, who knew a little history, looked at my frail form and big eyes one day as I pored over my chemistry tables. "Lady Jane Grey," he murmured.

I looked up Lady Jane in the *Encyclopedia Britannica*. Shy, virtuous. Queen of England and Ireland for nine days in 1553, only to be deposed—and subsequently beheaded—by Mary Tudor. A flower that briefly bloomed before it died and was forgotten. I wanted to ask my teacher why he had called me that. I decided not to.

Instead, I studied, I memorized. I drilled myself endlessly with sample exams from previous years. I barely cared when I wasn't chosen to be the class valedictorian—that honour went to another girl who, in the teachers' eyes, shone more brightly than I. All I cared about was making the grades I needed to get to university.

I wrote a poem for the yearbook of the graduating class of 1961 called "Call of the Westwind." I longed to write something true and profound, like T.S. Eliot. I wasn't very proud of the result, yet the poem spoke to my love of the land where I was raised and a nascent hope for the future:

> *I can hear the west wind sighing.*
> *O're the broad plain swiftly flying.*
> *Proud and free;*
> *O're the sleeping plain she passes,*
> *Stirs to life the slumbering grasses,*
> *Beckons me.*

Peter also wrote a poem for the yearbook—a poem of yearning and despair and hope. The penultimate line of his poem reveals the destiny he sought, for his people and himself: "For it is the Special Will of the Almighty: The Indian will roam again with nature."

A FEW WEEKS LATER, I stood in the little Pincher Creek post office, opening an envelope from the Alberta Department of Education with trembling hands. I stared at the numbers on the paper. There they were, higher than I had dared dream—stellar marks in chemistry and biology, followed closely by social studies, English, French, and math. Mom and Dad had always told me I would come out on top, and this piece of paper proved they were right. I was the best student in our class, or so the results of the departmental exams revealed.

Then the words of my grade eight teacher echoed, darkening my day: "You have an extremely high reading-retention score, but that won't do you much good. As a girl, you know."

I folded the paper and pondered my new problem. What would I do with it?

···

CHAPTER SEVEN

Into the World

W HEN I WAS FINISHING high school in the late 1950s, the world presented girls with five career options: teacher, nurse, secretary, telephone operator, and waitress. Correction—six options, if you included getting married and becoming a housewife. The last did not tempt me, even if it had been available, which it wasn't. Options four and five had been ruled out by my grade eight teacher; due to my abysmal alertness score, I knew I could never succeed as a nurse or a secretary. Maybe a teacher, but for some reason unknown to me, the tests did not recommend that, either. Uncertain, I plunged into the summer.

To make up for choosing a different class valedictorian, my teachers had put my name in for a Canada Council Award trip to the newly established Stratford Shakespearean Festival in Ontario.

Thirty or so graduating high school students interested in the arts from all across Canada would spend a week there attending plays and learning about the theatre.

To be honest, I had never thought much about the Canada that lay beyond Alberta's borders. I had memorized the basic facts in my social studies textbook—Canada was a country founded in 1867; it had ten provinces and two territories; John G. Diefenbaker was then prime minister; the St. Lawrence Seaway, being built far to the east, would transform the country—but they were meaningless abstractions I needed to learn to get through school. Mr. Richards's lectures on how the country ran seemed slightly more pertinent. "Three branches of governance," he intoned as he stood at the blackboard, "legislative, executive, and judicial. Judges have to be independent and impartial," he added. "That's why they have good salaries and can't be removed by politicians."

But apart from a smattering of historical facts and the rudiments of the country's constitutional set-up, I understood little about Canada except that it occasioned my father's rants about Ottawa always giving the West the short end of the stick. The East had always been a remote frontier to me. Now I would venture out into this strange and apparently hostile land and see it for myself.

Excitement overcame apprehension as the departure date approached. Alberta's allotment of deserving students mostly went to big-city schools with sophisticated arts programs. I was clearly the token country bumpkin. But that didn't prevent me from marvelling at my good fortune. Staring at the bus ticket to Calgary and the train tickets to Toronto and on to Stratford, I felt my heart pick up pace. I would travel three-quarters of the way across the continent. I would see the big city of Toronto. I would sit in the new Stratford theatre, with its elegant winged roof and glass porticoes, and watch the country's best actors interpreting the world's best plays. I said goodbye to my parents and a new baby brother—Ronald, a child of serene sweetness who entered our world on June 24, 1961—and set off in a mood of high anticipation.

The experience did not disappoint. I remember the endless stretch of the prairies—vaster than I could have imagined—the venerable stone buildings of Winnipeg and downtown Toronto, the tranquil beauty of the River Avon and its grassy banks, the exhilaration of the dramas in the playhouse.

The experience was also humbling. Everyone around me knew more than I did. My fellow students from across the country had acted in the Bard's plays. They knew the important lines by heart. Some had designed theatre sets; others had produced plays or made costumes or danced ballets. I, on the other hand, had briefly studied *The Tempest*. That was it. Nothing else. I was not merely playing the part of the token country student—I *was* the country student. The hesitant neophyte from a small town no one had heard of. I sank into the background as conversations I did not comprehend whirled above my head, declaiming this set or praising that bit of elocution.

The trip back to Pincher Creek was longer than the trip away, and I arrived home deflated, certain that I could never catch up with my sophisticated city cousins.

"How was it?" Mom asked as she drove me back to the ranch from the King Eddy Hotel, where the bus had dropped me. Her face looked sallower than it had three weeks before. My father's latest business venture—the one he was convinced would make him rich—was failing.

I thought about my mother's question and shook my head. How could I explain my sense of inadequacy? How, in the face of her hope, could I voice my fears and frustrations? And then, a childhood memory gave me words.

"Remember how you used to talk about your family's trip to California when you were ten? How amazed you were? How beautiful the flowers were, how tall the trees? How interesting and strange it all seemed to you, when you'd never been beyond Compeer?"

She nodded, a far-off look in her eye.

"It was like that," I said. "Very new, very different, very wonderful—as in full of wonder."

"And?"

"And I realized I don't know anything."

She downshifted to take a corner. I caught a brief smile on her face.

"I didn't know anything, either," she said at last.

As we followed the meandering road west to the ranch, I pondered my mother's words. The familiar scenes of my childhood once again unfolded before me—the waving prairie grass, the forest-clad foothills, the Rocky Mountains in all their slumbering glory. I would always hold this place, which had nurtured and formed me, deep in my heart. But now I knew these scenes would not be enough. The time had come to move on. The world was broad. Before me lay other landscapes, worlds I must explore.

···

CHAPTER EIGHT

Follow Your Bliss

THE SUMMER DREW ON. I took a job cooking for my father in his logging camp in the Porcupine Hills—hard, unrelenting work. But I didn't mind. Since childhood, my parents had drilled my brothers and me on the importance of "learning how to work." Back at home, the family was doting on my new little brother, Ron.

In the closing weeks of August, my future began to firm up. I had applied for admission to the University of Alberta in Edmonton. A missive from the post office finally told me I had been accepted. Subsequent letters told me that I had won a series of scholarships—an Alberta Hotelman's Scholarship and a Queen Elizabeth Scholarship—that ensured my immediate financial future. Mom's dreams of a university education for herself overcame her apprehension about the strange new world I was about to enter. Dad, sparing a moment from his business worries to listen to my plans, gave me a nod, which I took as his tacit blessing.

Excitement mounting, I purchased a little trunk and, one by one, laid my meagre possessions inside it. A couple of skirts, homemade. A couple of second-grade sweaters. One dress. Pyjamas, underwear, shampoo, deodorant, and a vial of Evening in Paris perfume. And the obligatory King James Bible.

"A chapter a day," Mom said, as we made our farewells in the Co-op parking lot, where I'd arranged a ride with three other students. Dad, as usual, was too busy to come. The west wind swirled the dust around our legs and into our hair. "And don't forget to go to church every Sunday."

"Sure," I said, desperate to shut down the stream of advice. I threw my luggage in the trunk of the guy's beater, a car that wouldn't have passed inspection had there been such a thing in those days. The Greyhound bus would have been safer, but it cost more. The boy who was driving the car had said I could come for ten dollars, but one bag was the limit.

I quickly kissed my mother goodbye before she could share with my fellow travellers her instructions to wash my hair once a week and look for a replacement Christian boyfriend for the one who had dumped me when I returned from Stratford two months earlier.

"Write every week," Mom hurled after me as I dived into the back seat. The boy driving looked at her, shook his head, and slammed the door, none too soon for me.

The journey was long. Two hundred and thirty miles north to Calgary. Two hundred more to Edmonton, the capital city of Alberta, population 261,000, plus 10,000 students who flocked to study there every September. With bags in the trunk and hanging off the roof, we followed the road signs because none of us had been this far north before. Correction: I had been to Edmonton when I was five to attend my aunt Doreen's wedding, but that didn't count for much when it came to navigation.

In the early evening, we reached our destination. After a long traverse of south Edmonton strip malls, we suddenly happened upon the university campus, an oasis of tree-lined streets and ivy-clad buildings. I had left the wind-parched plains of southwestern Alberta and arrived at the valley of the Saskatchewan River, lush with green turning gold. Green and gold, the colours of my new home, the colours of the University of Alberta.

I can't remember if I ate that night. All I recall is stepping out of the rickety car at a house whose address I clutched in my hand, and taking a deep breath. The chilly air was redolent with new scents and uncertain vibrations. Dragging my trunk behind me, I walked to the door, banged the knocker, and waited for what would happen next.

EIGHTEEN IS THE CRUELLEST age. One day, you're taking the world at a tilt. The next day, you're mired in a confused mix of anxiety and swirling hormones. In my first months at university, I was still a child most days. I dithered about everything.

I dithered about where to live. I had lined up a great place, only to waffle inexplicably and watch while another girl picked it out from under me. The landlady, feeling sorry for me, referred me to a nearby house owned by Mr. and Mrs. Bielenstein, Baltic Germans who had fled Estonia during the war and improbably ended up in this remote northern city. Mrs. Bielenstein surveyed my shabby clothing from beneath arched aristocratic brows and advised me that all her rooms were taken. Seeing my expression fall—my face has always been an open book—she conceded that she could show me a room that was too small for habitation. It was a former servant's quarters off the kitchen.

"Sixty dollars a month, room and board," Mrs. Bielenstein said.

"I'll take it," I said, and hauled my trunk through the door.

I was lucky. Mrs. Bielenstein was a formidable multitasker, doing stints of private nursing by night and managing the household—

herself, her husband, two grown children, and five boarders—by day. Breakfast and lunch we foraged for ourselves, but each night we gathered around the kitchen table for the dinner she had prepared. My fellow boarders were an eclectic mix—a farm boy from the north studying to be a teacher, a thin Brit doing his master's in geography, a German refugee who loved all things agricultural, and Gerhard, a handsome blond Baltic German engineer who was generous and treated me more like a younger sister than a stranger. The five of us shared meals and experiences and became friends.

I dithered about what to study. I could, despite my lack of alertness, try to be a schoolteacher. It was a practical goal, with a guaranteed job and salary at the end of three years. Schoolteachers did important work. It wasn't a bad life. All the rational arguments pointed in its favour. Not to mention the admonitions of my parents and every other adult who had opined on my future.

I was in the hall to sign up for the faculty of education when I pictured myself ten years on, standing where Mrs. Boyden and Mr. Semenoff had stood, trying to instil a passion for Shakespeare or algebra in thirty kids who'd rather be putting on makeup or shooting balls at the pool hall. Necessary? Yes. Rewarding? Maybe. Hard slogging? Definitely.

Maybe someday, an inner voice kept saying. Someday, but not yet.

"I don't know anything," I had told my mother. Now, as I fretted about what career to choose, my words came back to me. Before I made a choice, I needed to learn more about the world. More about the writers and thinkers and musicians and scientists who had left us the best of their wisdom. I left the lineup for education and crossed to the arts building.

Against all the odds and a great deal of contrary advice, I had decided to follow instinct rather than practical reason. Only later, when I encountered Joseph Campbell's work, did I understand why I did it. "We must be willing to get rid of the life we've planned, so as to have the life that is waiting for us," he wrote. "Follow your bliss." I followed my bliss and chose the wide-open world of arts.

My mother was stricken. "What will you do with a BA?" she asked in each weekly letter. I had no answer. But I had a conviction that I needed to explore the wide universe of ideas, and I had just enough scholarship money in the bank, touch wood, to get me through to spring. That was enough.

I enrolled in courses in modern languages (a little French and German wouldn't hurt), English, history, philosophy, and geography (this last one on the urging of my Brit co-boarder). The university added mandatory physical education. I dreaded the shouts of the daunting instructor and detested getting wet, but I learned to stay afloat in a lake, a useful skill at any stage in life.

I was diligent, never missing a class. I was studious, labouring six evenings a week and Sunday afternoons at the small desk at the end of my narrow bed to complete this essay or that assignment. And I was socially awkward, a country girl flailing in a sea of urbane sophisticates. No one took notice of me. No one particularly liked me, but no one particularly hated me. I was, in the true sense of the word, unattractive—incapable of attracting for good or bad, a solitary soul lost in a whirling social cosmos. In the dark of the night, I yearned for home, for familiar friends, for Mom. Yet I didn't allow myself to even think about going back. Somehow, I would muddle through. I would find my way, if not that elusive thing called destiny.

Music came to my rescue, as it would throughout my life. I tried out for the university's mixed chorus and qualified, despite my inability to read a score. Evidently I possessed something the esteemed director, Trevor Eaton, needed—an alto voice of no particular beauty, but strong and on key. Twice-weekly evening practices, concerts, and a tour of central Alberta were on the autumn agenda. I dipped into my fast-depleting scholarship money for the mandatory grey skirt and blue blazer, regretting my choices even as I handed over the precious bills. Once the money was gone, I would be sunk. My parents were mired in one of their perennial bad patches, with more debts than money. There would be no rescue of a child in frivolous pursuit of a worthless BA.

A frivolous pursuit that wasn't going well. In fact, it was going badly. Despite my increasingly frantic efforts, I couldn't make sense of anything, much less put it on paper. At the rate I was going, I would fail my courses or—in what amounted to the same thing—fail to get the scholarship money I needed to continue at university. I thought longingly of the faculty of education. By now, I would have been deep into learning how to run a classroom and on the road to a respected career. Instead, my feckless vanity had left me uselessly struggling with Chaucer and first-year German. I had made the wrong choice, and it was too late to go back. My father had always told me that university was overrated. Now I was about to prove him right.

A surge of fear hardened into determination. I would not drop out in ignominy. Desperately, I sought a respectable exit. I had emerged from high school with the unsubstantiated notion that I might, just might, be able to write. Perhaps I could go to work for a newspaper, like Matthew Halton, the namesake of my high school, or Ernest Hemingway. Maybe—more realistically—I'd have to settle for making coffee at the student newspaper. Who cared? I'd have saved face and saved my life. So, confronted with imminent academic failure, I signed up for *The Gateway*.

The newsroom was a crowded place, I discovered. All the important desks—sports, campus politics, social revels—had long been scooped up by more enterprising and efficient would-be writers. Desperately, I searched for an unoccupied niche.

"I'll write reviews of music and films," I told the editor.

"Sure," he replied cynically.

Undiscouraged, I started going to movies and student concerts and sending the editor reviews. I knew a little about music, but all

I knew about film were the weekly offerings of the Fox Theatre on Main Street in Pincher Creek. I borrowed tomes from the library and steeped myself in the work of Sergei Eisenstein and Akira Kurosawa and Satyajit Ray. I told myself that as long as I knew a little more than the average student reader, I could pass for an expert.

My English professor was less easy to fool. Every Monday, first-year English students were required to submit a five-hundred-word essay on whatever work we happened to be studying. Mine were tortured and muddled, filled with long passages beside which my teacher would scratch comments like "Incomprehensible," "What are you trying to say?" and "Just a lot of big words."

I despaired. How could I, an untutored eighteen-year-old from a small Alberta town, say something new or meaningful about *The Faerie Queene* or *Paradise Lost*? More to the point, how could I master the art of saying anything coherently? Every Sunday afternoon, I struggled to produce five hundred words on works I could not have cared less about. Every Friday, I shrank at my mediocre grade. I could not write; I could not even think.

Philosophy—a required survey course I had approached with a mixture of resignation and angst—saved me. My teacher was a lank, erudite Oxford graduate named David Murray. As I was bundling my books after class one day, he strolled over and, running his hand through his blunt-cut yellow mane, fixed me with his blue eyes.

"Your piece on Plato's *Republic*," he said. "It was really quite good."

Dumbfounded, I released my books and watched them clunk to the desk. "Really?"

"Really," he intoned. He had grown up in Halifax but had acquired a decidedly English accent during his years at Oxford.

He went on to discuss some passage I could have used to buttress whatever point I had been trying to make, but all I kept hearing were the words "really quite good."

"Have you considered studying more philosophy?" he asked as I gathered up my books again.

I left the classroom on a cloud. A professor had actually singled me out. At last, a ray of hope that perhaps I could think. It was a moment I never forgot, and a lesson I came to treasure. I did not know then that I would be in David Murray's shoes someday—did not know how important it would be to look, really look, at the young person before me and see her not for what she was but for what she might become.

MY ENCOUNTER WITH MY philosophy professor marked a turning point in my first-year university struggles. Thereafter, I focused on thinking—not just pursuing this thought or that, but thinking things through. And I focused on writing—not to string together fancy words, but to communicate ideas clearly and succinctly. Bye-bye to fuzzy thinking. Every word, every clause must carry its weight as you drive home your conclusion. And by the way, it's not just about getting there. Right and wrong count; learn how to figure them out.

My marks improved, and I got the scholarships I needed to come back for a second year. In that year, I became the arts editor at *The Gateway*. It was enough to get me a summer job at a real newspaper, the *Edmonton Journal*. I was excited—my first real job, my first paycheque, and, unfortunately, my first encounter with gender discrimination in the workplace.

I watched as the guys from *The Gateway* who went with me to the *Journal* were directed to desks in the main newsroom to write on politics, while I was greeted by the women's editor and led to a separate room with the words "Women's Pages" stencilled on the glass door. Beverley Gietz—would-be philosopher, amateur film critic, budding social analyst—longed to write about crime, corruption, and the pursuits of the powerful. Instead, she was condemned to pen pieces on church suppers and craft fairs. It was not that I disliked cooking, fashion, or home decor—indeed, I came to take modest pleasure in crafting stories on such matters. What rankled was the automatic assumption that because I was a woman, I could not aspire to "more serious" subjects, like what to do with the oil royalties that were rapidly filling the province's coffers, or how to interpret the plans of a young lawyer named Peter Lougheed, who was poised to defeat the Social Credit Party that had ruled Alberta for as long as anyone could remember.

I made the most of my situation. I hunted for social angles at church bazaars and hinted at the broader implications of warnings that it was a Catholic mother's duty to encourage at least one of her sons to enter the priesthood. I wandered the alleys of the summer fair to find a tassel dancer and wrote a gritty story on the plight of erotic dancers on the itinerant circuit. The piece ended up on the front page of the women's section (complete with a photo of my subject twirling her tassel) when my indomitable editor went on holiday and a feisty stand-in temporarily took her place. I was quietly pleased—until the managing editor boomed into the office and, flinging down a copy of the offending section, yelled at the stand-in, "What's happening to the women's pages?!" As he turned to go back to his male domain, he sputtered "And you" in my direction. It was clear he could not find— or dared not utter—the words to describe what he thought of me. As he retreated, I heard him muttering obsessively, "And you, you."

I would not do a repeat stint at the *Edmonton Journal*. Still, I am eternally grateful for the summer I spent there. I learned a lot about writing. We were five in the women's section: the editor and three young female staffers, plus me. I watched them work, I studied their craft. "It's simple," the senior of the three—a university dropout— told me. "You've got thirty minutes until press time. Figure out your lead. Write down the facts in order of importance. No long paragraphs. Don't omit critical names, places, and details. Simple, straightforward, lively. Tie it up at the end. And remember, however mundane the subject, you are writing a story."

When I started back at university in the fall, I applied the same technique to my exams. You've got an hour to answer this question, I told myself. Get the lead. Set out the facts and ideas in order of importance. Tie them together into a coherent whole. Wrap it up. Above all, tell a story. It worked.

My summer at the *Journal* taught me that I could profit from negative experiences. It also taught me that life wasn't fair for women. While I had always known that life wasn't fair for married women, consigned as they were to homemaking and childrearing and the constraints of married life, I had naively supposed that things would be different for women in the working world. Now I knew that was false.

The world was divided into two realms—one of men and one of women. Women were occasionally allowed to venture into the realm of men, but only to the extent required to accomplish what the men wanted or needed. For better or worse, I was committed to making deeper inroads into the realm of men. The way ahead would not be easy.

That was how it was in the early 1960s.

AFTER FINISHING UP AT the *Edmonton Journal*, I made a brief trip south to the ranch to visit my family and regroup for my third year of university.

One afternoon, I encountered my high school classmate George Crowshoe on Main Street. We stopped and chatted. He was at college in Calgary.

"How's Peter?" I asked.

"He went to Calgary, too. Trying to get his French so he can go to university and get to law school."

"Great," I said. "Say hi and good luck."

George nodded.

The next summer, I met George on the street again. He was still studying and doing fine.

"How's Peter?" I asked once more.

George was silent. "Couldn't get his French," he said at last.

I went home with a heavy heart.

"I'm going to be a lawyer," Peter had told me back in grade twelve. Now I knew he would never realize that dream.

Life wasn't fair for women. It wasn't fair for Indigenous peoples, either. Peter spoke two perfectly good Canadian languages, English and Piikani. But because he couldn't master a third, French, he was not allowed to go to university. He was denied his chance to study, to become a lawyer. That was also how it was in the early 1960s.

As things turned out, Peter Yellow Horn wouldn't let the lack of letters after his name deter him. He went on to become chief and lead his people in a fight against the Oldman River Dam, north of Pincher Creek, which would flood the valley where the Piikani had wintered and wandered from time immemorial. The Supreme Court of Canada, in a case on which I sat, faulted the environmental processes that had preceded the building of the dam. But it was too late; the dam had already been built, and the valley was no more.

Chief Peter Yellow Horn, Otahkoiikakato'sii, a respected leader of his people, died on April 6, 2013, at the age of seventy-one. After a service at the Anglican chapel on the Piikani reserve, his body was taken to a hilltop and placed on a raft of poles. His spirit was set free, as he had written in his yearbook poem so many years before, to "roam again with nature."

CHAPTER NINE

Love, Actually

"'TIS BETTER TO HAVE loved and lost than never to have loved at all," Tennyson famously wrote.

Love at its best is magic and inexplicable and overwhelming and tragic. It makes you hope, dream, and suffer. But it is infinitely worth the journey. Of all human engagements, love is the deepest. If you have not loved, you have not truly lived.

From high school on, I had boyfriends, some more serious than others. But nothing prepared me for Rory—Roderick Archibald McLachlin. Rory became a presence that weaved in and out of my life for forty years, giving it colour and strength and heft.

I met him in passing in the summer before I headed off to university. He had taken a year off from his own studies at the University of Western Ontario to travel west and ended up at Pincher Creek working in the construction of a gas plant. He boarded with my aunt Tina (she had looked after me in grade eight), and she introduced him to my parents, which in turn led to him working occasionally on our ranch. I retain a fleeting memory of a young man with long hair falling over his face. We said hello and moved on.

As often happened with workers on our ranch, Rory became embedded in the family. When I returned from Edmonton for Christmas in 1961, with three months of university under my belt, I stopped by to say hello to Aunt Tina at her farm east of town. Rory was there, with less hair and more face. A handsome face, brooding blue eyes and a quick, ironic smile. We chatted about literature. He had Aunt Tina reading *Anna Karenina*, but he seemed more interested in Hemingway. We spent a half hour dissecting *For Whom the Bell Tolls*, then I said goodbye and left, not expecting to see him again.

When I boarded the bus to head back to my first-year studies after the Christmas break, Dad handed me a letter he had picked up for me at the post office. I tore it open as I settled into my window seat. It was from the assistant editor at *The Gateway*, Bentley—good-looking, older, a star political science student. And to my surprise, he had written a poem for me and enclosed a necklace he had bought during a trip to South America. I looped the chain around my neck as if it were made of diamonds, and a heady feeling of astonishment and joy swept over me. I had admired Bentley from afar; now, miraculously, he was declaring that for him, the feeling went deeper. We quickly became a couple. Every Saturday night, we met to discuss books. I was young and chaste and those were different days. Reading was as far as it went. I was content. I liked his company and enjoyed basking in the reflection of his modest campus glory.

In the spring, Bentley invited me to his parents' ranch near Cardston, and one morning, he presented me with a diamond ring.

"I had no idea," I said, truly shocked. "I'm not ready."

Bentley was disappointed but undaunted. "Think about it," he said.

He drove me home to our ranch. Afraid he would raise the subject of marriage with my parents, I waved goodbye at the steps without inviting him in.

"How's it going with Bentley?" Mom asked once I was settled.

I shrugged. "He seems to be getting serious." I told her about the diamond ring.

From the corner of the living room, I heard a deep, familiar voice. "Tell him I'll match him diamond for diamond."

It was Rory.

In the days that followed, Rory and I became friends. We revived our common love of literature. He had spent a year at a tony school in Switzerland and worked his way through most of the twentieth-century classics, but around the ranch he prided himself on wearing workboots and handling tough jobs. He was intelligent, funny, and charismatic. We had long conversations. We got to know each other better, got to like each other.

But we were young and had our own plans. Rory would be going home at the end of the summer, back to London, Ontario, to finish his degree, and I would be going to Edmonton to my second year at university. My parents, who still dreamed I would marry a good Christian boy, watched our budding friendship with apprehension.

One summer evening a few weeks later, Rory and I were discussing summer jobs in his room on the lower floor of our house. The door was open, the conversation innocent, but it was enough in those strict times to provoke my father's ire. His figure loomed at the threshold. "Leave now," he said.

After a tender goodbye and a delicate brush of lips, Rory drove away in his used Ford. I cried a little and wrote a self-indulgent poem. I did not expect to see him again.

Back in Edmonton in September, I resumed my life. I couldn't bring myself to accept Bentley's proposal, however. I liked him, admired him. He was brilliant, intellectual, and now the editor of *The Gateway*—a big man on campus. That he had fallen in love with little ol' me amazed me. But I was only nineteen, more child than adult. Life lay ahead, untested, unexplored. And I knew in my heart that I did not love him enough to marry him. I broke it off. He was devastated, and I felt guilty.

Months later, he came to see me. "I know what I did wrong," he said. "I pushed you too fast."

I didn't tell him that slower might not have worked, either.

Freed from Bentley's shadow, I struck out on my own and began my stint at the *Edmonton Journal* after my second-year exams.

On a warm evening that July, Rory surprised me with a brief visit. I shook my head as I invited him into the house where I was staying. "Where did you come from?"

"Just passing through," he said. "Let's go for a drive."

"How's Bentley?" he asked later, as we walked along the river.

"We broke up," I replied.

"Good," he said.

I looked at him, wondering what to make of the word, but he only smiled and changed the subject. And he was gone as quickly as he had arrived.

IN MY SECOND YEAR of studies, I joined the World University Service and applied for a scholarship to attend a study trip to Algeria the following summer. To my amazement, I won. New horizons opened up before me—travel, discovery. Except for my trip to Stratford, I had never ventured beyond Alberta. Now I would fly to Europe and on to Algeria, all expenses paid, with a month at the end to travel Europe on my own.

Forty students from across Canada met for a week-long

orientation at a resort in Chantecler, Quebec. We didn't know it then, but among us were a number of people who would go on to notable careers, including David Dodge, later deputy minister of finance and governor of the Bank of Canada, and Raymond Chrétien, later ambassador to the United States, France, and elsewhere. I loved the Québécois food and the Laurentian Mountains. These were not the craggy peaks of the Rockies I had grown up with; they were older, worn down with the weight of ages. But there was beauty in that, too, I learned.

From Montreal, we flew to Paris. Once more, I marvelled—the most beautiful city on earth, someone had told me. I could not disagree. Then it was the train to Marseille, where we boarded a small ship for Algiers. I stood in the bow with a new friend named Sheila, watching the gleaming white walls of the Kasbah grow ever larger as we approached the African coast. There is something about coming to a city from the sea that no airport runway can replicate.

My time in Algeria was a magical journey through great and battered beauty, though some parts felt dangerous. We found ourselves plunged into post-revolutionary chaos. The long struggle for independence from France had ended only two years before, and a new regime that styled itself Islamic Communist had taken over under a leader called Ahmed Ben Bella. The underpasses were scarred with bullet holes, and in the university residence where we were housed, the plumbing was out of order and the electricity sporadic. We travelled on to the high hills of Tlemcen, where wine was still being made, and from there south into the Sahara Desert and its oppressive heat. After visiting Berber villages in the mountains, we reached our final destination: the eastern port city of Annaba, called Bône by the French.

On the third night of our stay in Annaba, a loaded Egyptian munitions ship blew up in the harbour. Exploding shells strafed the nighttime skies and we ran outside. As I lay in a grassy ditch, looking up at the fire, my brief life flew before me. I thought of Mom and Dad, and of Len, Conrad, Judi, and Ron. I thought of Rory. *Perhaps this is how it ends*, I thought.

And then the moment passed and we were scrambling out of the ditch and back to the city to see if we could do anything to help. We were greeted by chaos. The explosion had toppled the clay walls of the Annaba casbah; house upon house had fallen in a wave of collapsing dominos. The harbour was aflame. Everywhere people were screaming. One of us dived into the golden waters to rescue a drowning victim. Those with medical experience assisted in operating rooms in a hospital crowded with bloody and dying people. Others, like me, stumbled from place to place, trying to find anything useful to do. Eventually we made our separate ways back to our lodging and regrouped in the morning. No one had slept.

Most of us had cameras and had been taking photos since the first day of our trip. The cameras were doing double duty the night of the explosion. It should not have surprised us when uniformed men with machine guns interrupted our lunch the next day and forced us all to expose our film. The photos we had taken were gone. Back in Canada, the papers carried a six-line story beneath the understated headline "Algerian Explosion Causes Injuries and Deaths." It ran only once and attracted no editorial comment. Just another sad story from a faraway country.

Once the formal leg of the trip was over, we spent the final three weeks in Europe, roaming as we pleased. With little money, I made my way with a few other students through Italy aboard second-class trains. I stayed in student hostels, eating only when it was absolutely necessary. I wired my parents for more money, but it never came. *Europe on Five Dollars a Day*, a book I read before leaving, helped, but five dollars was more than I figured I had. I borrowed money from my friend and lost ten pounds.

By a twist of fate and generosity, I found myself transported from the gritty world of student trekking to the glitzy world of the über-rich at the Salzburg Festival. My philosophy professor, David Murray—the same man who had rescued me from the morass of my first-year confusion—was attending the famed Austrian music festival, and he found extra tickets for me. He introduced me to the opera, and I emerged smitten with it. Herbert von Karajan, Elisabeth Schwartzkopf, Hermann Prey—the names of the day—performing in *Elektra*, *Der Rosenkavalier*, and Schubert's lieder.

I had come from a world of violence in Algeria to a world of magic in Austria, the beginning of a lifelong romance with the opera. The music, the sets, the ethereal sounds of the human voice at its best—all these seized me in Salzburg in 1964 and never let me go. They have coloured my life and pulled me through some bad spots. In my work as a lawyer and judge, I witnessed injustices, deplorable behaviour, and unconscionable abuse. Life seemed dark and ugly at times. Whenever it was too much to bear, I would retreat home and listen to Lois Marshall or Jon Vickers or Jonas Kaufmann to remind myself that human beings are capable of not only evil but also other-worldly beauty.

MY EUROPEAN SUMMER IDYLL ended abruptly. One day I was in Salzburg, lost in the magic of its mountains and its music. The next I was on a plane, flying home to reality.

Months earlier, I had written a note to Rory, who was back at university in London, telling him about my trip.

"Stop over in Toronto on your way back," he wrote back.

Why not? I thought.

My heart lurched when I saw him across the airport arrivals area in Toronto, and I realized that for me at least, this was no longer casual. Somehow along the way, I had become invested in him, scary and improbable as it might be. He looked older and wiser than he had the summer before. Pushing his blond hair off his forehead, he put his arm around me and led me out of the airport. My heart lurched again.

We took the highway southwest to London. Along the way, Rory entertained me with sardonic stories about his parents—his father, a renowned surgeon inclined to heavy-handed discipline; his mother, an anaesthetist, a figure of reassurance and comfort. He was witty; he was funny. I sensed he was trying to put me at ease, but it wasn't working.

My apprehension grew as we threaded through a maze of suburbs and entered a parkland of elegant houses set in beautiful gardens. He was a city boy. I was a country girl. His parents were successful professionals. My parents had never finished high school. So what if I could manage rudimentary French and had learned how to properly hold a fork? His world was not my world. As the car nosed up the long drive towards his house, I could see how it would be. His parents would greet me politely, then look at my shabby dress and discount shoes and turn away. When the two-day ordeal was over, Rory would put me on the plane for home. And that would be it.

The doctors McLachlin were polite and reserved. They didn't say, "Come on in—just call us Angus and Sheila," as people out West did. Instead, they murmured polite hellos in modulated tones. *Minimum politesse*, I thought, as they installed me in the big upstairs bedroom that belonged to their absent daughter, Christine. As though intuiting the paucity of my wardrobe, Rory's mother pointed to the drawers where Christine's clothes were stored.

"Feel free to borrow slacks and a sweater if you need them," she said.

I repressed a flush of embarrassment.

Rory was kind. He took me to his father's farm west of the city and introduced me to the Labrador retrievers he bred and trained for hunting. The last evening, we dined with newlywed friends—one of them was Greg Curnoe, who would go on to artistic renown. Once more, I found myself lost in a world I knew nothing about. Chatter about colours and collages swirled about my head, punctured randomly by panicked cries of "Almost done! Almost done!" from the bride who was hosting us. Lost in a haze of red wine, no one seemed to notice that the chicken never did appear. I sat primly on the edge of my chair, afraid to speak.

"My father approves," Rory told me at the airport departure gate a couple of days later. Then he grinned. "Actually, what he said was, 'At least this one doesn't have round heels.'"

"Round heels?" I asked uncomprehendingly. Was he talking about my dreadful white pumps?

He put his arm around me and kissed me lightly. "Don't worry. It's a compliment. Off you go. Don't want to miss your flight."

I mounted the aircraft steps in a haze of tears. No close embrace, no mention of a future meeting. Not even a "See you soon." So much for that dream.

The plane rumbled and shuddered, and just when I thought it would never take off, it pitched into the air. I took out my wallet and counted my money. Eight dollars and some pennies. With luck, enough to get me from the Calgary airport to the Greyhound bus depot and buy me a ticket home. No hotel, no food. Just a long night waiting for the morning bus to Pincher Creek. I should have asked Rory for a loan, but I was too proud.

The stewardess—the term "flight attendant" had yet to be invented—came around with soft drinks and a tray. I stared at the mess she set before me and reluctantly forced myself to pick up my fork. These were the last calories I would see for twenty-four hours.

When I had downed as much as I could, the stewardess returned to collect the tray. She bent down beside my aisle seat. She was pretty— a kind face ringed with brown curls beneath her regulation hat.

"Is someone meeting you in Calgary?" she asked.

I cringed. She had taken it all in—my tears, my desperate money counting.

I shook my head. "I'm going to the bus station. In the morning, I'll catch the Greyhound to Pincher Creek."

She looked up and caught the eye of the other stewardess. I knew what was going through their minds: men, sometimes drunk, waited in the bus depot.

"You can't stay alone in the station all night," she said. "You can stay with us. We'll get you to the depot in the morning."

Once the plane had landed, my saviours waited while I collected my battered bag, then whisked me by taxi from the airport to their apartment. They pulled out their couch and bade me goodnight. In the morning, they drove me to the depot and I caught the bus. My heart might have been aching, but I was going home.

AS THE GREYHOUND ROLLED up Main Street to the King Eddy Hotel, I saw the town through new eyes. A clutch of drab farmers lounging at the storefronts. A pair of bowlegged cowboys exiting the City Café. Tumbleweeds rolling down the street. Somewhere a few miles away, my mother was pushing the speed limit to meet me and take me back to the ranch.

The town seemed smaller somehow, but there was goodness there, too. I thought of the stewardesses from the plane. I thought of Rory, gentle even as he let me go. I thought of Canada, my country— safe, reliable, and secure—where random acts of kindness were still possible.

....

CHAPTER TEN

Have You Thought about the Law?

IN SEPTEMBER 1964, I returned to Edmonton for the fourth and final year of my arts degree, confident in my identity as a serious philosophy scholar and intent on working hard and finding a place to earn my master's and PhD. My path in life was set. I would become a professor of philosophy.

It had all become clear in the days following my return from Europe to Pincher Creek. Chattering about the family reunion I had missed—hundreds of Gietzes congregated at the ranch while I was gallivanting in Europe—Mom slid in what she really wanted to know.

"So you stopped off to see Rory?"

"Yes."

She returned to clearing plates, more clatter than necessary.

"You don't have to worry," I said. "It's over."

I would put that dream behind me and pursue my career.

THAT YEAR, THE FAMILIAR autumn ritual of finding a place to live landed me in the House of Pius, a big three-storey home on a tree-lined street south of the campus. Pius was a wheat farmer from Saskatchewan. He had a lot of land. In the summers, there was lots of work on the farm. In the winters, very little. So when he'd reached his fifties, balding and thickening through the middle, he decided to spend his winters in Edmonton. To make the enterprise profitable, he turned his home into a boarding house for students—or more precisely, female students. No one knew if there had ever been a special woman in his life; no one asked.

The main floor of the house was the domain of Pius. The second floor was divided into six rooms, one of which was mine. On the third floor, under the attic, was a well-equipped kitchen where we girls could cook our meals.

The eldest of the tenants in the House of Pius was an English-woman who had spent two decades in Tuktoyaktuk in the High Arctic. Over toast in the mornings, she told me how she missed the north—the sense of community and belonging she had experienced there. The next room to mine housed the Engineering Queen—a designation given each year to the girl chosen by the faculty of engineering as their beauty queen.

The youngest of us was just nineteen and hugely pregnant. In an era when unwed mothers were often hidden and condemned, she bravely marched from class to class in bright tented dresses. She had broken up with her boyfriend in the spring, only to discover later that she was pregnant. We admired her courage and lived the drama of her choice. Would she put the child up for adoption, viewed as the "right" thing to do at the time? Or would she keep the baby? In the end, she decided to keep the child. A year later, I saw her with the baby, waiting for a bus. "Going great. Still studying," she said. And then with a frown, "Part time." I felt a pang for young mothers struggling to build a life.

As for me, I worked. I spent my waking hours marking first-year exams for extra cash and writing papers on esoteric philosophical subjects. My social life was confined to department parties. I stopped dating. But a minor note kept clanging whenever I thought about where all this was leading me. I found I was less enamoured of the linguistic philosophy that was increasingly dominating the field. I had always been attracted to moral and ethical philosophy—the questions confronting contemporary society. Algebraic formulations of linguistic constructions held no interest for me. And yet I carried on, ignoring the growing dissonance between my passions and the current academic trends. Offer letters from graduate schools came in, but I put them to the side of my desk. None of them felt right.

I left Pius's house in April, a month before exams. He'd asked me to come by one evening, then sat me down on his nubby brown couch and explained in kindly tones that my late-night typing was annoying my neighbour the beauty queen.

"Sure," I said. "I'll find another place."

I finished my term papers in a quiet high-ceilinged room in a university residence, where no one cared how late I typed. An aging professor developed a crush on me, which I politely rebuked after finding an enormous bouquet in my room. So much for romance. I got a job as a teaching assistant in the summer program of the newly founded philosophy department at the University of Calgary.

And then, out of the blue, Rory reappeared.

I heard a knock on my door one evening and opened it to see my Calgary landlady. She was profoundly deaf and I hadn't mastered sign language, but I could tell by her gestures that there was someone for me at the door.

I stepped back, surprised. Who could want to see me?

I came to the top of the stair, looked down, and saw him. He stared up at me solemnly—no wave, no word. And then he smiled that ironic smile I remembered so well.

My heart was in my mouth. After our awkward visit in London, I had convinced myself that I would never see him again.

"How did you find me?" I managed to blurt out.

"Not hard," he said. "I found Conrad working on the farm near Pincher Creek. He gave me your address for undefined future favours. I owe him."

"You could have written." I moved down the stairs and into his open arms.

"I decided to just come," he said. "How about a walk?"

After a desultory stroll along Seventh Avenue, we made our way to a pub. Over a glass of wine, he said, "Remember the time I took you to dinner at the Palliser?"

"Yeah," I said. It was the first summer after I turned Bentley down. "We drove all the way from Pincher Creek just for dinner in the grand dining room."

"Roast beef and caramel apple pie."

"Then we ran over a skunk on the highway just west of Fort Macleod. I had to throw out everything I was wearing. Even my nice blue coat."

"The car was never the same, either."

We moved on to discuss our school plans. He said he wanted to study zoology.

"Where?" I asked.

"Edmonton, of course. U of A."

"Great," I said.

"You don't seem enthusiastic."

"We seem to be at cross purposes. I won't be going back to Edmonton. I'm going to do a master's in philosophy somewhere else. Haven't decided where—England or the States."

As we talked about the schools that had accepted me, the concerns about philosophy that I hadn't dared articulate even to myself came out. Rory listened. And then, out of the blue, he asked the question that would change my life.

"Have you thought about the law?"

I stared at him. Of course, it made sense that he would put this question to me. He came from a line of professional women—his grandmother had been the bursar at the University of Western Ontario and his mother was a doctor.

"The law? Never."

"I think you'd be a good lawyer."

I shook my head. I had set my sights on a career in philosophy and worked hard to get this far. Besides, there was the gender barrier. In philosophy, I had found a place where women were treated equally to men. I knew there were women philosophers. I had never heard of a woman lawyer.

"I can't see myself as a lawyer."

"Think about it," he said.

Rory said goodbye and headed north to Edmonton that night. I waved him off with an affectionate smile but without illusion. He and I were and would always be just friends. Plan A—getting a grad degree—was still on track.

LATER THAT SUMMER, I finished my teaching assistant position and headed south to the ranch, the unanswered clutch of offers for graduate work in my bag. I need to make a choice, I told myself. But I could not. I plunged into chores on the ranch, too tired at night to think about whether Aberdeen was better than Ann Arbor. I'd toss a coin at the last minute and go where it led.

From somewhere in the back of my mind, Rory's words resurfaced. Perhaps, despite the lack of real-world examples, a woman could make a success of law. Maybe it would be a satisfying life—a life that applied abstract principle, the stuff of philosophy, to the concrete problems of people's lives.

In the dying days of August, I wrote a letter to the dean of the faculty of law at the University of Alberta—I knew there was a faculty of law and assumed there must be a dean. "Dear Dean," I wrote, "I would appreciate information about the study of law." I licked the envelope, stamped the letter, and dropped it in the mail slot at the tiny Pincher Creek post office, then drove to the Co-op to get the provisions I'd been sent to town to fetch.

Four days later, I once again found myself in the foyer of the post office, picking up the mail. Riffling through the usual pile of bills, I stopped at a white envelope with the return address "Office of the Dean of Law." I frowned. I had expected a big envelope filled with brochures and information. Maybe it was too late to apply for law this year.

I tore open the envelope, unfolded the letter, and stared at the simple message: "Thank you for your inquiry. I am delighted to advise that you are admitted to first-year studies in the Faculty of Law. Yours truly, Wilbur Bowker, Dean."

I reread the letter, dumbfounded. Even in those simpler pre-LSAT days, there were procedures to be followed. You weren't simply admitted to law school without ever having applied. Yet here was a dean in a discipline devoted to proper prerequisites and procedures, cutting through them all and simply saying, "You are admitted."

I thought about my love for philosophy. I thought about how it had welcomed me on equal terms to men. I thought about the law, a profession dominated by men, and about the hard business of serving clients and getting the job done. I thought about the gentle pleasures of discussing philosophical problems. I thought about the adventure of living in a different country, maybe a different continent. I thought about Rory in Edmonton.

A plan emerged in my mind. I would accept the offer to go to law school. I would give the law a week, two at the outside. If, at the end of that time, I decided it was not for me, I would quit, accept one of the philosophy offers in my file, and fly away to Aberdeen or Ann Arbor or Cornell.

On September 3, 1965, I once again boarded the Greyhound bus to the University of Alberta. I felt a sense of wrongness as I slid into the grungy seat. For years, I had looked forward to this as the moment when I would spread my wings and fly to far-off places. But here I was, making the long trip back to the same old city, the same old campus—headed north but going backwards fast. All to take on the law, a strange profession that, as far as I could tell, promised only disappointment for the few women who dared enter it. I opened my purse and fingered the offers from far-flung universities—my backup plan, still intact.

As the bus pulled out from the King Eddy Hotel, I remembered what my mother had said when I asked her how long it would take to count to one hundred: *They'll teach you everything you need to know*.

I had been going to school for sixteen years, and I still hadn't learned what I really needed to know—namely, what to do with my life. I had followed the expected paths for women, had gone beyond them, but I still felt lost. Now I was about to venture on a different path—a path beaten smooth by the footsteps of men but seldom trodden by women. The odds were not good, but maybe this time I would get lucky. Maybe this time, I would finally learn what I needed to do with my life.

PART TWO

....

THE LAWYER

Every individual is equal before and under the law and has the right to the equal protection and equal benefit of the law without discrimination and, in particular, without discrimination based on race, national or ethnic origin, colour, religion, sex, age or mental or physical disability.

—*Canadian Charter of Rights and Freedoms*, Section 15

CHAPTER ELEVEN

Law Studies

THERE IT WAS. NOT a proper law school building, just the top floor of the Rutherford Library. I had sometimes crammed for exams in its long halls as an undergraduate. Now I was climbing one further flight of stairs to the cluster of classrooms and offices that housed the University of Alberta Faculty of Law.

What am I doing here? I thought to myself. The two days since I dismounted the Greyhound bus had passed in a rainy grey funk. I'd found a room where I could temporarily park my belongings, and I'd checked out the whereabouts of the law school. The week before, I had sent a letter to Rory, care of the department of zoology, telling him that I had decided to try law, but I'd had no reply.

Now, on the first day of law school, I picked up my registration packet and looked at the class schedule—the first lecture would begin in an hour. These people meant business.

In the main corridor, I was startled by a booming hello. A long, homely face loomed over me. "You're the girl from Pincher Creek. I'm the dean who admitted you."

"Thank you," I managed.

It was my first encounter with the legendary Wilbur Bowker, who had been running the law school since time immemorial, or so people said. He had a reputation as a man who never missed a detail and never forgot a student's name.

"Good to have you here," he said, crushing my hand in his tight grip. I winced. It would be harder to escape this place than I had thought.

In the classroom—light pouring through its western windows— I found a seat not too far forward or too far back and looked around me. I was surrounded by a sea of men, punctuated here and there by a female face. I tried to count the women without being conspicuous— six, maybe seven, out of a class of sixty-five? How many of us would survive?

After introductory remarks designed to impress upon us the sacredness of a calling to the law, Dean Bowker dove straight in: "We use the case method."

I was used to lectures where professors laid out principles and propositions from textbooks. But here in law school, we weren't given texts. We were given casebooks containing rulings written by judges. Most of the judges were British. Here and there, a ruling from the Supreme Court of Canada cropped up, and even more rarely, one from an American jurist like Oliver Wendell Holmes or Roscoe Pound.

I had no idea what the dean was talking about, but I soon found out. The case method gave learning an immediacy I hadn't encountered before. Each case began with a story—"the facts"—and went on to discuss how the precedents and legislated enactments applied to those facts. Here were real people with real problems—money problems, business problems, life-and-death problems. To prepare for class, where the professor demanded that random students discuss the assigned cases, I had to first grapple with the human dilemma at the heart of each one and think about the implications of dealing with it one way or the other. Moral philosophy in action.

"*Donoghue v. Stevenson*," Dean Bowker's voice rang out in my third torts class. "The most important case in the history of torts, the law of civil wrongs and remedies. Be prepared to discuss it tomorrow. Duty of care. Who knows what that is?"

A thicket of keen hands shot up around me.

The most important torts case ever, no doubt produced by some earth-shaking catastrophe, I mused an hour later as I cracked my new casebook and started to read. I frowned with disappointment as I got into the judgment. On a Sunday evening in August 1928, Emma Donoghue took a train to the small Scottish town of Paisley and went with a friend to the Wellmeadow Café. The friend ordered a mix of ice cream and ginger beer for Emma. The waiter poured the ginger beer from an opaque bottle over Emma's ice cream, and Emma tucked in. When her friend poured the remaining ginger beer into a tumbler, a decomposed snail floated out. Emma claimed she felt ill from the sight and left the café complaining of abdominal pain, which continued in the weeks that followed.

Emma Donoghue sued the manufacturer of the ginger beer, a Mr. Stevenson. Mr. Stevenson responded that she couldn't sue because the law didn't allow an action for personal injury against a person whom the plaintiff did not know. The issue on the case was a question of law: whether, at law, Mrs. Donoghue had a cause of action. The facts had not yet proved to be true; that would happen only if the House of Lords changed the law and said she could sue a manufacturer whom she did not personally know.

But from this humble fabric, Lord Atkin of England's top court, the House of Lords, created a new doctrine that would forever change the law of tort. No longer was a plaintiff required to show that her injury fell within a preordained category of physical claims, or that the defendant knew her personally. All she need show was that her injury was reasonably foreseeable, and that the defendant owed a duty of care to potential customers, including her.

Why had Lord Atkin and his colleagues, armed with only this meagre, still-unproved situation, decided to create what Dean Bowker called the greatest advance in tort law of modern times? I thought about what the dean had said. They had done what they did because fairness and justice required it. They had done it because the old rules, based on medieval conceptions, no longer produced just results. In the age of impersonal mass manufacturing, the old rules were no longer fair. So the law adapted. I suddenly understood the power of the law to move with societal changes and make the world a better place.

It was heady subject matter for a young woman fascinated with rights and responsibilities. Philosophers debated these issues in the abstract. Judges made them the stuff of real life.

Torts wasn't the only place this happened, I quickly learned. Judges of constitutional law used the same methods to build the bones of the country. Criminal law judges shaped and interpreted the law to conform to contemporary views of right and wrong. Commercial judges defined and refined the principles on which businesses were run to meet the demands of changing economies. With each new case and class, I found myself increasingly captivated by the methods and the ameliorative power of the law.

But I still had misgivings. The judges whose decisions I read were all men. The lawyers who fought the cases were all men. My professors were all men, except for a newly hired librarian (a woman's thing). My classroom oozed male dominance. Even though I was sitting in the same room, I perceived a certain assumption—namely, that the men in my class would slip effortlessly into pre-eminent places in the legal establishment. Men were the natural heirs to the throne. Women were the odd gender out. The Other. What made me think I, a woman, had a place in the world of law?

AT THE END OF my first week, I assessed my options: I could continue with the law, taking my chances on a future in a male-dominated field, or I could cut my losses and find a secure sinecure in academe. I realized the two weeks I had allotted to assess whether the law was for me was far too short. The law's power to change lives, maybe even the world, fascinated me. But my mind was a jumbled mess of strange legal labels and bits of jargon. It was too soon to know if the law was for me.

I decided to compile a list of pros and cons, in no particular order, that would determine whether I stayed in law school or made a last-minute break for grad school. The first item on my list was the school itself. Rutherford Hall might not have been a real law school building, but it was dignified, lovely, and bright with light, a good place with a good vibe. "Nice space," I noted on the pro side of the balance sheet I was drawing up.

My work on the list was interrupted by an unexpected event—I learned that I was expected to attend a women's tea hosted by the dean's wife, Marjorie Bowker. It was a command performance—not attending would be a huge black mark on a girl's record. I had not come from a world of ladies' teas and didn't know the protocol, but I knew I had to go.

At the tea, I discovered that Marjorie Bowker was a lawyer and an ardent feminist. While she had not practised law, she kept herself involved through scholarship and law-related activities. The pleasant woman who greeted me at the door and invited me to take my coat upstairs to her bedroom was the first real woman lawyer I had ever met. Equally important, I found myself chatting to the other women in my class as I clung to my dainty china cup. Teas—now lost in the mists of time—are wonderful places to chat.

"Other women," I added to my pro list. I had been afraid I'd be the only woman in my class. Instead, I found myself part of the largest female contingent the law school had ever seen. And they were fascinating women. A medical doctor looking for a second career in the law. A divorcee and mother of two children, hoping to make a new life for herself. A timid girl from Saskatchewan. A stunning (and clever) blonde named Shirley. And Eleanor, a banker's daughter, who was to become my best friend.

"New interesting stuff" was the third item on my pro list. Once I got the hang of the vocabulary, it would be fun to find out how the Canadian constitution worked, when a person could be compelled to pay damages to someone she had injured, and what principles undergirded the criminal law.

"Stories," I wrote finally, underlining the word. I loved stories, and the law was full of them. Cases were essentially stories of people who had found themselves involved in conflicts, and how the courts had resolved those conflicts. The principles flowed from the stories. After four years of airy philosophy, I found this descent into the real lives of real people refreshing. I decided that if I did end up teaching philosophy, I would do it by stories.

It was the law's grounding in human behaviour and conduct (along with a small tick at the bottom beside Rory's name, even though I was still unsure what would come of that) that ultimately tipped the balance against the lengthy list of cons. The big moral questions of responsibility and power, guilt and innocence that had drawn me to philosophy were the law's concern, too, but in a practical way that had real consequences in the lives of women, men, and children.

I pulled out my grad school letters and penned polite thank-yous, advising that my life had changed direction and I had decided to study law. Not that the grad schools would care. It just felt good to say it like I really meant it.

Next, I phoned my parents—our weekly letters had been replaced by random calls—and told them about my decision. I sensed they were quietly pleased. They had long since given up advising me on what I should study, but becoming a lawyer was something they could understand and relate to. My father had always been fascinated by legal matters; he drafted affidavits and instructed the local lawyer on minor matters with great relish. "Good," he said.

Then I walked down the street to the house where my brother Len, who had just entered medical school, was boarding. "Good," he said, echoing my father. "I figured that's what you'd do."

Lastly, I told Rory, who had found me.

"I really like the law," I told him. I didn't want him to think I was doing this just because of him.

"I knew you would," he said.

I laughed. "Why didn't I just ask you instead of going through all the agony of deciding?"

"Because you have to do the agony," he said. "That's you. Now come here." He put his arms around me. "You are going to be one hell of a lawyer, my dear."

Rory had been dealing with his own challenges—securing a thesis adviser, figuring out a topic, getting to know the colourful students in the zoology program, and scouting out a place to live. He was charismatic, witty, and affectionate—and very, very smart. But I was learning there were sides to him I didn't fully comprehend—moments when he would withdraw and I couldn't reach him. They didn't worry me, though. Didn't we all have our moments?

I scrabbled together enough grant money to pay my tuition and moved into a shabby one-room apartment in an old house a couple of blocks from the law school. Somehow, I would find a way to make ends meet.

As the autumn progressed, I found myself increasingly at home in the ways and words of the law. But these were early days. My classmates were obsessing about the end-of-term exams. Myths and stories swirled. Rumour had it that any student who failed the Christmas exams would be invited to a chat with the dean to discuss alternative career options. I had failed journalism and cut my ties to philosophy. I had only one career option left.

So I spent most of my waking hours studying. I also spent time with Rory—he had taken an apartment with another biologist—when he wasn't off on some field trip or out of town. He took me to biology parties where great quantities of red wine were consumed and introduced me to his friends as his lady. But most of the time, I studied.

As I launched into the exams, I felt my confidence growing. The skills I had honed during my brief stint in journalism proved as useful in law as they had in philosophy: identify the issue, analyze the facts, put the arguments for one side and then the other, come to a reasoned conclusion. I returned to Edmonton after a Christmas holiday at the ranch to learn I had passed with flying colours. I immersed myself in my studies with renewed passion. Maybe, just maybe, I was on my way.

And then came a reminder that all is not fair in love, war, or law school. Although my marks put me at the top of the class, I was not chosen to be the editor of the law journal—a break with long-standing tradition. Instead, the honour went to a man, Jim Matkin. I was named notes editor, charged with revising short notes on current cases. No explanation was given for the deviation from the rule. I did not protest; I did not complain. But it cut deeply and left me apprehensive for my future. It had just been powerfully confirmed for me: law was still very much a man's world. Women could get good marks, but we couldn't be trusted to run things—not yet.

I realized that the struggle to be treated equally wasn't over, might never be over, and that being the odd woman out was often uncomfortable and sometimes downright difficult. No wonder wise women chose careers in fields where women already had parity, like nursing or teaching or secretarial work. When I spoke up in classes where men vastly outnumbered women, I felt like I was in the wrong room. An imposter. To be one of a handful of women in a crowded room is to be constantly, at some subconscious level, aware of your gender. When you speak up, you imagine, rightly or wrongly, that everyone is thinking, *The woman is speaking*. The more the gender numbers reach parity, the more you feel like a regular person. Not female, not male—a person.

Still another reality I needed to face: women were treated differently from men. I had been mostly ignored—a brainy, dowdy, rather strange intruder—but some of my female classmates had fared worse. A particularly attractive woman—great figure, long blonde hair—was singled out for sexual comments, even by some professors. Another seemed to be the butt of negative comments from some of the men, for reasons I suspected had to do with her personal life.

The men who taught us and the men in my classes were good people who by and large treated women respectfully and equally. Dean Bowker, a feminist before his time, backed up his unprecedented law school invitation to me with a sustained enthusiastic welcome; his wife later sat as a provincial judge in family court. Two professors, Trevor Anderson and Alex Smith, made a point of mentoring me and the other women. But other men proved less sensitive. That was how it was in law schools in 1965.

A decade later, the gender picture had radically changed. Women began to flock to the law, and their numbers reached, and in some cases surpassed, the halfway mark. My generation, it turned out, was a bridge generation—the link between past decades, when scarcely any women had ventured into the male domain of law studies, and the future, when women, driven by passion for social justice and the dream of better lives, would occupy the classroom in equal numbers.

Men marvelled at the transformation. Some quietly grumbled, while others predicted it wouldn't last. But second-wave feminism and the quest for an equal place in academe and the workplace had arrived. The world slowly began to wrench itself out of the old ways. Guys cut back on sexist talk, and profs stopped making dirty jokes in class. But like all social changes, the transition to a new gender-neutral order would prove halting, painful, and, in the end, elusive.

BEFORE I KNEW IT, the academic year was winding down. I confronted the perennial spring conundrum—what to do in the summer? Rory would be away at a biology station in Turner Valley. I needed a job, and I needed money.

I hit on a plan: I would get a master's in philosophy. The requirements were three upper-level courses and a thesis. I already had the credits since I had taken one extra course in my final year of my undergraduate studies and two during my summer as a teaching assistant in Calgary. Now seasoned at grant writing, I submitted a proposal for a master's degree focusing on the philosophy of law—or more particularly, a debate between two eminent scholars, Hart and Fuller, on the nature of law. Was it a rules-based system, as Hart contended, or a more amorphous social and moral discipline, as Fuller argued? I obtained a commitment of a generous grant of $1,000 a summer for two successive summers. If all went according to plan, my third summer would be spent working in a law office. People often marvel at the fact that I obtained a master's in philosophy while studying law. The truth is more prosaic, however—it was a make-work project.

I returned to the ranch with a suitcase full of books, but the reality was that I spent most of my days helping my mother, whose energy was declining. In the afternoons and evenings, I read philosophy.

And then I got my first legal job. Pincher Creek possessed only one law office, situated upstairs in the aging municipal building that also housed the public library of my youth.

I decided to drop by. Garth Turcott greeted me as if I were already a fellow lawyer instead of a student with one year of law school under her belt. "I'm swamped," he said. "Come back tomorrow. You can look at some of the files I never seem to get around to." Every law office has these files—dog files, they're called. They're opened in a moment of crisis—something must be done—but when the crisis dies down, they're forgotten, or perhaps just pushed to the bottom of a busy lawyer's list. It was pedestrian work, but it engaged me in a way nothing had before. Farmers who wanted to clear their land of long-paid mortgages. A family that needed a will. A personal injury claim arising from a motor vehicle accident left to languish while the plaintiff suffered. The files I looked at were old and tattered, and told stories from years ago.

Still, after my first day at Turcott's office, I drove home to the ranch in high spirits and felt my year-end bar review blues dissipate. I could do law, would do law, whatever others might think.

But could I still do philosophy? I found the debate between Hart and Fuller on the nature of law worth exploring, but when it came time to write my master's thesis, I felt that something was missing— something I was groping towards but unable to articulate. Justice, my heart told me, must be more than rules or the codification of moral intuitions. Justice must be a larger affair, concerned not only with regularizing and enforcing behaviour but also with basic fairness to every individual—a fairness that extended to social and economic realms. But in 1967, I lacked the means to conceive of or articulate such justice. I nevertheless completed my thesis and acquired my master's degree, satisfied but not elated.

···

CHAPTER TWELVE

Our Rightful Place in the World

Rory and I married the summer after my second year of law studies, on July 8, 1967. He was completing his master's degree, and I had one year left in law. We would finish our studies together, but first we would wed.

There was never a moment when he proposed on bended knee, never a time when I declared my undying love for him. What passed between us was at once more humble and more profound. Through times together and times apart, through moments of tenderness and moments of doubt, we both had come to understand that we were utterly committed to each other, and that the only way forward was together.

It was a simple wedding, held at the Pentecostal church on the east end of Pincher Creek. I wore a white suit and Rory looked smart in tailored grey. My friend Eleanor came down and stood at my side, and my brother Len stood up for Rory. My throat clogged as Rory and I said our vows. We looked deep into each other's eyes and swore to love and to cherish and to hold each other until death do us part. We both meant it.

Celebration followed. We retired to the ranch for a buffet meal. Grandpa Kruschell broke the strict teetotalling rule of the household by buying a case of rosé. "What's a wedding without wine?" he protested, and everyone seemed to agree. My brothers, who would themselves be married within a few years, watched with speculative interest. Judi and little Ron wandered from guest to guest, while Rory's parents genially adapted to informal Western hospitality. Mom and Dad, having long since lost their hope that I would marry a good Christian boy, gave us their blessing. They had always liked Rory; their concern was never him so much as where he might take me. But they had come to accept that we would be together, no matter what, and bowed to the inevitable with good grace. What else could they do? In the words of my brother Len, who'd developed a wicked wit, "Every so often, true love rears its ugly head." Nothing to do but accept and move on.

After the party, Rory and I climbed into his used Ford sedan and set out for our home in Edmonton, a newly rented apartment near the university, unaware that a mischievous brother had scrawled "Just Married" into the dust on the trunk. But I didn't notice the pavement beneath the wheels or fuss at the occasional honk from a passing car—I was riding on air. I had married the man I loved—a man who was brilliant, funny, and called me his "lady." A man who had pledged his future to my career as a lawyer. If his charismatic forays occasionally lapsed into dark moods, I wasn't concerned. He was loving, loyal, and infinitely supportive. And he always righted himself before long.

Together, we would conquer the world.

I GRADUATED FROM LAW school in April 1968 with the Horace Harvey Gold Medal in Law, given to the student with the highest grades, and launched myself into the real world. And a tempestuous world it was. Martin Luther King Jr. had just been assassinated, and the Tet Offensive was raging in Vietnam. Draft dodgers were fleeing to Canada, and Pierre Elliott Trudeau—who as justice minister had galvanized law students with his vision of a Just Society—was coasting to a June victory as the new prime minister. A fresh new wind was wafting through Canada's legal firmament. I felt elated and excited. Soon I would join this world as a real lawyer.

But my legal education, I quickly realized, was just beginning. I had studied contracts, torts, and constitutional law. I had mastered the rudiments of trust law, criminal law, evidence, and estate planning. I had learned how to analyze a complex bundle of facts and put a legal label on them. But I had no idea how to be a lawyer. How to deal with a client, how to draft a pleading, how to make a court application—of these and other skills fundamental to the practice of law, I was totally ignorant.

These skills would be acquired in the next year of my life—the year called articling, the one thing that now stood between me and the bar. First, I had to find an articling position with a law firm, then I had to complete the year's work to the firm's satisfaction, then I had to write another set of exams to show that I had mastered the rudiments of practising law. After I had surmounted all these hurdles, I would, with luck, be called to the bar, a full-fledged lawyer at last.

I screwed up my courage and drew up a list of firms—the best firms. After all, I had graduated at the top of my class. The best firms should want me. Still, I knew that the competition was fierce, and that all other things being equal, the firms on my list were more likely to hire a man than a woman.

Filled with trepidation, I dressed up in my only business suit, took the bus downtown, and presented myself at the first firm on my list. The groomed receptionist surveyed me coolly and ushered me into a small boardroom, where the senior partner soon joined me. Although it was the first time I had ever set foot on the premises of an upscale law firm, I felt reasonably confident. The partner I was meeting with was the lecturer in a course in which I had done well. The interview went swimmingly. We discussed issues of law, and he chatted amiably about the delights of legal practice. *I have the job*, I thought.

Then, just as we were finishing up, he asked, "Why do you want to practise law?"

I stared at him, stunned. I didn't know what to say.

Seeing my confusion, he stepped in. "I see from your CV that you're married."

What was said thereafter is a blank. All I recall is walking past the receptionist and out the door. I went downstairs and across the hall to my second interview, with Wood, Moir, Hyde, and Ross—a firm that had previously employed women—and got my articling position.

It took me a while to figure out what being a married woman had to do with wanting to be a lawyer. A couple of months later, a kindly mentor at my new firm explained that there was no longer a problem with women working as lawyers, but there remained a general view in the profession that married women should not work outside the home.

"We had a wonderful woman who worked here for many years—great clients, great practice," he told me. "But when she married, she resigned."

It was an unspoken rule—when a woman married, she was expected to give up all outside activities to focus on her husband and the home.

"Of course," my mentor said, "the world is changing."

He was right. The world *was* changing. Just not very fast. I arrived on the legal scene just as women were beginning to be accepted as competent and committed professionals. The operative word was "beginning."

Why did it take so long for women to gain a footing in the workplace and in the professions? Once we'd worked out that women could and should be equal, why couldn't we simply leap to liberty? The reality is that people take time to adjust to change. Social norms change slowly; real change is generational. In *The Second Sex*, French philosopher Simone de Beauvoir's great insight—an insight we're still struggling to come to grips with today—is that seeing women as the Other is hardwired into our psyches, social assumptions, and practices. The attitude is deep—indeed often unacknowledged—and resistant to change. We should not be surprised that for every step we take forward in the march to gender equality, we experience a backlash that sometimes becomes a backslide.

My mother grew up in the first wave of feminism—the fight to get voting and property rights for women. She embraced it. Her mother had scandalized the neighbours by insisting on driving her Model A Ford down the prairie roads. My mother followed in her wake, proudly (if badly) driving from the ranch to town. She also helped run the family business, which was no surprise. Farm women had long done that. Most important of all, she insisted on exercising her right to vote.

On election day, my parents would drive fifty miles to town and back to vote, and then my mother would announce over dinner that night that she had cancelled out my father's vote.

"Why did we bother?" my father would ask.

"To vote," she replied.

For her, it was an important act. For her, it mattered.

Although women were allowed to vote now, the ones I saw around me didn't actually seem to be living equal lives to men. They were staying at home with the children, obediently catering to their husbands' whims, watching each passing year whittle their dreams down to sad slivers of memory.

My skepticism as I was growing up had transformed into conviction when I got to university in the 1960s. Women were realizing that voting rights and the right to hold property hadn't changed much in their lives. What they needed was real, substantive equality—equality that ended discrimination and allowed women to compete as equals in the workplace and have whatever careers they chose.

The new thinking of second-wave feminism buoyed me. Here at last was the answer. We would not tolerate discrimination. We would insist on being treated equally. We would have the careers we dreamed of. We would have to live with the fact that the working world would still be male-dominated for the immediate future, but with our efforts, that soon would change.

On paper, all of this sounded good. Many men bought in, too. Liberal law firms embraced the new ethic—in principle. In practice, though, I was learning that reality often lags behind. Still, I believed it was only a matter of time until women assumed our rightful place in the world. With my husband at my side and an articling position in hand, I had found mine.

....

CHAPTER THIRTEEN

Into the Fray

I SHOWED UP AT WOOD, Moir, Hyde, and Ross on the appointed day in my newly purchased suit and black shoes, ready to get to work. It was a small establishment by today's mega-firm standards—just thirteen lawyers focused mainly on insurance law, with dabs of criminal law, commercial law, and this and that mixed in. The principal to whom I was articled was Arnold F. "Spud" Moir, the senior partner in the firm, known as a brilliant cross-examiner and master of the trenchant put-down. If I expected a greeting from him, however, I was disappointed.

The receptionist looked up from the panel where she was pushing and pulling at telephone connectors. "Oh, you," she said. After adjusting a few more knobs, she sighed, "I suppose I should show you your office."

I followed her around the corner to the last office at the end of the hall, where two identical oak desks were clumped in the middle of the room. I wondered at the arrangement—they hadn't told me they had taken on another articled clerk.

The receptionist tossed a file on one of the desks—"Mr. Moir wants you to have a look at this"—and left.

I was still wondering who the other clerk was when a woman with a narrow face and a halo of kinky red hair walked in. She slapped a court file down on the other desk, looked up, and glared at me.

"I'm Nina," she said. "Called to the bar. As of yesterday."

I realized how she had to see me—I was an unwanted intruder in what had been her office. Then she sighed, shook her head, and accepting the inevitable at least for the moment, plunked her slender form down on her chair.

I knew Nina, but only as a vague presence in the class ahead of mine at law school. Now, evidently, we were consigned to be desk-mates, even though every other lawyer (all of them male) had his own office. Despite having just been called to the bar, Nina, I would soon learn, was already deep into insurance practice. She managed dozens of files single-handedly, in addition to helping one of the senior part-ners with discovery and trial work on his more complex matters. She spent hours on the phone, arguing with this adjuster or that lawyer. She made it clear that if her conversations bothered me, the problem was mine. Most days, I took myself to the small firm library to work away on my memos there.

If Nina was galled by the expectation that she would be content to share her office with the new female articling student simply because she was a woman, she said nothing. In fact, we would eventually be-come friends. I learned that she had a quick laugh and was ready for anything—even the occasional foray to Elk Island Park to practise our mutually woeful golf skills. But as she glared in my direction that first day, I didn't know any of this. I just knew that I was an imposter.

I settled down to work and opened the file with trembling hands. My first file. I would do my best. I would show Mr. Moir. Staring up at me was a jumble of illegible notes. I leafed through them. The case was something about a mechanic's lien—a subject I had never encountered at law school. Near the bottom of the pile, I found the documents: a contract, something called a lien, and a sheaf of letters between increasingly testy lawyers. I concluded, with sinking heart, that Mr. Moir probably wanted a legal opinion. Somehow I had to figure out the problem and, assuming I got that right, take a stab at setting out the legal options. I went to the library, got out *Halsbury's Laws of England*—you never know what might help—and a few Canadian texts, and looked up mechanics' liens.

At four in the afternoon, still floundering, clutching my forehead to stifle a sharp pain that had just materialized, I was startled by the ring of the phone on my desk. So that's what it sounded like.

"Mr. Moir would like to see you," the receptionist intoned.

I picked up my file and made my way down the hall to my principal's corner office, where I knocked hesitantly on the door. A boom ensued from within. I took it as an invitation to enter.

Behind the dark wood desk sat a balding man of medium height and paunchy cheeks. "You must be the new one," he said, eyeing me with his keen gaze. "How are you making out on that memo?"

"What's a mechanic's lien?" I wanted to bleat. Instead, I said, "I've made a start."

"Well, carry on," he said, waving a hand to dismiss me. "By the way, we're in court tomorrow." I turned in the doorway. "Show up at nine thirty. I'll fill you in on the way to the courthouse."

And so my articles began. My main job, I discovered, was to follow Mr. Moir around and do whatever he asked. But along the way, I met and worked with other members of the firm—among them Joe Brumlik, a kindly elf with a genius for securing favourable settlements on insurance files, and John Weir, a shrewd litigator whose kind heart belied his curmudgeonly manner. They mentored me, taught me, and sometimes gently upbraided me. I lived and worked with a constant sense of inadequacy. The assumption was that I knew something. The reality was that I knew nothing.

"This kid had his leg burned off when his ladder touched a live wire. Draft a statement of claim," Spud Moir would command after morning coffee, handing me some notes on a napkin.

"Go down to speak to the trial list," John Weir would instruct. "And see that we don't get Judge X for the Smith case."

"Sit in on this discovery; it's a simple head-on collision. Make sure our client doesn't concede anything," Joe Brumlik would say.

I would leave their offices with my head reeling. What's a statement of claim? What's the trial list? What's a discovery and how do I keep the client from admitting anything?

Towards December, after I'd been floundering for more than six months, Mr. Moir announced that we would have lunch. In trepidation, I descended the elevator with him to the restaurant on the ground floor. I knew what was coming. He would politely tell me that despite my efforts, the firm had no place for a new lawyer, and I should start looking for another job in the spring.

The dining room was darkly lit, the tablecloth gleaming white. I was not surprised. "I can't stand eating without a white tablecloth," Mr. Moir had once said over a mid-trial lunch in a bistro. I ordered, knowing I would not be able to eat. Mr. Moir chatted about golf lessons. The food came. I picked up my fork, put it down. Waited.

Between bites, he looked up at me. "You're the best articling student we've ever had," he said. "We'd like to ask you to stay on."

And that was that. I carried on and completed my articles in a flurry of exams interspersed with dashes back to the office to deal with this memo or that piece of litigation. Today, law societies require a bar admission course or formal bar exams, which students may not pass. In 1969, the Law Society of Alberta contented itself with a series of lectures from senior practitioners spread over two weeks, plus a decent grade on a series of take-home exams. Admission to the bar, given a respectable effort, was a fait accompli. Life was simpler then.

I was admitted to the bar in May 1969, in a private ceremony in the Supreme Court of Alberta, presided over by one of the judges the firm most admired, Justice Peter Greschuk. The sun shone. The day was bright. My mother and father had made the long drive from Pincher Creek, my father proudly presenting me with a handsome briefcase to mark the beginning of my professional life. Rory beamed beside me. Having completed his master's degree, he had become deeply involved in a family land development project in Peace River in northeastern British Columbia, which took him away for big chunks of time. Immersed in my work, I hadn't minded his absences, but it was good to have him with me at such an important point in the adventure he had urged me to undertake.

Mr. Moir made a speech, describing my abilities in generous terms and including a personal note about my work ethic and sense of humour. I took the Bible in my hand and swore to uphold the tenets of the legal profession. Justice Greschuk declared me admitted to the bar, and the clerk declared court dismissed. The ceremony over, I turned to shake hands with the lawyers who had got me there, and to accept the embraces of my husband and family. I felt a deep sense of joy.

Somehow, with their help, I had done it. I had become a lawyer.

JOY COMES IN SHORT and fleeting bursts; the day-to-day slog of life goes on. The next day, it was back to work as usual. I returned to the office Nina and I had shared for the past year. *Surely*, I thought, *they'll give us each our own office now that I'm a lawyer, too*. I looked around. Still two desks. Still Nina's files on the desk across from mine. But Nina was nowhere to be seen.

I left the room to consult with another lawyer. As I came out of his office, I collided with Nina coming from the direction of our office, arms laden with a box heaped with files. She strode past, chin up, high heels clicking. I followed timorously and watched her march out the door. I went back to our office. Her desk was clear except for a few scraps of paper. Her files were gone. I suddenly understood.

Before long, the managing partner popped in. "Where did Nina go?" he asked.

"I don't know," I replied. "But I believe she thinks she's entitled to her own office."

He scowled, shook his head, and left. I heard office doors clacking open and shut as he made his way down the hall. A silence ensued—no doubt the partners were convening.

The white-haired managing partner once more darkened the door of our office. He was still scowling. "Get her back," he ordered.

"Why don't you?" I asked.

"Because she's in the ladies' room," he said. "We think."

"Very well."

I found Nina, as he predicted, in the women's washroom, leaning against the counter beside her heaping box of files. She was sending blue rings of cigarette smoke towards the ceiling fan.

"They want you back," I said.

Nina shook her head and blew another smoke ring.

"I think you'll get your own office," I said.

Nina stared at the wall. Then she ground out her cigarette in the sink. "We'll see," she said before she headed out of the washroom, leaving all her files exactly where they were.

I don't know what was said. But Nina got her office.

And so did I.

NINA AND I WERE among the lucky ones. We'd found a place in a law firm where women were respected and, in most matters, treated as equals. But that did not change the fact that the firm was still a man's place, and that men were entitled to behave however they wanted. The thoughts and feelings of a woman came second, if at all.

In 1969, the idea that sexual innuendo was inappropriate in a workplace setting hadn't yet entered law office culture. Women accepted comments about their appearance and clothing as the price to be paid for professional success. We became inured to sexual stereotypes and off-colour jokes. It came with the territory.

Women also got used to gossip—gossip that hurt. I came to work one day to find everyone talking about a judge who had dressed down a young woman in chambers for wearing a skirt he deemed too short. Months later, on a visit home, I discovered that my mother was deeply distressed because she had heard that I'd been chastised by a judge for wearing too short a skirt. I told her that it was another woman, not me, but I was never sure she completely believed me. That hurt. It also hurt that a lot of people out there were talking about me for something that had never happened. As I pondered the incident, though, what angered me most of all was the unfairness of putting down a woman doing a professional job because of the hemline of her skirt.

I experienced many things—downgraded treatment, exclusion from events at men's-only clubs, sexual innuendos in the library, unfounded gossip—and I survived. I put my head down and carried on. Certain men had certain attitudes, and the world was what it was. I felt there was not much I could do to change the office culture or a particular person's behaviour.

Three things carried me through. The first was a stubborn determination not to let the dark side win. I had worked too hard and too long to become a lawyer. I would not let a world that was stuck in denial defeat me. The second was the knowledge that not all men were chauvinists. Most of the men I encountered were prepared—spurred on by the occasional rejoinder—to treat me as a professional equal.

And a few of them even encouraged me and told me that I could be a good lawyer. They said positive things about my work to others. And they opened doors to new opportunities. The third thing that carried me through was the love and support of my husband.

"You're the hope of this family," he would say jokingly, but with an undertone of seriousness. "Someday, you'll be on the Supreme Court of Canada."

"You're crazy," I would respond, shaking my head at his flamboyant fancies. I knew better than to dream such a thing. I might be smart, but that did not negate the reality that I was just a small-town girl from Pincher Creek, trying to make it in a system with virtually no women on the bench. Still, Rory's confidence in me, irrational as it seemed, buoyed me and carried me through the tough times, for which I am forever grateful. The law was our shared dream; I could not let him down.

And so I set to work. Since Nina had resolved the double-office crisis, I now had the office at the end of the long hall to myself. Exerting an authority I did not have, I asked the office manager to move the second desk out and bring in a couple of nice chairs.

For my clients. When and if they came.

A few did come: walk-ins who were down on their luck and looking for someone—anyone—plus the odd legal aid referral. Most of the people I saw were referred to me by other lawyers in the firm.

Before long, the top drawer of my filing cabinet was filled with cases. I spent my days drafting pleadings, sorting documents, and holding clients' hands during examination for discovery. After lunch, I often found myself in traffic court on behalf of insurance companies that, not surprisingly, considered it advantageous to avoid convictions that might make settling their cases more difficult. I also often juniored another lawyer, usually Mr. Moir, in court. I watched how he opened a case, cross-examined a witness, put in documents, and made legal arguments. Occasionally, I was assigned a small trial or appeal brief on my own, where I could practise the skills I was learning.

The cases that stand out in my memory are those where I was able to help women find justice, such as the woman whose professor husband had consigned her to a mental institution. We secured her release and ultimately a divorce. Or the suit we brought for the archaic tort of breach of promise of marriage, on behalf of a woman who had been strung along for years by a defendant who promised to marry her, then left her for another woman. The defendant laughed at the suit, but in the end, the judge saw it our way and awarded significant damages to my client.

The work was sometimes boring—sorting through boxes of documents is nobody's idea of an exciting day. It could also be scary—who was I to decide on the wording of a statement of claim or what pitch we should make to the court of appeal? And always, it was stressful.

My days were filled with anxiety and my nights with worry. More than once, I found myself in the office on a Sunday checking whether I'd missed a limitation period or misstated a proposition of law. *You're paranoid*, I told myself. But I knew I couldn't stop checking and re-checking, couldn't stop worrying. I practised law. It was my identity. I must do it perfectly—no slip-ups, no mistakes.

Practice took me to the office Monday to Friday, and when Rory was out of town dealing with the family's Peace River venture, as he often was, Saturday mornings, too. The routine was the same every day, except when I went out of town for a trial or discovery. Shower, dress, get to the office by eight. Have a cup of coffee and a piece of toast in the cafeteria with other lawyers of the firm. Take the elevator up to the office. Check the day's schedule. Rush off to the courthouse. Go to a discovery. Draft a statement of claim. Bury myself in the library to research a point of law. Find time for a quick lunch—maybe with someone, maybe alone. Then back to work. Interview a client. Work the phone with an opposing lawyer.

Not that it was all work. Around five, lawyers back from court or discovery or wherever their day had taken them drifted towards the company library. They would pour themselves a drink—you could tell how a person's day had gone by the amount of rye in the ginger or rum in the cola—pull up a chair to the long table, and hash over the events of the day. Exchange tidbits of legal gossip. Vilify the judge who had just tossed them out of court. Discuss the repercussions of Pierre Trudeau's long-overdue overhaul of the Criminal Code—the first step in a drive to bring the archaic concepts of criminal law into sync with modern norms.

Early on at the firm, I was handed a file on a woman charged with the offence of vagrancy, known as Vag-C. "What's vagrancy?" I asked the assembled group. "Being in the wrong place at the right time," came the reply. I must have looked puzzled. "Prostitution, my dear," an older lawyer explained with a wink.

The overhaul would stop short of criminalizing the sale of sex, but it confined it to the streets by outlawing "bawdy houses" and making it an offence to provide services like rooms or cars to a prostitute. While criminalizing the solicitation of sexual services, it left the use of those services legal. Sex workers could be criminals, but johns could not. The law was still unable, it seemed, to call the sale of sex what it was—prostitution—or assign legal responsibility for it in a fair manner.

Years of legal debate on the issue culminated in 2013 with *Bedford v. Canada*,[1] a case I would preside over as chief justice of the Supreme Court. I believed we should strike down the provisions on the grounds that they endangered prostitutes by preventing them from talking to potential clients and depriving them of the rudimentary protections of a place to conduct their business. As I penned my reasons, I cast my mind back to the library explanations of Vag-C so many years before. Perhaps, at long last, we were finally bringing the law governing the sale of sex closer into the twenty-first century.

Sometimes as we gathered around the library table to discuss the law, a deck of cards would appear and a round of blackjack would be played. Gradually, people would trickle out and drift home. Or head back to their offices to finish an uncompleted task or pack a briefcase for after-dinner work.

I learned more of the practice of law around that library table than in my office. And I learned that law is not just a job—it is a way of life, a profession, a social activity that knits individuals into a cohesive whole and makes the entire venture sustainable.

At the end of my first year of practice, I paused to assess where I stood. I had undergone the most stressful year of my life and come out the other end. I had thought a thousand times, *I can't do this. I can't sustain this. I'll collapse of anxiety or go mad.* I recalled with horror the day when, overwhelmed by fear, I found myself paralyzed before the judge, unable to open my mouth. No harm was done—I recovered and said what was needed—but I resolved I would never let such a thing happen again.

And here I was, more or less sane, sleeping, eating, and looking forward to each day. I often felt inadequate. And I missed Rory. But the practice of law left no time for self-indulgence. Deal with the crisis, get the job done. Into the fray and on. This became the mantra for the rest of my life.

CHAPTER FOURTEEN

···

Strange Comfort

For two and half years—well, three and a half, counting articles—I practiced with Wood, Moir, Hyde, and Ross in Edmonton. For almost the same amount of time, Rory had been commuting between home and Fort St. John in British Columbia. Every second weekend, he made the long drive south to Edmonton. We would indulge ourselves at the movies and dinners out, and occasionally we found weeks when we could take a trip or just be a normal couple at home. Our life was one of extremes—we lurched from highs to lows and back again. We never fought, and our commitment to each other remained strong. But the long weeks apart were hard for both of us. We longed for each other's company, for an ordinary marriage.

"You could practise law in Fort St. John," Rory ventured.

"No," I said. "I like what I'm doing here." To go from a big-city practice to a small-town firm seemed like a step back.

Still, the idea lingered. On a trip to Fort St. John, I investigated the possibility of joining a law firm there. When I asked David Levis, the senior partner of Levis and Herdy, the biggest firm in town, if there might be a role for me, he enthusiastically said yes. Back in Edmonton, I pondered the options and decided to accept Mr. Levis's offer. I loved my husband and was tired of being alone. Maybe I would come to like small-town practice.

But first I had to gain admission to the British Columbia bar. While the regulations required a period of articles for applicants who had practised less than three years, the Benchers—an elected group of lawyers who governed the practice of law in the province—waived the requirement in my case.

I flew south to Vancouver to be called to the BC bar. This time it was a mass call. I was sworn in, along with fifty or so other applicants, in a courtroom ceremony. In the women's robing room of the stately pillared courthouse, I was approached by a distinguished-looking barrister. She stuck out her hand. I looked at her stern face and cropped grey hair, uncertain what to expect.

"I'm Mary Southam," she said. "I'm a Bencher. You should know that I didn't vote for you."

I recognized the name of the only female Bencher. *Not a great beginning*, I thought with a sinking heart.

"Well, I'm glad the others did," I managed in response.

Then Miss Southam—as she insisted on being called—surprised me again. After we'd shucked our court regalia, she said, "Let's go for coffee at the Georgia."

As we sat sipping our coffee in the dark-panelled room that seemed to be the local legal haunt, she suddenly stood up.

"Excuse me," she said.

I watched as she made a beeline to a nearby table, where a former classmate of mine was being feted by his parents and fiancée. He was still sporting the black vest and white tabs that lawyers wear beneath their gowns. I had occasionally seen this happen in Alberta, too.

"Young man, take your tabs off," Miss Southam said in her deep, clear voice. "You should know better. Tabs are not to be worn outside the courthouse."

My classmate reddened, then blanched as he reached to detach the offending neckwear. I thought about fleeing, but Mary Southam was triumphantly marching back to our table, a look of grim satisfaction on her face. *Who is this woman?* I thought. I folded my body into my chair in a futile attempt at invisibility, but not before my hapless classmate, recovering from his embarrassment, shot me an accusing look.

So it came that I was introduced to Vancouver by none other than the redoubtable Mary Southam, renowned barrister, famed straight talker, and stickler for court etiquette and the strict application of the rules (which explained why she hadn't voted for me). It was the first of many coffees we would share at the Georgia Hotel.

Only later did I realized how much Mary Southam's occasional presence in my life had meant to me. Here at last was a role model— a woman who had made it on her own by dint of intelligence, courage, and resilience. All the odds were against her, yet she had pushed on and succeeded. I could never be like her, I thought to myself. But the mere fact that she was there, a leader at the male-dominated bar, sent a powerfully positive message. The fact that the men she went up against quaked with fear in her presence was only icing on the cake.

Armed with my BC practice certificate, I returned to Fort St. John, only to find that the person I had been looking forward to working for, David Levis, had been appointed a judge. To replace him, the firm brought in Dennis Mitchell, a lawyer from nearby Dawson Creek. Dennis, formidably bright, was as sharp a litigator as he was a solicitor. He took me under his wing, and Rory and I became fast friends with him and his wife, Ruby. But within months,

Dennis decided to return to Dawson Creek, taking with him the litigation work I loved.

I plowed away on pedestrian files, less and less content. The scenery was beautiful, the country wild and wonderful. But the town was rough, crammed with hotels and bars fuelled by the oil industry, and the legal work ran to a disappointing mix of boom-and-bust business transactions and drunk-driving charges in provincial court. At the same time, Rory was souring on land clearing and feeling unsupported by our business partners. I watched his frustration mount to the point he could not go on. Eventually, we decided we would wind up our affairs in Fort St. John and move to Vancouver, where I would find more interesting work and he would pursue a PhD.

I flew down to Vancouver and put out feelers. None of them connected. The big firms were not vying to hire an unknown quantity from Fort St. John, even if she did have good marks and a letter of recommendation from an Edmonton law firm.

Dennis Mitchell came to the rescue. He had once worked at Bull, Housser, and Tupper, a blue-ribbon Vancouver law firm. Dennis introduced me to Bae Wallace, who was putting together a team to take on a marathon case arising from the construction of the W.A.C. Bennett Dam, west of Fort St. John, on behalf of BC Hydro.[1] I met Bae in the dining room of the ubiquitous Georgia Hotel.

During our meeting, he pulled out a cigarillo and asked, "Do you mind?"

I cheekily replied, "Not if I can smoke one, too." I didn't smoke, but on that occasion, I forced myself to take a deep drag.

Bae Wallace hired me. Rory and I rented a spacious apartment on the top floor of a building at the edge of the University of British Columbia. Rory decided to take a year in education, which would allow him to teach in case the PhD didn't work out.

The Bull, Housser, and Tupper team assembled for the conduct of the litigation had set up a war room in the Georgia Hotel, across from the courthouse. I was responsible for reviewing the discovery transcripts and expert reports, and preparing for the upcoming trial. I spent long hours there and in the firm's offices, but when I did turn out the light and head home, Rory was there.

Like so many before us, Rory and I fell in love with Vancouver. From the balcony of our Point Grey apartment, we could see the ocean and the thin blue line of the peaks of Vancouver Island to the west. And from my glass-walled office at Bull, Housser, and Tupper's new downtown premises, I looked north to Coal Harbour and the mountains of West Vancouver. I had come to love the quiet beauty of Edmonton, the river snaking through the lush valley, green by summer, white by winter. But not since my days on the ranch had I lived and worked in the midst of such spectacular beauty as Vancouver afforded.

We fell quickly into the pace of our new life—a pace that felt less rushed than it had in Edmonton. People in Vancouver understood that it was fine to leave the office early on a spring afternoon to take out the sailboat, or to adjourn a case to ensure a propitious start to a weekend of skiing at Whistler. Senior lawyers like Bill Esson and Harvey Bowering never seemed too busy to stop and share a story. On the weekends, there were concerts and plays to attend. And there was family—my father's sister Millie, who lived with her husband and children on a leafy Kerrisdale Avenue, welcomed us with Sunday dinners and invitations to their cottage at Gower Point. Rory was looking forward to starting PhD studies in the spring. The future once again looked bright.

JUST WHEN ALL SEEMED perfect, the storm clouds bunched in anticipation of the winter rainy season, and I received the news that my mother was gravely ill.

My father's bewildered voice over the phone betrayed his devastation. "She collapsed in the bathroom. They're taking her to Calgary. I can't get up there right now. I have to stay with Ron." My youngest brother, Ron, was only eleven.

I booked a flight to Calgary and packed my bag. Rory and I drove to the Vancouver airport in stunned silence. We could not conceive of life without Mom, my beloved mother. I found her in the hospital in Calgary, heavily medicated and mute in her bed, awaiting diagnosis.

I could do nothing for her, so I rented a car and headed south to Pincher Creek. Before driving to the ranch, I stopped at the local clinic and demanded to see my mother's doctor. The nurse ushered me into a small room. Within minutes, the doctor knocked and entered. The slope of his shoulders and the abject tilt of his head told me more than I wanted to know.

"A stroke," he said. "Maybe something else."

"Like a brain tumour?"

He nodded.

"Were there any signs? I mean, she's been having headaches for years, and sometimes seeing spots."

The doctor shook his head. "You have to understand," he said. "Your mother is an emotional woman. I put it down to anxiety, hysteria."

"You never did any tests?" I asked incredulously.

He shook his head. "I gave her Valium," he said.

I stared at him, choking back outraged anger. "You gave her Valium?"

"You have to understand," he repeated.

I did not understand, not at all. Blinded by tears, I fled the clinic and steered the car up the winding road to the ranch. I had seen this happen before, too often. Women stumbling into the law office, high on Valium. Women dealing with injuries from car accidents, high on Valium. Women checking into addiction centres to overcome their dependence on Valium. Valium—the drug of choice in the 1970s, the cure for hysteria. For women only.

I flew back to Vancouver on Sunday evening, but the next weekend, and almost every weekend after, I was in Calgary. One day, walking into the ward where my mother was recovering from surgery to remove the massive tumour the doctors had discovered at the base of her skull, seeing her in her wheelchair with bandaged head and sunken face, I felt the room swirl. I fell in a faint. When I came to, I was in a wheelchair, too. I was mortified at my weakness and distressed to be adding to the nurse's burdens. "I'm sorry," I managed.

"Stop it," the nurse said with a kind smile as she wheeled me to my mother's side. We sat like that for some minutes, mother and daughter, side by side in wheelchairs. There was a strange comfort in it.

My mother was a brave woman, never one to shrink from hard questions. And now, in her final days, she did not shrink from the ultimate question. From the time she met my father, she had been a Christian believer. Her most passionate desire was that those she loved—her brother, Len; her sister, Doreen; her children—share her faith. Yet now she faltered.

In her delirium, she questioned the value of her life. "A big boot," she whispered, conjuring up some image of futility deep in her brain. "Pouring in, pouring out. No God," she said. "No God."

Tears welling, I, who had since youth found belief difficult, struggled to ease the desolation of her soul. "God is there," I insisted. "Perhaps not as you once imagined him, but he is there, in what we see, in what we do. He is there. He is here." Suddenly Albert Camus's pronouncement came to my mind: "We do not believe; we choose to believe." Mom had always just believed. Now she had to choose.

My mother, Eleanora Marian Kruschell Gietz, died on December 19, 1972, in the Pincher Creek Hospital—the same hospital where she had given birth to me and my four siblings. Her passing was serene, according to my father, who was with her. She had faced her doubts and demons, and at the end of her difficult journey, she had chosen to believe and found peace. She was only fifty-two.

The little church was packed for her funeral. People wept, and messages of condolence poured in. She was a good woman. She had lived a good life. She had not achieved fame or wealth, but she had listened and sympathized. She had touched people's hearts and made them better.

Back at the ranch, the family huddled in grief. My sister, Judi, in her first year at the University of Lethbridge, and little Ron, only a child, sat in distraught silence. Christmas had always been a time of gifts and joy in our home. Now celebration seemed incomprehensible.

And then we realized that celebration was exactly what Mom would have wanted. We packed ourselves in cars and went to Lethbridge to buy gifts. "Making Christmas" is what my father had called my mother's furious holiday preparations. In this time of our desolation, we would make Christmas in her honour, or try to.

....

CHAPTER FIFTEEN

Back to School

To BUILD A HOUSE is no small thing. I have always cared passionately about architecture. My surroundings—where I live, where I work—matter enormously to me. It isn't a question of status; I'm not house-proud. It's a question of seeing order, calm, and, if I'm lucky, a bit of beauty around me.

I have lived in log houses without electricity or running water. I have lived in bungalows with high windows that shut out the light. I have lived in small rooms and basement apartments, in an old house on the banks of the North Saskatchewan River where we froze in the winter, in a lofty apartment with a view across the Strait of Georgia to the shadow of Vancouver Island. Different spaces that touched my soul in different ways.

One day, I returned from work, unlocked the door, and stepped back in shock. Every inch of our Vancouver apartment was crammed with furniture. Rory's grandfather had passed away, and his mother had put the unclaimed contents of his two-storey stone house in London, Ontario, on a moving van with instructions to deliver it to us in Vancouver.

I recalled the telephone conversation with Sheila. "Would it be all right to send you some of Rory's grandfather's things?" she asked. "Don't feel obliged to keep anything. You probably don't want to spend your precious time dusting Victorian whatnots."

"Sure," I said. I had imagined a chair or two, a few knick-knacks. Now here I stood, unable to navigate through the hall to the kitchen.

When Rory arrived home, we set about trying to make some order of the chaos that had invaded our home. A big couch was crammed against the living room wall; an oak table crowded our dining space. A real bed frame and dressers replaced mattresses and boxes in the bedroom. We stuffed the old pieces we wanted to keep into somebody else's locker downstairs.

Exhausted, we plunked ourselves on the Victorian chairs and looked at each other. It was okay. Some of the pieces were quite lovely, and more important, they were imbued with family memories. But the furniture just didn't work in our spare apartment. This stuff cried out for a house.

I became obsessed with the project of finding a house. These were the days before the Vancouver real estate boom made starter houses unaffordable. We didn't have much money, but we found a new build in Burnaby, where the prices were reasonable, and moved in.

In 1976, we started planning to build a dream house closer to my work and UBC, where Rory would be studying for his PhD. Not a large or elaborate house—we couldn't afford that—but comfortable. We sold our starter home and bought a lot near the University Endowment Lands. Rory oversaw the construction. As though planning for doomsday, he reinforced every wall. The world will fall around us, but this house will stand, he seemed to say.

Rory planned and planted. "You do the cooking; let me look after the garden," he said, "and I promise you roses six months of the year."

"It's a deal," I said. I didn't know much about gardening, but I had been cooking as long as I could remember.

Rory kept his promise, and so did I.

Teaching was one of the five careers a woman could choose, my school counsellor had told me back in Pincher Creek. I had chosen a general arts degree that led to the law instead. The study of law had brought me joy, and the practice of law gave me deep satisfaction. Yet the idea of teaching still lurked in the recesses of my mind.

I decided to try my hand at teaching a law course. It was not unusual for practising lawyers to teach a course or two on the side. Vancouver, like Edmonton, had a long tradition of cross-town lawyers teaching at the university law school. I had enjoyed listening to these experienced teachers when I was at school; they brought stories and perspectives that reflected not just book learning, but what really happened in the trenches. And although I was enjoying practice, part of me yearned for more scholarly pursuits. I sensed yet another landscape and decided to explore it.

I ran into the dean of the UBC law school, Bertie McClean, an avuncular Northern Islander, at a legal event. In the course of our conversation, I opined it might be fun to teach a course at the school.

"I can arrange that," he said with his broad grin.

And he did, although not quite in the manner I had imagined.

"FIRST-YEAR CIVIL LITIGATION," said Bertie, smiling and rubbing his hands together when I drove out to the university for our first formal meeting. "Just the course for you."

I hesitated—I'd had in mind something grand, like torts or trusts, and I knew civil litigation was not a choice subject—then I thought, *What the heck*. "Fine," I said, and signed up.

What I failed to realize was that civil litigation was the bane of the law school. Students hated it; teachers avoided it. I understood why Dean McClean had smiled and rubbed his hands.

With no choice, I dug in and prepared my notes. There was no textbook—just a dog-eared collection of cases some despairing teacher had put together years before. The subject matter was technical—how to file a writ, how to bring motions, how to draft pleadings—and included the arcane science of what you must put in this document and must never put in that one. Affidavits of documents, oral discovery, how to set down an action for trial—in short, the bewildering mess of tedious rules that govern the mechanics of what lawyers do to get a civil case to trial. The challenge was simply stated: communicate all this to sixty-five first-year law students who had never seen the inside of a courtroom.

I sat at home in the evenings—my teaching was extracurricular, so I couldn't work on it at the office during the day—and tried to figure out how to make the mass of procedural detail interesting to a bunch of first-year students who were coming to law school to learn how to change the world, or at least set a few fires in it. Kids who didn't know what a statement of claim was, and probably didn't care. Kids who, without a basic understanding of the court process, would find the morass of special rules incomprehensible. Kids struggling to make sense of the arcane processes of the law, just as I had a decade earlier.

As I had when I contemplated a career teaching philosophy, I decided my only hope was to tell stories. Stories of real people in real cases who needed their day in court. "It's like hockey," I told my first batch of students, seeing their eyes already beginning to glaze over. "It's all about winning. But you can't win unless you understand the rules." It went better than I'd dared hope. The students—some of them, at least—bought into my hockey metaphor. They hung around after class to discuss what would happen if you did this or that. At the end of the course, I got a stellar student endorsement.

I enjoyed the experience and found myself thinking about taking a break from practice to teach full-time for a while. I wanted to try it, but I didn't want to leave the practice of law. With mixed feelings, I discussed it with the people I worked with at Bull, Housser. "If you want to give it a try, go ahead," they said, and they gave me a fine send-off complete with an engraved silver bowl and an invitation to continue working on files on the side. So I accepted a position as a tenure-track associate professor with the law school. It was 1974. The law school would be my life for the next seven years.

I PLUNGED INTO LAW school life. I found it a sociable place, inhabited by a suite of young professors around my age. Some, like Jim Taylor, a lawyer who started teaching the same year I did, became lifelong friends.

My disappointment was that the two courses I really wanted to teach, torts and constitutional law, had long ago been appropriated by other professors. I wrote an article on damages in tort—ever since that lecture on *Donoghue v. Stevenson* in my first week of law school, I had been fascinated by the legal consequences that could flow from a simple act of negligence, like leaving a dead snail in a bottle of ginger beer. Although my article was published in the *Canadian Bar Review* and cited favourably in a seminal Supreme Court of Canada decision, I was not allowed to so much as put my head in a torts classroom. So I settled for second best: evidence law and contracts law, supplemented over the years by a host of subjects that no one else wanted to teach, like copyright and creditors' remedies (the stuff of mortgages, liens, loans, and how to get your money back when things go bad).

Getting excluded from the courses I wanted proved to be a blessing in disguise. First, I came to love my new subjects, particularly the law of evidence. The rules of evidence—what goes in, what stays out—are fundamental to just outcomes. As I had learned on day one of law school, every case starts with the facts. The judge builds her decision or the jury renders its verdict on the facts. And those facts are determined by the rules of evidence. Evidence that is unreliable, unduly prejudicial, or protected by confidentiality must be kept out. But at the same time, undisclosed evidence may thwart the search for the truth. The rules that maintain the proper balance between these two goals had fascinated me ever since law school, where I had chosen a problem of evidence as the subject of my first published article. Now I found my passion rekindled.

Second, although I was unaware of it at the time, my grounding in the rules of evidence provided the perfect training for a future judge. I knew something about how to run a trial. I knew what should go before a jury and what should not. I could go into chambers and work out the priorities between feuding creditors or understand a copyright argument.

Immersed in my new life and taking on new courses every year, I worked crazy hours. I gathered case materials, prepared lectures, spent endless hours with students, marked exams in December and May, and then started the process of preparation, teaching, and marking all over again. I was constantly beset by guilt—there was always another case to consider, another article to read, another perspective to absorb. Two things helped me carry on. The first was the love of the law. I loved the courses and the details and intricacies they evoked. Tackling each new course was like exploring a new country—looking for familiar landmarks, noting new features. I became a geographer of these new legal landscapes. And the second was the students. They came in many sorts and sizes, and with diverse expectations. Gratifyingly, about 50 percent of my students were women—a huge advance in the short span of the decade between my own law school experience and my experience as a teacher of law. Thing were changing in the world, and for the better. True equality could not be far off.

Many of my students became my friends. They kept turning up throughout my life, in satisfying incarnations. One, Hugh Stansfield, became chief judge of the Provincial Court of British Columbia and a champion of alternative courts to help mentally ill and addicted young people. Another, Kim Campbell, went on to become a federal justice minister and the first female prime minister of Canada.

WHAT I LOVED MOST of all was helping my students learn to think like lawyers—the ultimate object of a legal education. Good lawyers develop a unique analytic ability to figure things out, to take the complicated situations humans create, analyze them, and disentangle them so that they can be understood and managed. Laws change. The world changes. Learning a mass of facts about the current state of the law won't get students far in the real world. What they need to learn is how to think like a lawyer—to pick out the relevant facts, apply the appropriate legal principles, and come up with an answer.

Among the most monumental changes in the law in the 1970s was the way it regarded women. In 1970, Germaine Greer published *The Female Eunuch*, making her a household name and ushering in second-wave feminism. Greer systematically deconstructed what we mean by womanhood and femininity, and argued that women are forced to assume submissive roles in society to fulfill male fantasies of what being a real woman entails.

The book was an instant bestseller. *The Female Eunuch* and the feminist thinking it inspired quickly impacted criminal law and the law of evidence, my principal field of academic interest. Law professors and students began to view in a new light the legal rules that surrounded sexual assault—rules that tragically too often reflected the preconceptions and interests of men, more than the reality of the crime and its impact on the victim. Women demanded that the law of sexual assault be reformed and the rape myths that riddled it be removed. They were heady days to be an academic teaching the law of evidence.

In my early years in law, I strove for perfection and flagellated myself when I fell short, as inevitably happened. Sometimes the quest for perfection almost paralyzed me. *I can't do it*, I would think. *I have to be perfect, and I'm not.* Years later, it came to me that the singular obsession with perfection that had bedevilled me for so long was a uniquely female trait. The men around me never obsessed about whether they were perfect—they just got on with the job at hand. Women of my generation had subliminally absorbed a message—we were allowed into a man's world by grace, but to keep our place we had to be perfect. The inference was lethal: If we were not perfect, we were not worthy. If we were not perfect, we deserved to fail. Better to get out with grace while we could.

Teaching law energized me. It was hard work, but my love of the law and the creative act of teaching carried me on. Along the way, I absorbed an important truth about life—perfection was unattainable. I developed a revised set of self-directives: Accept imperfection. Embrace risk. Have the courage to fail and the strength to pick yourself up and start over. Do your best and move on.

My parents, Ernest and Eleanora Gietz, on their wedding day, November 28, 1942.

Me, two years old, pushing on the gate to new adventures.

Dad, me, Len, and Mom on an outing in Waterton Park. With my hands on my hips, I imagine I was thinking, "Let's get this picture over with so I can get back to the swings and slides and have some fun."

Here I am, the big sister, with Conrad and Len at our kitchen table.

Grade twelve at Matthew Halton High School. This was the year when I began to give serious thought to what I could do with my education.

Ready to ride my horse, Promise.

My high school graduating class in 1961. I'm third from the right in the second row, Diana is on the far right in the third row, and Peter is third from the left in the back.

Me in my University of Alberta bachelor of arts honours garb in 1964.

On a lark in 1962, I let a photographer take this glam photo,
which I promptly buried—it definitely didn't feel like me!

Rory, the biologist, in 1966. He entered my life in the summer of 1961 and changed it forever.

Rory, in the hills west of Turner Valley in Alberta.

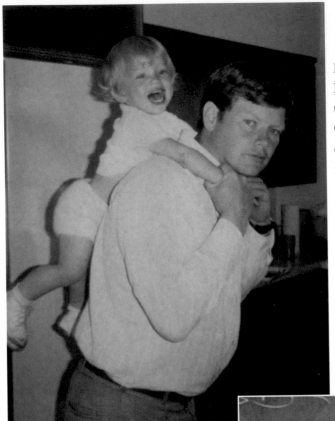

Rory and Angus, 1977. Proud parents, we traveled to London, Ontario, to introduce our one-year-old to his father's family.

My seven years as a lawyer at the University of British Columbia deepened my understanding of the law and helped me be a better judge when I unexpectedly found myself named to the County Court of Vancouver in 1981.

Me at 24 Sussex Drive with Prime Minister Brian Mulroney,
who appointed me chief justice of the BC Supreme Court,
and, later, justice of the Supreme Court of Canada.

Celebrating my sister Judi's wedding on June 16, 1984, in the lush garden Rory created. He promised me roses six months a year and he delivered.

....

CHAPTER SIXTEEN

Parenthood

O<small>N MAY 11, 1976,</small> my son was born. We called him Angus, for Rory's father. For me, it was a distinctive, strong name, fitting for the robust little boy who emerged from the womb fighting. Rory and I rejoiced together in the birth of our son. My father, alone at home in Pincher Creek, sent twenty-five red roses to the hospital.

The word "miracle" is much overused. I reserve it for two events—childbirth and parenting. The emergence into the world of a new being whom two people have mysteriously created—them and yet not them—passes understanding. With time and trouble, one can describe the processes involved. But emotionally, it is a miracle. Or so it seemed to me.

The second is the bond between parent and child that emerges over time. I experienced that miracle and live it today. Angus and

I know each other, understand each other, and love each other in a profound and inexplicable way. We are simply there for each other, part of each other, for better or for worse. We understand that it will always be this way.

Parenthood was also hard work. Struggling to be an adequate lawyer and law teacher, I now found myself also struggling to be an adequate parent. First there was the business of learning to be a parent. Learning the myriad physical tasks of feeding, bathing, and changing dirty nappies, not to mention the sleepless nights and bouts of colic. Learning to be patient, to endure, to not worry obsessively. Learning about how parenting was affecting me as a parent.

In my adult life, I had always been optimistic, upbeat. I had never, apart from times in my youth, experienced prolonged sadness or feelings of futility. I had what I wanted, what I had never dared dream of—a strong marriage, a child I loved, and a fulfilling profession.

So it came as a shock to realize, in the month after Angus's birth, that something wasn't right. Even as I cradled my perfect child, I would wipe tears from my cheek. What was happening to me? For nine months, every part of my being had strained to accomplish a single goal—to bring a new being successfully into the world. Now, the task accomplished, I felt empty and exhausted. Outside my window, the clouds seemed omnipresent and the rain endless. I looked at the child in my arms and knew, with a certainty that defied logic, that I would not be able to give him what he needed, that I would fail as a mother.

I thought back to the only other time I had faced depression, during my winter of snow on the ranch. Then, like now, I had struggled with changes within me that I didn't fully understand. Then, like now, I had been beset by feelings of doubt and inadequacy. Then, like now, I had found myself unable to understand or articulate my anxiety and fear. I had come through that, I reminded myself; I would get through this.

I remembered what I had learned practising law and teaching: perfection is a chimera. Just as I had made mistakes in law, I would make mistakes as a mother. When I did, I would pick myself up and move on.

So I did. The first step was to reclaim my other life as a teacher of law. I could not be a good parent unless I myself was fulfilled. It was the summer, and there was no need for me to be back at the law school—I could prepare my courses as easily at home as in my drab university cubicle. Yet my survival instinct told me that set-up wasn't working. I found a lovely lady to look after Angus for three mornings a week, and on those days, I returned to the law, read the latest Supreme Court cases, discussed them with colleagues—in short, I got back to the profession that had become part of me.

My depression lifted. Maybe it would have passed anyway, but the experience brought me to a realization about myself: I needed an external world around me. Even more importantly, I needed my work and its intellectual explorations. I needed the law like I needed food and water; without it, I withered and sank into sadness.

With reluctance and some guilt, I came to accept that this was my personal reality. I watched mothers who found total fulfillment in parenting with admiration, envy, and occasional pangs of guilt. I longed to be like them. But I could not. By September, I had found a full-time caretaker for Angus and was back at the law school five days a week. I might not be a perfect mom, but together, our little family would move forward.

JUST AS MY SKIES were beginning to brighten, tragedy struck once again. Angus was a year old, and we had made a trip to London, Ontario, to visit Rory's family. The flight east had been delayed by six hours, and we arrived exhausted. I went to the downstairs guest suite for a nap. An hour later, Rory awakened me and whispered that my father had passed away.

My mother's death had broken my father's life. He had tried to put it together again. The ranch had sold to French interests, and at last there was money. For the first time in his life, freed from the grind of work, he had been taking vacations. He had even remarried. But he'd never recaptured the magic he had known with my mother.

I felt a profound sense of sadness at his passing. Sadness for gifts unused, dreams unrealized, words unsaid. Sadness for the loss of him. He had trouble putting feelings into words, but I had always known, deep down, that he was in my corner no matter how unexpected my choices or strange my fancies.

The official cause of my father's death was heat stroke, brought on by spa treatments for rheumatism and hoeing in his garden. The unofficial cause was unhappiness. There is more than one way to die of a broken heart.

I had lost both my parents much too soon. Both had possessed enormous gifts—gifts that life and circumstances had prevented them from fully realizing. The Christian parable of the talents came back to me. Human beings are given certain talents, some more than others. Whatever our endowment, it is our task in life to develop those talents and use them to make the world a better place. My parents understood this. Both had great dreams in their youth. But life— the grind of family and incessant work—had got in the way, until the dreams dimmed and finally ebbed away. I looked at my son and vowed it would not happen to him.

Still, it was hard work ensuring that my child always had what I wanted for him. Like other young parents, Rory and I struggled with the problem of childcare. Rory juggled completing his PhD, environmental consulting, and overseeing the construction of our home on the edge of the University Endowment Lands in Point Grey. For Angus's first two years, we found childcare with the wives of graduate students, who would take in an extra child for additional income. Angus, beginning to talk, burbled about "Mommy Chung," his caretaker; I was just "Mommy." I swallowed a pang of jealousy and smiled. When this wonderful caretaker moved on, he went to the campus townhome of a friendly family. Their son, Ugo, became Angus's playmate and best friend. Angus would dash from the car when I dropped him off in the morning, calling, "Ugo, Ugo!" The warm embrace of these caretakers and their families eased the guilt I felt as I pulled away from the curb and headed to my books and classes.

We graduated from home care to co-operative daycare as Angus neared his third birthday. While there were trained workers on staff at the daycare, parents were required to chip in several hours a week and to help with weekend cleaning. The daycare was only a few blocks from the law school, so I did most of the co-operating. The ever-changing parent rota required me to dash from classes in a panic and terminate student interviews mid-stream. On one occasion, a business lunch went later than anticipated and I was late for my shift in the play yard. I arrived to the crisp reprimand of the daycare supervisor and the glares of the other mothers on duty. Miserably, I did the walk of shame to the nursery and set about changing the nappies of howling toddlers. Maybe I rated an A-plus at the law, but I was scoring a D-minus at parenting.

Things improved when Angus moved to the upper daycare next door. It was co-operative, too, but the hours were fewer, and Rory and I had more control over our shift times, allowing us to share the duties. The daycare employees were professionally trained, and I watched with admiration as they handled this or that problem and advised parents on the particular needs of their children. They understood childhood behaviour and genuinely loved children.

Angus, an affectionate child, had developed the awkward habit of opening a conversation with other children with a punch to the shoulder. The daycare workers did not content themselves with sitting him on a chair for five minutes—the usual discipline—and discussed it with Rory and me. "The children aren't afraid of him," they explained, "but we can't have this behaviour."

"Why do you hit other kids?" I asked my son.

"Don't know," came the answer.

Rory and I conferred on our own. We decided that while we might be physically absent for most of the day, we could be virtually present. Each day when we picked up Angus, we would ask how things had gone. If he'd had to sit on the chair, we discussed why after dinner.

A few weeks later, the daycare workers called me in for a meeting. With dread in my heart, I entered the tiny office. "Angus has improved," they said. To my relief, they reported that his conversation-opening gambit of a swift right had disappeared.

"Not to pry," said one of the workers, "but are things going better at home?"

I looked at her in bewilderment. "Things have always been good at home," I told her. "What's changed is that we've been having discussions with Angus about his conduct. Whenever he has had to sit on the chair, we ask him what happened."

The worker shook her head dubiously. "He's too young to internalize," she said.

I smiled and let it go. It was the only time my opinion ever differed from theirs.

AS I STRUGGLED TO combine a full-time career with motherhood, I found myself musing on the difficulties that mothers encounter in the working world.

Equality is an elusive concept, slippery and multi-layered. As a schoolgirl, I thought equality meant getting an equal break with the boys. Gender-neutral departmental final exams ensured that I did.

As a university student, I thought equality meant equal evaluation and equal marks for equal work. Due to fair professors, I passed the bar and moved ahead. As a young lawyer, I thought equality meant being given an equal chance, but being judged by a different standard. Because I wore skirts, I had to be better—not just marginally better but a lot better—to succeed. Again, I eked through.

Now, as a mother, I gave the word "equality" yet another dimension. I had always understood and accepted that "equal opportunity" implied "equal performance." What I had not appreciated was that "equal performance" is too often interpreted as "identical performance." To that point in my career, I had been able to deliver identical performance—showing up for work or court or class at stipulated hours, doing as much as if not more than my male counterparts, contributing to the incidental social activities of whatever work unit I was part of. But now, I found myself asking new questions.

How can the mother of a sick child always show up to work at the appointed time? How can she consistently—day after day, year after year—perform exactly like her male counterparts? Faced with all the demands on the home front, how can she ensure she is going the expected extra mile by organizing and participating in after-hours work events? When would we move beyond the assumption that women bear most of the responsibility for the care of children and the home?

I was lucky—I was a well-paid academic who could afford day-care and help, and I had a secure and reasonably flexible job. I had to be at the law school for classes, meetings, and other prescribed events. But otherwise, I could be where I needed to be. If I found my dual role challenging, what of the mothers struggling to make ends meet while working in rigidly structured jobs behind cash registers or banks of phones? And how much worse must it be if the wages one earns are pegged below those of men, simply because the job in question is mostly performed by women?

In 1973, while I was still coming to grips with these problems and the gender inequality that confronted me at every turn, a revolution was born. It was called *Murdoch v. Murdoch*.[1]

James and Irene Murdoch were people I could relate to. Like my parents, they operated a family ranch in the Porcupine Hills, just north of Pincher Creek. They ran their joint venture just as my parents and the parents of all my friends ran theirs: as a complete and equal partnership. Mrs. Murdoch did the cooking and housework, looked after the children, and, when she could spare a moment, worked in the fields. Their venture grew and prospered.

Twenty-five years on, when the marriage failed, Mrs. Murdoch left with the children and sued for half of the family ranch. After all, she was an equal partner in the enterprise, working side by side with her husband to build up the equity. Her husband offered a monthly allowance for her and the children. No way, said Mrs. Murdoch. I'm entitled to an equal share of the property.

Court after court rejected her. There was no legal basis for her claim, they said. The property was in her husband's name. To claim a share, she needed to show that her husband held the property in trust for her. But under the existing law, Mrs. Murdoch could not establish a trust.

Mrs. Murdoch, no doubt by now deep in debt, pursued her case to the Supreme Court of Canada. The court sat with only five members (not atypical before automatic rights to civil appeals in certain categories were eliminated in 1975).[2] In a four-to-one decision, penned by Justice Ronald Martland, the court affirmed the trial judge's determination that Mrs. Murdoch's contributions were merely "the work done by any ranch wife."[3] Mrs. Murdoch had made no financial contribution.[4] She and her husband had not intended to create a trust.[5] Following English jurisprudence, Justice Martland concluded there was no resulting (or informal) trust that required Mr. Murdoch to share the property with his wife.

The court's newest justice, Bora Laskin, wrote a passionate dissent. He detailed Mrs. Murdoch's equal contribution to the ranch and ruled that justice required she be accorded a share of the property. The English law was inadequate, Justice Laskin argued—under Canadian law, the property should be impressed with a trust in Mrs. Murdoch's favour.

The decision made waves. As future chief justice Brian Dickson would subsequently recall, "Bora, for his dissenting judgment, was declared the folk hero of Canada, and very much lauded and applauded, whereas the others were somewhat criticized and denigrated."[6] Less than three months later, Prime Minister Pierre Trudeau defied tradition by elevating Justice Laskin to the chief justiceship over his more senior colleague, Justice Martland, whom most expected to get the job.

The *Murdoch* decision stirred the Canadian conscience. Outraged women, joined by many men, publicized the case across the country. Advocates began demanding that husbands and wives be given equal rights to property acquired during the course of the marriage. Legislators listened. Province after province passed legislation setting a baseline of equal distribution of matrimonial property on the breakup of a marriage. Skeptics predicted equality would be the death knell of marriage and family. Both have survived.

Mrs. Murdoch, the catalyst of this momentous change, did not benefit. After her defeat in the Supreme Court of Canada, both she and her husband petitioned for divorce. Mrs. Murdoch sought maintenance, which is exactly what it sounds like—just enough to get by on. After yet another court proceeding, she was awarded a lump sum of $65,000 in lieu of support payments for herself and her children.

The *Murdoch* case marked a turning point in equality for Canadian women—not because of the court decision, but because of the outrage it produced. While wives could now expect to share equitably in property acquired during a marriage, the case did not herald complete economic equality for women in Canada. Since the 1950s, legislation had begun to proclaim the right of women to equal employment benefits, yet little had changed. Sure, women were working outside the home. The problem was that they weren't getting paid what they should for that work. But pay equity was next on women's agendas.

In 1983, a young judge named Rosalie Silberman Abella—who would years later be promoted to the Supreme Court—was called to head up the Royal Commission on Equality in Employment. Her report concluded that great and persistent inequities existed. Women faced higher unemployment than men. Those who had full-time work in 1982 earned an average of sixty-four cents for every dollar men earned, while women's incomes overall were 54.6 percent of men's.[7]

"To argue, as some have, that we cannot afford the cost of equal pay to women is to imply that women somehow have a duty to be paid less until other financial priorities are accommodated," wrote Judge Abella. "This reasoning is specious and it is based on an unacceptable premise: the acceptance of arbitrary distinctions based on gender as a legitimate basis for imposing negative consequences, particularly when the economy is faltering."[8]

Judge Abella also observed that among eleven Crown (government-owned) corporations, women enjoyed as few opportunities for advancement as they had five years earlier. In 1978, just 1.1 percent of those in the upper-level management ranks were women. By 1983, that number had risen to only 3.7 percent. In middle management, professional, semi-professional, and technical positions, the data were no less dismal.[9] "There is no disputing that sex-role stereotypes have affected labour market decisions, thus limiting women's options and expectations, and shaping their behaviour," Judge Abella noted.[10]

Though she called for "a massive policy response to systemic discrimination,"[11] it was not forthcoming. While the 1977 federal

Canadian Human Rights Act required "equal pay for work of equal value," provincial human rights codes in 1983 did not. Instead, "equal pay for equal work" was the standard for only the 11 percent of the workforce that was under the Canadian Human Rights Commission's jurisdiction.[12] And so it remained. Twenty-five years on, only women in federally regulated industries and in the province of Quebec enjoyed a statutory guarantee of equal pay for work of equal value.[13]

Since the Abella Commission concluded its work, women have been bringing pay equity issues to the courts. In a steady stream of rulings, the courts, some of which I have been a part of, have supported them. In 2011, as chief justice, I surprised the assembled lawyers in the Supreme Court by giving a quick, unanimous judgment from the bench in the longest-running pay equity challenge in Canadian history—twenty years in the making. The court decided that women who had been paid less than men for equivalent work between 1982 and 2002 would not wait an hour longer for their victory.[14] And in 2014, I was part of the court that allowed an appeal by British Columbia's teachers' union, which had argued that a school board's refusal to "top up" birth mothers' government maternity and parental leave benefits amounted to unlawful discrimination.[15] This case, too, the court decided with a brief oral judgment from the bench, shortly after the hearing.

We are making progress, but half a century after I started my legal career and four decades into the fight for pay equity, the most recent statistics show that women still lag behind men, earning just eighty-seven cents on the dollar in 2015.[16] Women still earn less than men, and women who are mothers earn less than women without children.[17] Indigenous women and women of colour fare even worse. We still have work to do. So let's get on with it.

I had my work set out for me, so getting on with it is exactly what I did. As Angus got older, Rory assumed primary on-call responsibility. Angus went to after-school care. Just in case something went wrong, Rory put a cord with a key and his name and address around his neck before he went to school. Latch-key kid—the phrase still evokes a spasm of guilt. In my anguished state, I counted up the waking hours of each week and wrote down how many of them I spent with my child. To my surprise, it turned out to be half. Not great, but not terrible, either.

We were a happy family. Each night, we read stories. Each summer, we took a long vacation on Pender Island, spending our days exploring the shore for sea creatures and fishing in little wooden boats the resort supplied. Rory taught Angus all the Latin names for the things he saw—one entire summer was spent obsessing over jellyfish, which Angus insisted on calling *Cyanea rosea*. We took two road trips, one to Disneyland in California and another to Texas to visit my brother Len and his family. Angus didn't mind the long stretches on the road; he would sit in the back seat reading his favourite books and using coloured markers to create characters for new stories he imagined.

Rory and I were exacting parents. We were proud of our amazing child and determined to equip him with everything he needed to succeed (and a number of things he did not need). We imposed rules (sometimes too many) and discipline (sometimes too much). We subjected him—and ourselves—to endless rounds of activities and programs.

With Rory's encouragement, Angus developed a knack for soccer. Unafraid and incapable of flinching, he was a good enough defence player to make it into an elite Vancouver soccer league. And he showed an early passion for music, which was to occupy our weekends with lessons and recitals. He started off with the group Yamaha organ program. He chafed at the organized group activity but loved the music. "He should take private lessons," the teacher said. She taught him one-on-one for a while, before he moved on to a teacher who held a position in the faculty of music at the university.

The first time we greeted his new piano teacher at her house,

Angus cocked his head at the music emanating from her stereo. I identified it as Mozart. But he did better. "Symphony 41," he said. "The *Jupiter*." The teacher and I looked at each other in astonishment. Where had he picked this up? Rory and I usually had the radio tuned to CBC's classical channel. Angus had been listening, really listening, and learning.

"He has perfect pitch," the teacher told me later. I recalled Grandpa Kruschell's passion for the trombone and marvelled at the wonder of talents popping up two generations removed.

Was I a perfect parent? Certainly not. Was I an adequate parent? I came to believe I was. I once asked a stay-at-home mother who had raised five fine human beings to adulthood for her opinion on the elements of good parenting. She gave me a faraway look, and then she said, "Parenting. Two things are essential: strength of character and unconditional love."

Maybe it's that simple.

Long after my child was grown and on his own, the question of whether I was an adequate parent still haunted me, and so I asked him. Angus gave me a strange look, then smiled.

"Get over it, Mom," he said. "You were there for me. It was okay." And then he hugged me. A long, wrapping hug that I never wanted to end.

Perfection in all things—especially in parenting—is unattainable. You just do your best, no matter the inequalities and injustices of life, and enjoy the miracle.

PART THREE

THE JUDGE

The *Canadian Charter of Rights and Freedoms* guarantees the rights and freedoms set out in it subject only to such reasonable limits prescribed by law as can be demonstrably justified in a free and democratic society.

—*Canadian Charter of Rights and Freedoms*, Section 1

....

CHAPTER SEVENTEEN

The New Judge

IN THE LATE FALL of 1980, I looked at my calendar one day and saw that the law school was holding a reception I needed to attend at the faculty club across the way. In my rush, I read the time as five instead of five thirty and arrived early. One other person was there— Allan McEachern, chief justice of the Supreme Court of British Columbia.

The chief justice had the battered face of an ex-rugby player and a crooked smile. His eyes were wary and weary but kind. He was not large, but he was a force of a man, renowned for his courage and devotion to justice. I had done a legal opinion for him on a murder case and knew him slightly.

"Never a bad thing to be early," he cracked.

Little did he know how many times I had raced in late for a

lecture or meeting. We chatted for a while, and then he asked me a question I never thought I would hear.

"Have you ever thought about becoming a judge?"

I should have said something like "How interesting." Instead, I laughed and blurted, "Never!"

Which was the truth. I had begun to think about going back to practice—doing a few cases on the side while continuing to teach. But judging? Never. Complicating the matter was the fact that I had been writing some fiction. Ever since my university days, I had toyed with the idea but never attempted it. Rory and I devoured fiction. While still in Edmonton, we had discovered an unknown (to us) writer named Alice Munro. Or rather, Rory had discovered her.

"You have to read this," he said, handing me a copy of *Dance of the Happy Shades*. So I did. The intricate turns of the lives that Munro's short stories explored, the unspoken drama of the ordinary life, the sheer beauty of the language—it all captivated me. I knew I could never write like that. But perhaps I could write something.

I was overloaded with teaching, parenting, and my share of the homemaking. I told myself to forget this strange compulsion to write fiction, but I couldn't chase away the idea. I started to type on my old Olivetti each evening after Angus was in bed. A character emerged— a feisty female criminal lawyer I called Jilly Truitt. I created a story to go with her. I knew the plot was sketchy, the writing too sentimental. But on a lark, I submitted my manuscript to a McClelland & Stewart competition for first-time novelists.

I didn't win, but Anna Porter, the legendary publisher, asked to meet with me on a trip to Vancouver. I dressed up in my best jacket and made my way to the eighth floor of the Vancouver Hotel, where Anna, suffering from a wicked cold, told me that while there were problems with the story and most of the details, she liked my character and liked my writing. "Rewrite it and we'll publish it," she said.

"Sure," I replied, elated.

And then, just as I was contemplating the pursuit of my literary dream—something I had never thought possible—there came an official offer to join the County Court of Vancouver. (In those pre-application days, the "tap on the shoulder" method governed judicial appointments.) There was no way I could combine writing with judging. A few judges had written short stories, poetry, or nonfiction. But balancing a career as a novelist with the calling of a judge was, for me, unthinkable.

I had other concerns, too. The county court did important civil and criminal work, but it didn't deal with the big commercial and criminal cases or the cutting-edge legal issues of criminal law. Would the routine nature of the work satisfy me? And if it didn't, what then? The tradition was that judges didn't leave office. I had no guarantee of promotion to the BC Supreme Court. Would I be happy spending the rest of my life as a county court judge?

I sat down at the kitchen table with pen and paper. Just as I had when I was dithering about continuing in law school, I listed the pros for judging on the left side of the sheet and the cons on the right.

The pros:

1. Interesting and challenging work. Instead of reading and analyzing what other judges had written, I would get to do the writing.
2. A significant increase in salary and a generous pension.

The items on the con side were more amorphous, but no less compelling:

1. The probable end of my dream of writing fiction.
2. The distinct possibility that I would not be good at judging, or that I would pass muster but for the rest of my working life remain at the starting-level position I had been offered.

3. The fact that my life on the bench would be long indeed. I was only thirty-seven, and early retirement would not be an option.
4. The apprehension of once again entering a man's world, where as a woman my future was uncertain. The only woman on the court—of fifty or so judges—was Patricia Proudfoot.

In the end, the pros won. When I received the fateful call from Justice Minister Jean Chrétien, I said yes. I joined the county court. I went down to Matz & Wozny Court Apparel and had a new striped skirt and gown made. On April 22, 1981, I put them on, took the Bible in my hand, and was sworn in as the second woman to join the County Court of Vancouver. Rory watched proudly with little Angus, not quite five, at his side. I thought of Mom and Dad, and how proud they would have been to see their daughter on the bench.

As I readied myself to take my oath, I reflected on why I had been asked to become a judge. An academic with limited experience and no stature at the bar, I was entirely devoid of the usual attributes for a judge. And at thirty-seven, I was too young.

As expected, the men who'd supported my candidature—Allan McEachern and my mentor, Bae Wallace—denied this. They had worked with me and were fully confident that I would make an excellent judge. But deep in my heart, I knew exactly why my name came up in 1980, a time when public attention was increasingly drawn to the fact that there were virtually no women on the bench. The federal government had decided the country needed more women judges. Yet, not many women had been called to the bar for the requisite ten years or more. Contrary to the usual pattern, I was asked to become a judge *because* I was a woman.

I was sworn in as a judge at 10:30 a.m. Tea and cookies and re-served congratulations—early days, too soon to know how this would turn out—occupied the remainder of the morning. The *Vancouver*

Sun announced on the inside pages that a woman had been appointed to the county court. In the corridors of the courthouse, lawyers exchanged uncharitable whispers about the new judge with better legs than legal qualifications. In the afternoon, I heard my first case.

It was a simple case—Chief Judge David Campbell had decided to ease me gently into my new role—a dispute between a homeowner and a flooring company about workmanship. I did my best to look like a judge and appear competent, even though I knew nothing about how to conduct a trial or flooring. The next morning, when I was gowning up for the completion of the case, the clerk advised me that it had settled. I was stricken. Clearly, I had failed.

"They thought they were better off to settle than to trust the new judge," I quipped.

The kindly clerk saved my judicial career. "Oh no," he said. "Just the opposite. You were listening and asking questions, and they started seeing each other's case in a different light. Before you knew it, they were talking settlement."

I had learned my first lesson in judging: listen. If you think you know the answer, you probably don't. If you think you are the smartest person in the room, you're probably in the wrong room. Listening will help you get the right answer. And even if you don't get that far, listening in itself is an important part of the trial process. And I learned something else—in this job, as in all those that had come before, I should not be too quick to brand my efforts with failure.

The next months were a time of intense learning. The judges of the County Court of Vancouver were a wonderful lot who did everything they could to help me find my way. "If you don't know what to do, adjourn," Dave Campbell told me. "We'll help you out. Remember, you are in charge." It was good advice. Although I seldom had to adjourn, I took all the tips I could get around the lunchroom or over coffee, and I always tried to remember that nothing would happen that I couldn't control.

I learned that while the main job of a judge is to hear the evidence and come to a decision, there were two other things that were essential. First, a judge must run the case in a manner that is both fair and efficient. A judge must never berate or bully, even when she thinks a lawyer is being obstreperous or going on at undue length. But she must also ensure that time isn't wasted and the trial runs smoothly. That means she must be efficient. I decided that when evidentiary issues arose in my courtroom, I would rule on them as quickly as possible to keep the trial moving. Second, I learned that a judge should give clear, concise reasons for her decision. The cases in county court weren't usually complex, and often I could deliver judgment orally from the bench. Sometimes, however, the case demanded careful and scholarly writing. There was not much time allocated to this vital activity—one week in every four—so I took to writing my reasons at home at night, after Angus was in bed.

Angus's daycare workers were excited by my appointment and asked me to come to talk to his class about life on the bench. I fretted about how to communicate the art of judging to preschoolers. But Angus came to my rescue. "Wear your costume," he said, referring to the blue-and-gold robes that I had worn on my swearing-in.

The summer flew by. I found I was enjoying my new job and gaining confidence with every trial I had and every decision I wrote. I decided that whatever my misgivings going in, I liked being a judge on the County Court of Vancouver.

But it was not to last. In the fall of 1981, after only five months on the county court, I received a phone call from Jean Chrétien once again. "We would like to move you up to the Supreme Court of British Columbia," he said.

"When?" I asked. I was hoping he'd say, "In a year or two, when you've gained a little more experience."

"Immediately," he replied.

Just when I thought I might be able to manage my job on the

county court, I was being asked to take on new challenges for which I felt ill prepared. My mind raced through the duties I realized I'd have to take on but knew little about—how to run a jury trial, how to deal with a class action, how to manage the chaos of Monday morning chambers (where the judge had to deal with everything from mortgage foreclosures to complex procedural problems in a matter of minutes). But then the noise in my head quieted, and I remembered the lessons I had learned—embrace risk; have the courage to fail.

"Thank you for your vote of confidence," I said. "I'd be delighted."

And that was that. I was sworn in as a judge of the Supreme Court of British Columbia in September 1981.

I QUICKLY SETTLED INTO the routines of the supreme court—jury trials, civil and criminal; chambers motions; intricate problems of law, trusts, and business. I loved the work. Every day I observed humanity in all its forms, from the depraved to the noble. Many days, I had to decide fascinating issues of evidence and the law. My colleagues were fine people who put justice—in philosopher John Rawls's sense of fairness—above all else.

Rawls's ideas resonated and shaped my personal instincts about justice, formed during my years in law school and in practice. Justice was essentially about fairness, and equality was central to what was fair. Society should accord individuals maximum liberty, I believed, limited only by the imperative that one person's liberty should not infringe another's. People should be treated equally, but equality did not mean simply treating likes alike, as Aristotle had posited. Beneficial inequalities should be tolerated in order to help the less well-off, not make it harder for those without resources to occupy positions of power and influence. These were ideas that would profoundly influence my approach to judging, and each conversation with my colleagues provided me new insights and wisdom.

I was grateful, too, that Allan McEachern, my chief justice and the man who had first asked me to consider judging, was wise and considerate.

During my first weeks on the court, I ran up against a difficult problem and went to Allan to seek advice. He listened patiently and, when I was done, gave me his crooked smile.

"Do the right thing," he said.

The message was profound: You are the judge; you and you alone are responsible for the decision. And by the way, do the right thing. Whenever I faced a difficult decision, I remembered his lesson: take responsibility, search the law and your conscience, and above all, do the right thing.

The job involved a certain amount of travel to outlying districts. I didn't ask for special treatment, even though being away from home with a young child was difficult.

"I'll assign you to some out-of-town sittings," Allan told me. "I don't want people to think you aren't doing your share. But they'll be less than some of the other judges." Then he smiled. "Don't worry. When Angus is a little older, I'll even things out and make you do double duty."

I started slowly and floundered more than I wanted to, but no one died, and no one, to my knowledge, was wrongfully convicted on my watch. Gradually, I learned the business of judging. Case after case came hurtling at me, one lined up behind the other, and the heat of the trial demanded on-the-spot decisions. I picked up my pace, I learned, and I realized one important thing.

"You were right again," I said to Rory across the breakfast table one Saturday morning after an exhausting week. "I love being a judge."

....

CHAPTER EIGHTEEN

Growing and Grieving

Bᴇ 1983, ANGUS WAS in grade two French immersion, engrossed in his piano studies, and gaining a local reputation as a mean soccer defenceman. Rory was dividing his time between parenting and environmental consulting. On weekends, we explored the wonders of the Pacific Northwest. I was two years into my job on the Supreme Court of British Columbia, and I was still loving it. Life was good.

"You should be using a computer—it's called word processing," Rory observed as he watched me write out my judgments and reasons. Most judges wrote their judgments in longhand; some dictated them into tiny recorders. In the 1980s, no judges used computers.

I thought about it and decided he was right. It was the early days of word processing; computers were just beginning to replace the memory typewriters that were still the norm in British Columbia courthouses. Using a computer would be quicker than writing long-hand or dictating. It would also produce a better result by allowing me to move around or edit blocks of text. Finally, it might just save me waiting the days and sometimes weeks it took for our shared secretaries to get to the junior judges' cases.

I didn't dare ask my chief justice for a computer—I knew there was no court budget for one. So I went out and purchased my own, then set about learning how to use it by taking evening classes. I was fortunate that I could type—due to a dearth of optional subjects, all Pincher Creek students had to learn to use a typewriter. Once more my humble origins proved useful.

My secretary, Aline, and I worked out a routine. I would produce printed reasons for judgment on my daisy wheel printer. She would then append the style of cause and technical matters. In ancient court files, you can still uncover the strange amalgams of font and typeset produced by our collaboration.

Slowly, I realized that lawyers were talking about me in revised terms. The "new judge in skirts" was earning a reputation as a serious jurist who ran a trial well, got her rulings out promptly, wrote clear and concise reasons for judgment—on a computer, no less—and, most important, strove to be fair. Did I sometimes fail in one or more of these ambitions? Certainly. Did the court of appeal overturn my rulings on occasion? Definitely. Still, I was doing well enough. I had proved myself.

It came as no surprise, therefore, when, in 1985, I was asked to become the first woman to sit on the British Columbia Court of Appeal—the highest court in the province. I accepted, but not without qualms. I would be leaving a job where I alone ran the courtroom and called the shots for a court where I would sit as one judge of three or five, with no guarantee that my view would prevail. I knew from experience what it felt like to be the only woman around a table of men—the outsider, the imposter (although no one would be so impolite as to say so). There had been women on the county court before me, and women on the Supreme Court of British Columbia. But no woman had ever breached the hallowed halls of the British Columbia Court of Appeal. Who knew how I would fare?

I suddenly felt the weight that comes with being a first. Everyone is waiting and watching—some rooting for you, and some secretly hoping you'll fail. And the future of those who follow rests on how you do. A line from Kermit the Frog's song from Angus's favourite show, *Sesame Street*, kept ringing in my ears: "It's not easy being green." It's not easy being first, either, I realized.

What's more, I was apprehensive about the change in work that elevation to the court of appeal would bring. I knew with certainty that I would miss the trial process, miss the witnesses and the drama of watching the evidence unfold. My short time as a trial judge had made me a firm believer in the jury system. I saw first-hand how seriously the jurors took their duties, how perceptive they were in sorting out truth from lies. I felt the sense of ownership in the justice system it brought to the public. I would miss all that.

Life in the court of appeal did indeed prove to be different from life as a trial judge. Instead of running the trial, I took a back seat to the presiding judge. Instead of never knowing what was coming next, I had a predictable range of legal issues and time to think about them in advance. Instead of worrying about who was telling the truth and finding facts, my new job was to accept the facts as found by the trial judge and figure out the law that applied to them.

The chief justice of the court of appeal, Nathan Nemetz, was a clever and wily jurist. He was not given to writing long legal treatises, but he was almost always bang on in his decisions. My problem, I discovered, was that he sometimes went too fast for me. As the three judges gathered in the corridor before entering the courtroom, the chief would say, "Not much in this one, right? I think we can proceed directly to the respondent." Proceeding directly to the respondent was a sure sign that the appellant's written argument, or factum, hadn't shown anything wrong with the decision on appeal, and the appeal, barring some surprise, would be dismissed.

"I'm sorry, Chief," I would say in my most deferential voice, "but I've looked at the material and I think I need to hear from the appellant. I think there may be a problem . . ." My voice would trail off under the chief's glare. But the rules were the rules. If one of the three judges wanted to hear the appellant, the appellant would be heard. The chief's face would gradually morph into a sad sigh at the prospect of a longer hearing than he felt necessary, and more often than not, he proved right in the end. Occasionally, though, the appellant's arguments swung the case in a different direction, and I felt vindicated.

I slowly warmed to appellate work. I was fascinated by how legal principles adapted to new situations, allowing the law to grow within its natural limits. This was the bailiwick of the court of appeal. As I gained seniority, I found myself writing for the court on important issues like the interpretation of the *Canadian Charter of Rights and Freedoms'* guarantee of equality or the right to a fair trial.

Adopted only four years before, the Charter was the centrepiece of the *Constitution Act, 1982*, a package that patriated our constitution from the United Kingdom to Canada. It guaranteed the rights of Indigenous peoples, as well as a catalogue of other rights, including democratic rights like the right to vote, freedom of religion, freedom of expression, mobility rights, protection from unreasonable search and seizure, liberty, fair trial rights, protection against cruel and unusual punishment, and equality rights. While guaranteeing these rights, Section 1 of the Charter also provided that the government could limit them, provided the limit was justified in a free and democratic society.

The *Constitution Act, 1982* changed Canada from a parliamentary democracy to a constitutional democracy. This meant that all laws and government actions would henceforth have to comply with the Charter and other guarantees. It would now fall to the courts to determine whether a disputed law or government action complied. This placed the courts at the centre of questions of constitutional validity on a host of new issues, whether they liked it or not. It also confronted jurists with the task of interpreting a new document with new guarantees, with little or no precedent to guide them. It was challenging and fascinating work. We all understood that the ultimate interpretation of the Charter's provisions rested with the Supreme Court of Canada, which had been Canada's apex court since 1949, when appeals to the Judicial Committee of the Privy Council were abolished. But before a Charter challenge reached the Supreme Court, it had to pass through the provincial appellate courts; the judges of these lower courts had no choice but to jump into the fray and do their best.

On BC's court of appeal, I found myself wading into debates on the scope of the Charter's provisions. What did the presumption of innocence and the right to a fair trial mean? How broad were the guarantees of equality and free speech? I fell to the work with gusto and a sense of rare good fortune that chance had placed me on the court of appeal at this exciting jurisprudential moment. It was heady stuff for a girl who had once wondered if she would ever find a place in the law.

LIFE WAS GOOD BEYOND my wildest imaginings. But there were clouds clustering so slowly I hardly noticed them. Rory wasn't well. He would fall prey to severe flus that sent him to bed for weeks and to mysterious stomach ailments that put him in hospital. He always recovered, always resumed more or less normal life, but the bouts of illness became more frequent, and they were increasingly followed by debilitating fatigue. Nothing serious, we told ourselves. Nothing we can't deal with.

I don't recall when I first suspected that Rory was seriously ill. Was it his gradual loss of energy? The increasing number of minor illnesses as his immune system began to fail? His desperate attempts to complete lingering projects on ever-lengthening lists? Or the periods of anger and depression that came with more regularity?

In the late summer of 1986, Rory took Angus and me along on a field trip to the interior of British Columbia. It involved digging a pit to record soil strata—an afternoon under the hot Osoyoos sun. That evening in the motel, he collapsed. The next morning, I drove us home, appalled at the spectre of the man beside me in the passenger seat. He had been seeing his doctor, but no diagnosis was forthcoming.

In the weeks that followed, he would manage bouts of activity, only to fall into fatigue and depression again. I sensed that something was very wrong but was helpless to discover what. He kept seeing Dr. Fritz, and Dr. Fritz kept prescribing new treatments and panaceas.

And then tragedy struck. It was the spring of 1987. Late in the morning, as I emerged from court, the clerk slipped me a note: "Call your husband." I frowned, thinking it must have to do with Angus, since Rory was the contact parent when I was on the bench. I wasn't alarmed. At the noon break, I returned to my room and shucked my gown. The note fell out of my pocket. I called.

"I have cancer," Rory said. "Mouth cancer."

I slumped over my desk, a stone in the pit of my stomach. The fears I had subconsciously repressed, the scenarios I had refused to contemplate as I blithely pursued this case or that line of law, flushed to the surface and sabotaged my power to think. It was a diagnosis that shattered our dreams.

"I'm coming home," I whispered.

"No, finish the case. We'll talk tonight."

My colleague Bill Esson found me at my desk, still leaning over its leather top. I had known Bill from my days at Bull, Housser, and Tupper, and over the years, we had formed a deep friendship. "Come to lunch," he said. "We'll talk."

I sobbed through lunch, venting my fears. Bill listened and grieved with me. "You should not assume the worst," he said. But in my heart, I knew.

That night, Rory told me that his dental surgeon had noticed an abnormal growth in his mouth, taken a biopsy, and found what the doctors had missed. Cancer. The post-diagnostic trajectory was predictable. Massive surgery in May. A summer of attempted recuperation. Early hope in the winter. A setback in the spring, with new cancer in the lungs and then, in the summer, the bones.

For a year and a half, our little family lived with the reality of cancer—moments of optimism and hope dissipated with news of each setback. Rory and I resolved that while we would try to be optimistic, we would never tell Angus a lie.

"Daddy's sick," we told him. "The doctors are working to make him better."

Angus accepted this with round, frightened eyes, saying nothing. Perhaps he had no words for what he was feeling. Perhaps he had resolved to be brave and not add to our burden.

Once, near the end, Rory asked that Angus and I lie on the bed beside him. So we did, two parents with their child between them. Time passed. Rory seemed to drift into sleep. I feared that this was difficult for Angus and whispered that he could go if he wished. He slipped off the bed. Rory stirred a few minutes later. "Someone's not here," he whispered. He had not seen Angus go, had not felt him leave. He simply knew one member of our small family was suddenly missing. Such was our bond.

Rory didn't ask for much. Etched in my mind is a memory of him shortly after the initial diagnosis, standing beside the kitchen table, body rigid with grief, tears in his eyes. "I only want six more years," he said. "Six years to see Angus grow up. Six more years."

But it was not to be. Rory accepted his fate with grace and equanimity. "Someone has to occupy the low end of the bell curve," he said with an ironic smile, a scientist even at the end.

IN SEPTEMBER 1988, AS Rory lay dying, Prime Minister Brian Mulroney, who had swept the Progressive Conservative party to power in September 1984, called. I had taken the summer off work. It was the traditional vacation period of the court of appeal, still observed in those days of lighter caseloads. Aware of Rory's illness, my chief had quietly freed me from my duties on the court. So the call came to my home.

A call from a prime minister, I have learned over the years, is a complicated thing. It's not just a matter of "Hey, somebody get the phone." The prime minister's switchboard contacts you in advance to advise of the impending call and to ensure that you are on hand to receive it. The appointed time comes. You wait. Eventually, the telephone rings. You pick up the receiver and a disembodied voice intones, "Please wait to be connected to the prime minister." Once again, you wait. Finally, the voice of the man—there has been only one female prime minister, my friend Kim Campbell, and she never had occasion to call me during her brief time in office—comes on the line. A call from the prime minister is the modern equivalent of the forelock-tugging walk up the red carpet to the king's throne in medieval times. It is a matter of precise protocol, and it takes a while.

Not so with Prime Minister Brian Mulroney.

The telephone rang in the next room, my home office. A deep, plummy voice sounded in my ear.

"Hello, this is Brian Mulroney."

I dropped the receiver, then caught it in mid-air. "Yes, Prime Minister."

After polite enquiries as to my health, which I assured him was fine, he got to the point: he wanted me to be the next chief justice of the Supreme Court of British Columbia. The redoubtable Allan McEachern would move up to head the court of appeal and become chief justice of British Columbia, and I, the prime minister said, would replace him as head of the trial court.

I had a sinking feeling in my stomach. No, not now. I was happily ensconced on the court of appeal, immersed in fascinating legal issues thrown up by the Charter—issues like whether imposing mandatory retirement[1] or barring a non-citizen from practising law[2] violated the right to equal treatment. The job of chief justice of the trial court was heavy on administration—something I had never done much of—and light on the law. I had a young son and a terminally ill husband. I was sagging with sadness. I didn't need any more complications.

"I am deeply honoured that you would think of me," I told the prime minister. Indeed I was—honoured and surprised. "But I can't consider this. Not now."

"Why not?" he asked.

And so I found myself explaining that my husband was dying, and that I had a young son to get through the ordeal. I did not have the mental space or serenity to consider changing jobs. And if I could somehow muster the required reflection, my instincts told me the answer would have to be no.

"Respectfully, Prime Minister, may I urge you to consider someone else?"

"I understand. Completely. Your priority must be your husband, your family. But perhaps you could discuss it with Rory?"

"No, Prime Minister, that's—that's not possible." We exchanged a few polite words and hung up.

That's that, I thought with relief as I put down the phone. It's not easy to say no when a prime minister asks you to take on a responsibility. His judgment that you are the person for the position deserves deference, whatever your personal misgivings. But I had done it, and it was the right decision. For five months, I had been sleeping only five hours a night. I ate little and had lost fifteen pounds. I was exhausted and felt my mind fraying as I lurched from crisis to crisis on sheer willpower and the need to be there for Rory and Angus.

But that was not that. Each day at around two in the afternoon, Prime Minister Mulroney would call again.

"How is your husband today?" he would ask.

"As well as we can expect," I would say. Then, half-unwilling, I would find myself responding to his sympathetic queries, sharing details with him that I spared even my sister, Judi.

On the fourth day, when I returned from the prime minister's call to Rory's bedside, I found my husband awake and lucid.

"Who's been calling so often?" he asked.

"The prime minister."

"What does he want?"

"He wants me to be chief justice of the Supreme Court of British Columbia."

"What did you tell him?"

"I told him no."

Rory's eyes closed and I saw him slipping back into unconsciousness. I had lost him again. Then I felt his hand squeeze mine.

"You should take it," he said.

I could have dismissed his words. I could have made a different decision. But in reality, I could not. The person who cared for me more than anyone else, whose judgment and advice had never led me astray, had given me his opinion. With his words, the decision was made. If the prime minister still wanted me, I would accept.

The next day, I waited for the prime minister's call, but it didn't come at the usual hour. *Good*, I thought. *He's given up.*

Then the phone rang. Prime Minister Mulroney's deep voice came on. "How's Rory?"

"Fading," I whispered, choking on the word.

"Have you talked to him about the appointment?"

"Yes."

"What did he say?"

I thought of Angus. I thought of myself. I thought of the huge administrative burden of running a court of fifty-odd independent judges.

"He said I should take it."

"That is good news," said Mulroney. After a pause, he added, "Thank you. I know this is a sacrifice. You won't regret it."

Rory died on September 14, 1988, age forty-seven. It all seemed so unfair. Dr. Fritz tried to console me, but nothing could change the tragic reality.

Rory asked that his ashes be scattered in Howe Sound. On a perfect September day, Angus, a tow-headed twelve-year-old, and I boarded a sleek craft borrowed from a cousin for the occasion. We carried a small box. The boat threaded its way between the islands of the Strait of Georgia, which Rory had always loved. As we approached the Narrows, where the islands almost touch, the boat throttled back. To the east, a pod of orcas surfaced.

Together, my son and I let Rory's ashes float onto the water and slowly streak towards the whales. We said nothing. No words, only tears. We waited until the sun on the water faded and they could be seen no more. Only then did we make our way back home.

THE PRIME MINISTER WAS wrong. There were times when I did regret taking on a new job within days of my husband's death. But he was also right. In the end, I did not regret my brief time as chief justice of the BC Supreme Court.

The months after Rory's death were difficult.

Physically difficult. Nights when I could not sleep. Days when my mind wandered absently and my memory failed me. A cold that came with the late-November rains lingered. Unable to contemplate Christmas in our empty house without Rory, Angus and I flew to Texas to spend a week with my brother Len and his family. I thought the warmth and rest had cured my cold, but it returned with a vengeance on the flight home. I cancelled all evening events—and there were many that came with the job of chief justice. I was worn out. The months without sleep or proper nutrition had depleted my immune system. Preoccupation with death and loss undermined my ability to concentrate. I had held it together for a long time, but now I was paying the price. I nursed myself back to health with tea and lemon and focused on healthy living. For Angus. For myself.

Professionally difficult. The new job entailed hours of meetings. Meetings in person and on the phone. Meetings during the day and often after dinner. Meetings about a myriad of vital matters—setting hearing schedules, talking to unhappy judges, badgering the attorney general for money to buy computers for the judges, and introducing myself to local bar associations.

One matter consumed an inordinate amount of time and emotional energy. Following the lead of provinces like Ontario and Alberta, the government of British Columbia had decided to merge its supreme and county courts. For decades, the county courts and the supreme court had divided the litigation load, with the county courts hearing less serious criminal cases and simpler civil disputes. But over the years, changes to the Criminal Code had increased the jurisdiction of the county courts, blurring the time-honoured division of labour. Having sat on a county court, I knew the good work it did and was personally unconvinced that a merger would improve matters.

But there were strong arguments for merger. More to the point, the attorney general had decided the merger would happen, and so it would. Ever the realist, I wanted to navigate the process in a way that would not leave the court divided and embittered, as had happened in Ontario and Alberta. Other judges, however, saw the matter differently.

Facing division among the judges of the supreme court, I adjourned all cases one afternoon and convened a meeting. I set out the issue and turned the floor over to them. Just when I thought tempers were spiralling out of control, a respected senior justice stood up and quietly reminded us all that our job was to provide the best possible justice to the people of British Columbia, under whatever court structures the government, working within its constitutional jurisdiction, chose to put in place. Tempers cooled, reason prevailed, and the merger went ahead without further incident.

The administrative burden of my new job meant I did not have much time to sit on cases. But I knew I must, as much to preserve my sanity as to maintain morale on the court. I knew from watching Allan McEachern and Nathan Nemetz that a chief justice must lead by example and shared experience. And I was following in a tradition of chief justices who had taken on the toughest, most high-profile cases on the docket.

So I took on the politically charged *Dixon* case.[3] The issue was whether British Columbia's electoral map, which featured significant divergences in population between districts, violated the right to vote of the *Charter of Rights and Freedoms*. The arguments were fascinating and took me deep into the principles of electoral equity and representative democracy. I would squirrel away a few hours from my administrative load each day to immerse myself in writing my judgment. In the end, I decided that the province's electoral districts did indeed violate the Charter guarantee of the equality of voting power. I signed my reasons with a flourish, satisfied that they were a good piece of work. Despite all that had happened, I could still do law.

Yet the months that followed Rory's death were emotionally difficult. I thought I understood grief. I had grieved the loss of my mother, then that of my father a few years later. But I had no inkling of the complexity, profundity, and endurance of the loss I would feel with the death of my husband and partner of twenty-two years. A friend gave me a book about the five stages of grief. I seemed stuck in phase one—unable to fully comprehend that Rory was gone. At night, I was beset with lifelike dreams of Rory that left me sweating in terror.

Not long after Rory died, I went to the government office in Kerrisdale to renew my driver's licence. I stood before the clerk at the wicket. The form asked me to check a box for "married" or "single," and I couldn't decide which to choose.

"I'm recently widowed," I told the clerk.

She gave me a sympathetic look that had the air of experience. "You don't get more single than that," she said.

You don't get more single than that. More single than childhood. More single than young adulthood. More single than spinsterhood or bachelordom. I had loved and lost. You don't get more single than that, or more alone.

The emptiness that pervaded our home reached its hollow tentacles beyond me. I tried to carry on as normal, go out for treats, arrange parties for friends. Angus went along with it, but he refused to speak about his father's passing and would sit for long minutes staring into space with his dog at his side, closing in on himself and his inner preoccupations. Anxious about Angus's well-being, I took my concerns to a child psychiatrist. He had a long talk with Angus and then with me. "He's fine," the doctor told me. Grieving, but nothing to worry about. Still, worry I did.

Even the cat grieved. During Rory's illness, our plump Siamese had spent endless hours in his lap as he rocked in his recliner. After his death, the cat declined. Slowly he changed—stopped eating, stopped hunting, stopped begging us to take him on our laps. Endless trips to the vet produced no clear diagnosis. The compassionate veterinarian volunteered to take him in over the Christmas holiday. When Angus and I returned from visiting Len's family in Texas, the vet informed us that the cat had died. Maybe something viral, he said.

I knew better. The cat had died of grief.

··

CHAPTER NINETEEN

The New Justice of the Supreme Court of Canada

IT WAS APRIL 1989. By happy coincidence, a legal conference I wanted to attend in Sydney, Australia, coincided with Angus's school spring break. "Would you like to go to Australia?" I asked him.

His eyes lit up. For the first time in months, I looked at him, really looked. He was almost thirteen, and sometime in the past year he had changed from a child to the beginnings of a confident young man. "Let's do it," he said.

"We'll take a week after the conference to see a bit of Australia," I said.

"Can we dive on the Great Barrier Reef?" he asked. "Cool stuff down there." Our early trips to Pender Island had instilled in him a love of the ocean and all its creatures.

"Absolutely," I promised.

Our travel agent laid out an itinerary: Sydney to Canberra; Canberra to Melbourne; Melbourne to Adelaide; Adelaide to Uluru; Uluru to Townsend and diving on the reef; Townsend to Brisbane; Brisbane back to Sydney and the airport. All by air. Just manageable in our two-and-a-half-week slot, with luck and flawless execution.

Luck deserted me the second evening in Sydney. As I sat chatting with a colleague in a restaurant, a thief slipped by and lifted my purse. With it went our passports, my credit cards, and all my cash. Naively, I reported the theft to the police, who offered sad smiles and took my name. I despaired. On my first big trip as a single parent, I had managed to maroon us in a foreign country. We had no money, no way to continue our trip, and no way to get home.

After the initial shock wore off, I set to fixing the situation. I cancelled the credit cards, and Angus and I visited the Canadian High Commission consulate officers, who took our photos and issued us new passports. A generous Canadian colleague lent me seven hundred Australian dollars to tide us over. And I discovered that I had fortuitously left my bank card in my hotel drawer, which would allow me to withdraw cash as Angus and I toured the country. We were back on track.

It was a cathartic, unforgettable trip. In Sydney, Angus, ever independent, spent two hours each morning running in the park that lay above our hotel in the Rockeries. In Canberra, we woke up on Easter morning to deserted streets. In Melbourne, we marvelled over the art that decorated the buses, the elegant boulevards, and the gutsy restaurants. We (well, I) used Adelaide as the base for a wine tour in the Barossa Valley. Uluru—also on Angus's must-see list—stunned us. If the innkeepers along our route entertained suspicions about the strange woman who paid for everything in cash travelling with a twelve-year-old boy, they were tactful enough to keep their speculations to themselves.

It was near the end of the trip, in Townsend, that Prime Minister Mulroney's office finally caught up with me. It was hard to reach people on the move in the days before iPhones and laptops.

"Someone from Canada has been trying to reach you," said the clerk at the desk of our hotel as she looked at a note on our reservation. "Your credit card, please."

"I don't have a credit card." I dug into my wallet. "How about cash? In advance."

She slid a bill from the top of the wad I proffered and fingered it delicately, checking for counterfeit. "I suppose so," she said.

Late that evening, a ministerial aide from the justice department called.

"Whew!" said the young man. "I've finally found you. I was about to give up. Where have you been?"

"Travelling," I offered vaguely, wondering what judicial appointment to the BC Supreme Court could be so urgent that he needed to speak to me in Australia. "What's this about?"

"I have to ask you a question," he said, moderating his tone.

"Fire away."

"If you were offered a position on the Supreme Court of Canada, would you accept?"

I was stunned. I knew that Justice William McIntyre, the British Columbia member of the Supreme Court of Canada, had announced his retirement, I'd never imagined I would be nominated in his place. Just seven months earlier, the prime minister had appointed me to a different job, one I had barely begun. I managed a response. "I would need to think about it."

"No problem. The prime minister wants to announce the appointment in the next two days. I'll call you tomorrow." The line went dead.

Angus emerged from his room. "What's up?" he asked, eyeing the phone in my hand.

"The prime minister wants to know if I would accept a place on the Supreme Court of Canada, if asked." I shook my head. "I think I should say no. I'm barely into my new job in Vancouver. And it would mean moving to Ottawa." I looked at him. "We've been through too many changes lately, you and me. For you, this would mean a new school, new kids. It's too soon for another change."

He nodded. We went to bed.

I woke up early the next morning and went to the small sitting room that divided our bedrooms. I had spent most of the night tossing and turning. I would say no. I had to say no. It was too much, too soon. This was no time to uproot and take ourselves to the other side of the continent. A few years on, perhaps. Now? No way. Angus's nod had settled the matter.

As I looked out over the grey ocean skies to the dock and the helicopter that would shortly ferry us to a floating hotel for diving, I heard Rory's voice in my head, telling me that I would someday be on the Supreme Court of Canada.

I had laughed at his crazy speculations. "They'll never ask me."

I was wrong and Rory was right. But he wasn't with us anymore. There would be no happily ever after.

I looked up. Angus was standing before me, very straight and tall. He pushed his blond hair aside and looked me in the eye. "Mom," he said, "you should do it. You should say yes."

I felt myself choke. And then I folded him into my arms.

The prime minister's call came in the middle of the next night. This time, the formal protocol of the PMO switchboard had been fully engaged. The ship was abuzz. It's not every day that the prime minister of Canada sets up a telephone call with a guest on a floating hotel in the middle of the Pacific Ocean. The call came later than expected, though, and when the phone rang, I was startled awake from a deep slumber. In the inky dark, I knocked the phone off the table, retrieved it, and fumbled for the right end of the receiver.

I heard a distant voice: "What's going on? I think we've lost the line."

"Hello," I said.

In due course, Prime Minister Mulroney's plummy voice came on the line. "Don't you judges ever stay at home?" he asked. "I've just spent two hours trying to reach Chief Justice Brian Dickson in Vienna, and now I find you—I don't know where. On a boat on the Pacific?" And then I heard his famous chuckle. "As you probably know, I want to invite you to become a justice of the Supreme Court of Canada."

"I would be honoured, Mr. Prime Minister."

We chatted a bit about the court and the vital role its judges play in Canadian democracy, particularly since the *Charter of Rights and Freedoms* had been adopted. The Charter had been in place for only seven years at that time, but already it was evident that it was profoundly changing Canadian law and society. The justices of the court had done much work in building upon its provisions, but more remained to be done. I had wrestled with Charter issues in the BC Supreme Court and the Court of Appeal, secure in the knowledge that if I got it wrong, the judges upstairs would fix it up. Now I was being asked to join the final court, where the buck on pressing legal issues stopped. Was I up to it? Did I want this heavy responsibility?

"Congratulations and good luck," said the prime minister before I could let second thoughts interfere, and then his voice was gone.

When Angus and I emerged from our cabin at seven the next morning, we were greeted by an array of bunting and balloons hanging from the ceiling and every available wall sconce. Evidently, my Aussie friends had been listening in on the prime minister's call. "Congratulations to the New Judge of the Supreme Court of Canada!" a twenty-foot banner proclaimed.

I love Aussies.

My life had just taken a radical shift—one that would take Angus and me across the country and bring me a new position replete with responsibilities I had never imagined. It had all happened so quickly. I pushed my way through the balloons and banners and accepted the hugs of my shipmates in a blur of unreality. Today I would celebrate; tomorrow I would face the consequences of saying yes to the prime minister in the dark of the Pacific night. Angus and I would head back to Canada and a life forever changed.

CHAPTER TWENTY

A New World on the Ottawa

T HE SUPREME COURT OF Canada sits on a bluff overlooking the Ottawa River. As befits the highest court of the land, it lies close to the Houses of Parliament and the key executive offices of government.

The building that houses the Supreme Court of Canada is a rare thing—an architectural mishmash that has achieved iconic status. It was designed in the 1930s by the renowned Montreal architect Ernest Cormier in the art deco style. Cormier spared no detail or expense in his quest for a building of classic simplicity—grand staircase, Grecian columns, a grand hall (*la salle des pas perdus*)—lit by glass windows echoing the contemporary abstraction of Mondrian. In keeping with the art deco style and modern aesthetic, Cormier ordered a flat roof.

Legend has it that each day during construction, Prime Minister Mackenzie King passed the building as he walked his dog, watching it slowly rise from the barren field of grass where it was set. The prime minister had been intimately involved in the design, reviewing the detailed plans, making this change or that. He had left the flat roof intact. But as the court took shape—or so story has it—he decided that the flat roof would not do. Not grand enough, not regal enough. Not fit for the Supreme Court of Canada. He called Cormier in and demanded a roof in keeping with the neo-Gothic peaks of the Houses of Parliament and the nearby Justice Building.

Whether Cormier protested is lost in archival mist. It seems inconceivable that he did not. But Prime Minister King, as was his wont, had his way. In due course, a steep copper roof, as tall as the stone façade of the building itself, rose towards the skies.

To architectural purists, the roof—replete with gargoyle-like curlicues—is an abomination. Justice (later Chief Justice) Antonio Lamer summed up the view of many when he dubbed the roof the court's "dunce cap." But to most Canadians, including me, its silhouette has become synonymous with justice.

And now it was to be my home. At least for a while, or so I thought when I first arrived there in April 1989. Little did I dream that I would pass twenty-eight years of my life in the imposing precincts of Cormier's supreme courthouse.

I had been to Ottawa twice before—once as a twenty-one-year-old student attending a conference, and once as a new judge on my way to new judges' school at Lac-Sainte-Marie to the north. I knew nothing about the city, though, and I had never even seen the Supreme Court Building.

A man in a dark jacket who identified himself as a court attendant met Angus and me at the Ottawa airport on a cold Saturday afternoon. In Vancouver, the cherry blossoms had just finished blooming; in Ottawa, there was still snow on the ground. I shivered inside my summer coat. Someone should have warned me.

The attendant drove us to the Minto Place Hotel, and Angus and

I checked in to the suite that had been reserved for us. The next day, I walked down Lyon Street to Wellington. There, across the street and a swath of yellow grass flecked with streaks of snow, sat the Supreme Court of Canada, the grand lady of my dreams. I had no key, no way to get inside. But my view of the outside sent a shiver through my body that had nothing to do with the bracing west wind. The Arthur Erickson–designed courthouse that had been my home in Vancouver was low-slung and bedecked with plants—a place of human dimensions that wrapped you consolingly in its beauty. This building was august and forbidding. I approached and inspected the brass doors at the top of the long flight of steps.

Tread carefully and enter at your own risk, they seemed to say.

"Too late," I murmured to myself. *You must have been mad, that night on the boat when you said yes to Prime Minister Mulroney.*

It was indeed too late. Contingents from the West had already arrived for the impending ceremony, and more were en route. All was set and ready to go. I, the centre of all the preparation, had no choice but to show up.

On Monday, April 17, 1989, before a packed courtroom, I was sworn in as the sixty-fifth puisne judge of the Supreme Court of Canada. My voice trembled with emotion as I repeated the oath in French and English. I walked to the desk, took the pen, and signed. The deed was done.

I mounted the stair, took my place at the end of the bench, and looked down the long curved plane of wood. Eight judges—six male, two female. My eye halted at Claire L'Heureux-Dubé, dark-haired and smiling, at the other end of the dais, then moved back to Bertha Wilson, the first woman to be appointed to the Supreme Court of Canada.

Bertha returned my look and leaned forward. "Three down, six to go," she whispered sotto voce in her Scottish brogue.

Speeches followed. The minister of justice and representatives of the bar took their turns, struggling to find something auspicious to say. I had been a judge for only eight years. I was a decent judge, they said. I wrote clear reasons. The treasurer of the Law Society of British Columbia, Paul Beckmann, decided to forego the bromides. "The new justice," he intoned dryly, "is noted for two things. First, it was evident looking at her career that she couldn't keep a job. Second, she had made it through the court system faster than most cases."

His remarks brought the house down.

Chief Justice Brian Dickson, a jurist I had long revered, welcomed me, and then it was my turn to speak. I looked out at the bench where my family sat. Angus sat proudly beside my sister, Judi, who had flown out from Vancouver for the occasion. I spoke of my mother and father, who had taught me the values of integrity, hard work, and responsibility. Choking up a little, I spoke of Rory—the only person who had foreseen this day. I pledged to give my new position my very best.

The day concluded, as swearings-in at the Supreme Court always do, with a dinner for members of the court, active and retired, and their spouses, held in the judges' dining room, a capacious oak-panelled room on the third floor, overlooking the river and the Gatineau Hills. The room had once been used for interlocutory hearings but was converted to a dining room in the seventies, under Chief Justice Bora Laskin.

As I walked into the elegant space, which was gleaming with candles and flowers on white linen, I felt the last of my anxiety ebb away. Judges welcomed me, my family beamed. Angus, eyes wide, looked at me and said breathlessly, "Wow."

I didn't know what lay ahead. But I knew I would give it everything I had.

A FEW WEEKS LATER, I flew to Edmonton to speak at a legal conference. I was not a seasoned orator—I had done very little public speaking in Vancouver—and consulted some of my new colleagues on how to go about it. "Say something funny at the beginning," they advised. "Something that will make them chuckle. Then you can get on with the serious stuff."

After I was introduced as the recently appointed third woman on the Supreme Court of Canada, I stood up and launched into my opening story.

"Let me tell you what Justice Wilson said when I took my place on the bench after signing the oath," I said. " 'Three down, six to go.' " I even rolled my r's.

A few people laughed, and I got on with the serious stuff. I thought nothing more of it until the next morning, when someone brought me the *Edmonton Journal*. There, at the top of the op-ed page, was a letter from an irate citizen. "How dare the new justice suggest that the Supreme Court of Canada should be composed entirely of women," the writer fulminated.

Judges wisely let disparaging comments lie and decline to reply to criticism, however unfair it may be, but had I been allowed to respond, I would have pointed out that for more than a century, the Supreme Court of Canada was composed entirely of men and had somehow survived. Was it so outrageous to think the court might survive nine women for a while? More seriously, I would have argued that it is important to have both men and women on Canadian courts, both to provide female perspectives on legal problems and to reassure women that they are fairly represented.

The furor over my comments took me back to a family law case I had heard as a trial judge on a sleepy afternoon in 1984. The issue was how to divide the contents of the family home and a few other assets. The wife was represented by a woman lawyer. The court clerk and court stenographer were also women. The husband sat alone at the counsel table on the left side of the room.

The wife testified, answering the questions put by her lawyer.

When she finished, I looked at the husband. "It's your turn now," I said.

He seemed to have trouble getting to his feet—a lawyers' term for addressing the court. I assumed it was because he didn't have a lawyer. I explained that the case was not complicated, and that I needed to hear his side of the matter.

When he finally composed himself, he swept his eyes across the occupants of the courtroom—all women. "Frankly, Your Honour," he said with umbrage, "I feel a little outnumbered."

I assured him that I would not hold his gender against him. He got on with his side of the story, and in the end, I ordered that the property be equally divided between wife and husband. I thought nothing more about the incident until later that evening, as I reflected on my day. A thought struck me: How many women, throughout the centuries, had stood before all-male courts and felt a little outnumbered?

The courts belong to the people and should reflect the people. No one should be obliged to go before a court that seems distant and alien. This truth applies not only to women as judges but also to minorities. For too long, Indigenous peoples have felt that the courts are not theirs—that they don't represent them or understand them.

What we now need is diverse representation on the bench. It may take time. But we should do all we can to get there.

My installation as a justice of the Supreme Court was accomplished and the party was over. The people who had gathered in Ottawa to fete my appointment had packed their bags and gone home. Angus and Judi had flown back to Vancouver; he would stay in her home to complete his school year.

I returned, alone, to my serviced flat at Minto Place, just up Lyon Street from the courthouse. I wandered from tiny room to tiny room, unable to settle or sleep. I missed Angus, I missed my friends, I missed my house. Even in the dark days, when Rory lay dying, I had not felt so alone.

But I quickly became acquainted with my other new home, the court. The building wraps itself around a central core, which houses the main courtroom. The justices' offices occupy the second floor, stretching in a U shape around it. The court had only seven justices when the building was designed, so the architect planned for seven justices' chambers, with two additional rooms thrown in for symmetry.

Everything at the court, I quickly learned, depended on seniority, including the size and location of one's office. As the junior judge, I got the junior office, which meant that I was relegated to chambers at the end of the east wing. My new room was long and severe. Instead of the glorious bank of windows of my capacious Vancouver office—possibly the nicest chief justice digs in Canada, if not the world—I now owned a single long window.

"You will grow to like this office," Justice McIntyre, who was in the process of emptying his desk, consoled me. "I could have moved out long ago, but I liked it and decided to stay." He was a large man in every way: in body—he stood well over six feet—in mind, and in spirit.

"Really?" I responded skeptically, looking around at the barren walls.

"It has a big cupboard," he said with a wry turn of the lip. "That's a great advantage."

I must have looked puzzled.

"For the books," he explained. Then he sighed. "You'll find out soon enough. Parties' books. Interveners' books. Hundreds of books—fifty for this case, forty for that. You need someplace to keep them."

I felt a flutter of panic in my stomach. "You read them all?"

"Let's just say I look at the relevant passages." He smiled. "Did you know that Supreme Court judges possess proficient reading-retention scores?" he continued. "They ran some tests for language-training purposes. Amazing scores, apparently."

My mental clock ticked back to that bleak day in grade eight when my teacher had told me I was fit for nothing useful.

I nodded to Justice McIntyre. I had just found the answer to my teacher's question: it's useful if you get yourself appointed to the Supreme Court of Canada.

I did grow to like my new office. It had dark panelling, a fireplace that I was not allowed to use, and a magnificent view of the Peace Tower. The fact that Mrs. Johnson, my assistant, was in a separate room next to a stairwell I regarded as a minor inconvenience. I counted myself lucky. I had shared a secretary throughout my eight years as a British Columbia judge, except for the brief months I had been chief justice. To have an assistant all my own was an immense privilege. Not to mention the court staff, who seemed determined to do whatever they could to assist me in settling in.

In the spring of 1989, each justice had two law clerks. I was inheriting two from Justice McIntyre—Arthur Grant and Sandra Foweraker—and I learned that in the fall, the number would go up to three. I could not believe my good fortune. I would soon learn that clerks were not a luxury but a necessity in keeping up with the heavy caseload of the Supreme Court.

Lawyers love to speculate on the role of clerks at the Supreme Court of Canada. Over late lunches, they are given to debates on whether the bright young graduates who win clerking positions have too much influence. Several books by ex-clerks of the Supreme Court of the United States—describing how they influence the certiorari (leave to appeal) process, sway outcomes, and write reasons—naturally spawn questions about the role of clerks in the Supreme Court of Canada. Is it the appointed justices who decide the cases? Or is it the "clerkery"?

From the perspective of my twenty-eight years on the Supreme Court, the answer is clear: it is the justices and the justices alone who determine which cases get leave to appeal and how the cases heard are decided. Law clerks assist the judges, to be sure. They prepare preliminary memoranda on each case. They may suggest how they think the case should be decided. They may even, depending on the judge, play a role in drafting memoranda and decisions. But in the final analysis, it is the justice who makes the decision.

When I started at the court, I sat down with my new group of law clerks to discuss how we would work. "I'm the judge," I told them, "and I will make the final decisions. I don't want you to tell me how to decide the case. That's not your job—it's mine. If you feel the outcome is clear, by all means tell me, but the final decision is mine, not yours. And while I may ask you to help with reasons, filling in background or authorities, I will do the writing." It was a conversation I would have each autumn with my new cohort of clerks.

Judgment writing is the best part of judging, I always felt. Setting out the relevant facts, working through the pertinent cases, analyzing the statutory provisions at issue—these are the essence of judging. The process of putting these things on paper is an integral part of determining the proper outcome. In most cases, I began drafting reasons with a sense of what I thought the answer would be. But the process of writing clarified the rightness or wrongness of my initial inclination. In some cases, it even led to a different result than I expected. Judges sometimes say, "It just won't write." What they mean is that in the process of drafting reasons to support their initial view, they come to the conclusion that the initial view was wrong—that the facts and the law, rigorously examined, lead to a different conclusion.

Nobel Prize–winning economist Daniel Kahneman, in his book *Thinking, Fast and Slow*,[1] describes good decision-making in terms of two mental functions—fast thinking, the instinctual gut feeling about the right outcome, and slow thinking, the meticulous checking and elaborating that tests the initial intuitive conclusion. This insight is central to good judging. Experience and listening to the evidence and submissions usually point a judge to the correct answer—fast thinking. But before making her decision, the judge has to go further and methodically examine the basis for the decision—slow thinking. And that's the process of writing a judgment.

My "clerkery," as I dubbed it, would become one of the most rewarding aspects of my time on the Supreme Court of Canada. Collaborating closely with these bright young spirits not long out of law school forged bonds that continued unbroken long after they moved on to other endeavours. The eighty-six clerks I have worked with became eighty-six firm friends. Every five years, we had a clerks' reunion. Among my most precious memories are afternoons in the garden of my home, sharing memories with past and present clerks while little grand-clerks shrieked through the ferns or commandeered the tree house.

With the new judge in place, Justice McIntyre packed his papers and prepared to fly west. After more years of exile than he had promised his wife, Mimi, they were headed home to their beloved Vancouver. I'd known him for only a few days, but as he made his final farewells, I felt a pang of loss. He knew so much that I needed to know. As he was leaving, I asked, "If you had one piece of advice for me—only one—what would it be?"

He looked at me, then turned his gaze to the window. The spires of the Parliament Buildings shone in the pale April sunlight. Finally, he turned back.

"Find some outside interests," he said, his voice rough. "Otherwise, this job will consume you."

He nodded. I was dismissed. Case concluded.

CHAPTER TWENTY-ONE

···

Changing Minds

I TOOK JUSTICE MCINTYRE'S ADVICE to heart. I held the old-fashioned view that I would stay on the court, health permitting, until mandatory retirement at seventy-five. The *Supreme Court Act* requires the justices to live in or near Ottawa, which meant that I would be in the city for almost thirty years. If I was to survive and stay healthy and happy, I needed to make a life here—one outside the court. Second—and I admitted this was something of a long shot—I figured that outside interests would make me a better judge by keeping me close to the real-life concerns of Canadian women and men. I resolved not to distance myself from the community but to become part of it. I would make friends outside the legal world. I would participate in local events. I would take an active part in the school community. And when Angus returned, we would explore the Ottawa Valley together and get to know our new environment.

The first step was to find a house. I set one requirement: our new home must be within walking distance of Ashbury College, the school Angus would attend starting in September. Unfortunately, this slotted me into a pricey real estate market. Rory had always said, "Never buy an old house." That advice was more pertinent than ever, now that I was on my own, with no time to handle domestic malfunctions. But old houses were all that were available.

After touring and rejecting a long string of properties, I finally found a not-so-old house (1960s instead of the usual 1940s); it was classic red brick in the Georgian style, set on a beautiful lot in the north part of Rockcliffe Park. It was bigger than Angus and I needed, and more expensive than I wanted, but it had good vibes. Deep in my bones, I felt that if Angus and I were to thrive here, we needed the comforts of a home we could love.

What I saw at the court only cemented those feelings. The other judges I met and worked with at the Supreme Court of Canada in the spring of 1989 were, to borrow the words of one English novelist, "paler and tireder." Two recent appointments, Justices Charles Gonthier and Peter Cory, still exuded energy, but on most days, the old hands fit my novelist's stereotype.

Judging doesn't look hard. The judge sits on an elevated chair, listens, makes some marks on paper. Then she goes to her office and makes some more marks on paper. A good part of the time, she stares absently out the window as she ponders this or that option. Occasionally, she attends a meeting with law clerks or other judges. Soft touch, the observer may think. But I had long since discovered that judging is hard work—the kind of work that can leave you pale and tired.

"You will find the workload here unlike anything you have encountered before," Justice Bertha Wilson told me. "Endless hours of reading and preparation for each case, tough debates with colleagues on difficult legal issues, [and] long days and nights of writing and rewriting reasons for judgment." She gave me a contemplative look. "I made a rule for myself. I stop working at nine at night."

Wow, I thought. *This is a new reality.*

I told myself it couldn't be that bad, but I quickly learned that Justice Wilson was right. A new routine imposed itself on my life. Up at seven. Out for a jog. Shower, change, and walk from my flat to the court. A day crowded with intense work—hearings two weeks of the month, writing the other two weeks. Home at six or seven for dinner, followed by more reading. The arrival of Angus and our black Lab, Cass, changed my workday routine slightly—up at seven to walk the dog, shower, change, breakfast, and school drop-off on the way to the courthouse. Home at five, dinner, and into the den to finalize preparation for the next day's case.

"It used to be worse," Justice Antonio Lamer assured me. "In the early days of the Charter, we had hundreds of cases on the docket. There were no precedents, no rules to tell us how to interpret them. We still had the old procedural rules that allowed unlimited time for hearings and oral applications for leave to appeal in every case. And," he added, "we didn't have three law clerks like now. One, and then later two."

"I don't know how you did what you did," I said, thinking of the excellent body of work the Supreme Court had put out in that period, laying the foundation for all the Charter jurisprudence that would follow. The advent of the Charter had deluged the court with a flood of new and complex work. Cases came in escalating numbers, demanding answers—answers that would affect thousands of lives and shape the law of the future. Like swimmers tossed into the deepest part of a lake, the justices had struggled to find sure ground, with no map to show them where it lay. They had worked late into the night, week after week, year after year, without respite, reading and rereading, writing and rewriting. The work demanded energy, creativity, and, above all, wisdom. I thought about their struggles and resolved never to complain about my workload again.

The Charter blitz of the 1980s had taken its toll. Justice Gerald Le Dain, a formidable intellect, suffered a breakdown that led to his departure from the court. Justice Willard "Bud" Estey retired. Justice Lamer himself looked old and tired, and Justice Wilson bore debilitating arthritis with stoicism. Justice John Sopinka, a brilliant trial lawyer and academic, carried on indefatigably, as did Justices Gérard La Forest and Claire L'Heureux-Dubé. The burden had also been wearing on Chief Justice Dickson, who, although he still rode his beloved Morgan ponies every morning, suffered shoulder and back pain. *How will I fare?* I wondered.

By the time I arrived, the court was in the final stages of implementing the changes required by the initial onslaught of Charter litigation, including time-limited hearings and intervener processes.[1] The remaining concern was the heavy load of pending judgments and the stubborn backlog of old cases.

"Remanets," I kept hearing at each court conference. "How many remanets do we still have?" It wasn't a word I knew. I had to look it up. "Archaic term for backlog," I read, derived from the same root as "remainder." Justice Lamer was leading a drive to get dead cases (abandoned appeals) off the books by issuing notices to quash. The justices began to talk about the light at the end of the tunnel. But it was not until my second year at the court that the remanets dwindled to insignificance.

The other remaining problem was the amount of writing, much of which was done at night or on weekends. At the time, there was no set method of assigning cases. Justices interested in writing for the majority would signal this at the end of the court conference. Usually, others would acquiesce, but when they wanted a case, senior justices did not hesitate to pull rank. I was prepared to spend much of my first year at the court writing insignificant judgments that no one else wanted. Yet the work was anything but simple. Even the cases that seemed mundane on the surface concealed complexities I had only imagined in the lower courts. I felt inadequate to the task. But I had been asked to do it and had agreed. There was only one way to go, and that was forward.

One case in particular piqued my interest—*R. v. Hebert*, a confessions case.[2] The issue was whether a jailhouse confession made to a cellmate who turned out to be an undercover policeman was "voluntary" and hence admissible in evidence against the accused. It was an issue I had mulled over in my years as an evidence professor. Did "voluntary" simply mean free from overt promises or coercion? Or did the concept of liberty and presumption of innocence endorsed by the Charter mean that the person confessing must actually have intended to confess to the police?

After the hearing, we adjourned, as usual, to the judges' conference room to discuss the case. The tradition was that the junior judge—me—should speak first. It wasn't easy, knowing that eight other judges might follow with chilling exposés of the failings in my argument. But I launched forth. I went through the analysis I had prepared of the pros and cons for admitting the confession. The other justices followed in order of precedence. While the issue was difficult, most seemed to favour holding the confession admissible. Chief Justice Dickson spoke last. At the end, he said, "Why don't we let Beverley have a go at this one?"

Walking on air, I returned to my office and set to work. I decided I would try to write for the position the majority had endorsed at conference, holding the confession admissible. But the deeper I got into the issue, the more it seemed that fairness required a test that looked not only at the external pressures the police had brought to bear, but also at whether the accused person, in his own mind, intended to confess. How could a statement obtained by a trick be called "voluntary"?

With trepidation, I circulated my draft a few weeks later. I was certain that the majority would reject it, and that I would be left with an elegant but unimportant set of dissenting reasons. Not a stellar start. But to my surprise, the other judges, one by one, indicated they would concur. Chief Justice Dickson wrote me a note: "Congratulations on an excellent piece of work," it read. "It is no small achievement for a new judge to persuade her colleagues to change their minds."

I held the note to my heart. Years later, when I was chief justice, I would recall it and remind myself of the importance of a word of encouragement to a new and uncertain justice.

But my new chief justice could also be exacting. A handsome man with military bearing—he had lost a leg in the Second World War and walked with the aid of a prosthesis—he set high standards for the court and its justices. He had long been one of my legal heroes, writing groundbreaking decisions in clear, compelling prose. He took time to make me feel at home and give me advice—advice that sometimes cut.

One of the extra duties justices were required to perform was to give royal assent, or formal approval, in their capacity as deputies of the governor general. This involved a trip to the Senate and a ceremony of some formality. I sensed there were protocols I should know about and went to the chief's office to ask for advice.

"What would you recommend I wear?" I asked.

He looked up and down my outfit of the day—a long-sleeved green knit dress with a black stripe down the middle.

"Not that," he growled.

Ever the military man, Brian was a stickler for propriety. I never wore the dress again.

....

CHAPTER TWENTY-TWO

Morality and the Law

At the end of June 1989, the court adjourned for the summer recess. I flew to England in July to attend the Cambridge Lectures, a ten-day lecture series for judges and lawyers held at Queens' College. I had attended once before, in 1983, and I immediately relaxed into the quiet routines of English academe.

I had arranged for Angus, who had been staying with his uncle Sandy, Rory's brother, on his farm near London, Ontario, to join me so that we could take two weeks after the conference to travel through Europe before returning to our new home in Ottawa together. Angus was scheduled to arrive a few days before the conference ended, and I took the train from Cambridge to London and then the Tube to Heathrow to meet him. I stood at the arrivals gate and watched my blond-haired boy, now thirteen, shift his backpack and march down the ramp towards me. His face was unreadable. Was he glad to see his mother? Or would he rather have been back in London or Vancouver?

"Hey, Mom," he said, as I put my arm around him.

I felt his apprehension, and I wondered if it was mixed with secret, unacknowledged resentment at the new direction his life had taken. I remembered my own inner turmoil at his age. I squeezed the spare muscle of his body to me and breathed a wish for the best.

A few days before, I had mentioned to Frank McArdle, the executive director of the institute sponsoring the lectures, that I was going down to London to pick up my son.

"My son and I will be in London for the weekend," he said. "If you like, we can drive you and Angus back to Cambridge on Sunday."

I thought of lugging Angus's bags on and off the train. "That would be so helpful," I replied.

After Angus arrived, he and I overnighted at a fusty but well-located hotel on Jermyn Street.

"We're getting a ride back to Cambridge with Frank McArdle," I said to Angus that evening.

"Who's he?" Angus asked.

"You'll find out," I said. As indeed he would.

The next morning, we descended the stairs from our little suite. Frank and his son, Jim—a lawyer like his father—were waiting outside, just as promised.

Frank looked at Angus as I struggled to get my bag through the hotel door. "Help your mother," he directed.

It was a good ride north to Cambridge. Frank, whom I barely knew, took charge of everything, including my son's conduct. "Don't talk to your mother that way," he instructed after a mildly impertinent remark, following up with a comment that made us all, Angus included, laugh. By the time we turned off Silver Street through the gates of Queens' College, we had settled in as friends. Angus heaved my bag out of the trunk without being asked. Frank settled Angus in his room, and Jim gave him a white chef's hat so he could flip hamburgers at the barbecue the next night.

On Wednesday, the conference ended and my trip with Angus was supposed to begin. There was just one problem: I hadn't planned ahead what we would do. "How about a bus tour?" I asked my son.

"No way," said Angus.

A friend and former executive legal officer at the Supreme Court, James MacPherson, suggested the Alps. Angus's eyes lit up. "The Alps it is," I said.

He and I packed our bags and headed south to London and across the English Channel to Paris. From Paris we took the train to Grindelwald, in the Swiss Alps, where we spent four days hiking and climbing. As we took the train through the mountain valleys to the tiny town, Angus's eyes widened. Before our trip was over, he had learned the names of all the major peaks and climbed a number of them. He immersed himself in books about great climbers and visited their graves; most of them had died much too young. The danger of the mountain cliffs, the precariousness of life in pursuit of a dangerous passion, death itself—these were things my son, a child on the brink of adulthood, a young boy who had recently lost his father, was pondering. I suppressed a pang of apprehension and decided to steer him to lighter pursuits.

"Time to move on," I said on the third day. It was beautiful in Grindelwald, but the mood was dark. Besides, I was sore and stiff from climbing the Rothorn the previous day.

"Where will we go?" Angus asked. Clearly he would have stayed in Grindelwald forever.

"Italy," I said. He gave me a dubious look.

"Venice, Florence . . ."

"Museums," he grumbled, but packed his bag.

We travelled by train, stopping in Zurich, spending three days in

Venice, and ending up in Florence. Before moving on up the coast to Monte Carlo, France, and home, I decided it might be a good thing to check in with the court. Mrs. Johnson answered the phone.

"Thank goodness you called. We've been looking for you everywhere. I'll put you right through to the chief justice's office."

"Where have you been?" his assistant demanded. "The chief justice has scheduled an emergency hearing for next Monday. You need to be back."

Evidently I had misunderstood. Even on holiday, a justice needed to put the court first.

Two days later—four days earlier than planned—Angus and I touched down in Ottawa. My court attendant met us at the airport and drove us home.

As we pulled up to the red-brick house I had chosen two months earlier, anxiety balled in the pit of my stomach. I had seen the house only twice before—once on the initial showing that led to my offer, and once with the inspector I had hired to vet it. The possession date had occurred while we were in Europe. I had left detailed instructions with the movers as to what to put where, but it was too much to hope that the house would be in a habitable state. The things we loved would be piled up in heaps here, scattered helter-skelter there. Another set of confused circumstances to negotiate as my son and I worked our way to a semblance of our old ordered life.

I opened the door, took a deep breath. No boxes, no piles of furniture. There they were: our familiar sofa and chairs in the living room; our table in the dining room. Upstairs our beds were set up and made. Even our clothes were stowed in the drawers.

"It's just like home," Angus said as he walked from room to room.

In the backyard, he stared up at a huge Norway maple. "I need to make a swing," he said. "Can we go to Canadian Tire?"

Our first trip was not to get food but to buy a hank of rope. Angus spent the next three hours fashioning a swing that could carry him halfway across the back garden.

"Great views from up there," he said, coming inside only for a snack.

"If you say so," I said.

Angus didn't leave our new home for three days.

TWO DAYS AFTER TOUCHING down in Ottawa, I was back in court hearing the emergency case that had prematurely ended my holiday. I wasn't the only one whose vacation had been interrupted by *Tremblay v. Daigle*.[1] Justice Lamer had got the call as he was manoeuvring his boat under the Brooklyn Bridge. He docked the boat and flew home.

What made this case so important that the chief justice called a special mid-summer sitting and assembled his judges from far and wide? I had expected a matter of high constitutional urgency. What I discovered was a dispute between two former lovers.

As it turned out, it was actually a very important dispute in legal terms. Chantal Daigle was Jean-Guy Tremblay's girlfriend. She became pregnant. Things turned nasty. Jean-Guy allegedly beat Chantal. She told him the relationship was over and she was getting an abortion, and she left. Jean-Guy retaliated by seeking a legal injunction against her obtaining an abortion. He argued that he was asserting the fetus's rights to be protected. He also suggested that as the father, he had the right to insist that the child be born, against Chantal's wishes.

Abortion rights were a hot issue in 1989. The 1969 amendments to the Criminal Code had restricted legal access to abortion. In 1970, the Abortion Caravan crossed the country to protest the restrictions— a trek that ended with twenty-five women chaining themselves in the gallery of the House of Commons that May. Parliament did not remove the restrictions and litigation followed. In 1988, a divided Supreme Court had held in *R. v. Morgentaler* that the Criminal Code requirement of approval of therapeutic abortions by hospital committees violated a woman's rights.[2] However, the *Morgentaler* decision did not resolve the status of fetal rights or the issue of whether a woman could be required to carry a fetus to term against her will. In separate reasons in the *Morgentaler* case, Chief Justice Dickson had described the impact of the law on the bodily integrity of women in a physical and emotional sense,[3] while Justice Wilson had criticized the majority reasons for stopping short of recognizing a woman's right to control her own body.[4] "[T]he flaw in the . . . legislative scheme," she'd written, is that it essentially "assert[s] that the woman's capacity to reproduce is not to be subject to her own control. It is to be subject to the control of the state . . . She is the passive recipient of a decision made by others as to whether her body is to be used to nurture a new life."[5]

So in the summer of 1989, the issues of fetal rights and a woman's right to control her reproductive functions were at the top of the public mind. It was no surprise, then, that Chief Justice Dickson convened a special sitting of the court for a case that squarely raised these issues.

We sank into our places at the long bench, opened our red leather books, and prepared to listen to the lawyers. The Court of Appeal of Quebec had granted the injunction, so it fell to Ms. Daigle's lawyers to convince the court why this decision should not stand. They argued forcefully that the decision was for Ms. Daigle alone to make. She sat pale and silent on a bench at the back of the courtroom awaiting the court's decision.

The bombshell hit after lunch. Ms. Daigle's lawyer stood up. "I have a preliminary matter," he announced. "I have just learned of a development that conscience requires me to disclose to the court." Every justice leaned forward. And then he told us that unbeknownst to him and in spite of the injunction, Ms. Daigle had already obtained an abortion.[6]

I saw the tide of red anger creep up Chief Justice Dickson's face. "The court will adjourn," he stated. We all filed out.

What is said between judges in the conference room of the Supreme Court of Canada remains confidential. But to say the chief justice was displeased and all the other justices upset is only to say what became clear later in court. Ms. Daigle, at great inconvenience and expense, had continued to press the urgency of an immediate hearing when the issue on the case was moot. Lawyers have phrases for this, like "lack of candour" and "abuse of process."

Yet in the end, the court decided to complete the hearing and rule on the issue of the legal status of a fetus. The issue before the court was not confined to Mr. Tremblay and Ms. Daigle; it was important to women and men throughout Canada. And when one put oneself in Ms. Daigle's shoes, some of us argued, her conduct could be seen as more panicked than contemptuous, less a slap in the face of justice than the action of a woman running out of time.

The experience of sitting on *Tremblay v. Daigle* taught me several important lessons about judging in the Supreme Court of Canada. The first lesson was that while it is the duty of the Supreme Court to resolve disputes between either citizens and citizens or citizens and the state, an equally important function is to settle the difficult points of law that society and the legal system throw up. Ms. Daigle's case may have been moot, but resolving the issue she raised was important to the broader Canadian public.

The second lesson was that for time-sensitive cases, prompt hearings and decisions may be necessary to ensure that justice is done. Chief Justice Dickson was right to summon the court for a summer hearing, given the urgency of the issue. And the court was right, given the broader importance of the issue to the Canadian people, to issue a prompt judgment, even though it was moot in the particular case. Prompt justice is an important component of access to justice—it is the right of every Canadian.

The third lesson I learned was that even in the Supreme Court and even on a highly charged moral issue, judges were capable of putting aside their personal views and deciding matters objectively in light of the Constitution and the prevailing law. When *Tremblay v. Daigle* was decided, a number of the justices were practising Roman Catholics, and their religion taught that life begins at conception. Yet that did not prevent them from asking the central legal question—does the law, viewed objectively, recognize fetal rights?—and answering it honestly. Canadian judges are not MPs or clerics; they do not vote on politics or moral edicts. Their ultimate commitment is to the law.

The final lesson I learned was that perspectives matter. Judges of different backgrounds and genders ensure a deep and full discussion that gives due weight to the concerns of each party. One of the dangers judges face is that they may overlook or treat too lightly a particular fact or situation. A balanced bench guards against the problem of missing perspectives.

In the end, the court in *Tremblay v. Daigle* unanimously affirmed that a fetus has no legal status in Canada, either at common law or under the civil law of Quebec,[7] and that a man, while claiming to be protecting fetal rights, cannot obtain an injunction to stop an abortion and compel a woman to carry his child.[8] The decision clarified the law on the issues that had been put before the court. The aftermath was for others to navigate.

The abortion debate moved back to Parliament. The next year, Prime Minister Brian Mulroney's government attempted to fill the legislative void by passing a bill that would have re-criminalized abortion. Only when a doctor determined that a woman's physical, mental, or psychological health was threatened by her pregnancy would an abortion be considered legal. The bill, however, died in the Senate.

The process had been convoluted but democratic. Three

institutions—the courts, Parliament, and the Senate—weighed in. In the end, Canada was left without a law prohibiting abortion. Some saw this as unsatisfactory—indeed immoral. Others applauded the fact that the law would no longer dictate to women what they could or could not do with their bodies.

Jean-Guy Tremblay's suit to prevent Ms. Daigle from obtaining an abortion was not the end of his involvement with the court system. In 1999, he was convicted on two counts of assault in the violent beatings of his girlfriend and her close friend in Calgary.[9] In the course of the sentencing proceedings, it was revealed that his criminal record included eleven adult criminal convictions, most of them attacks on former girlfriends. He was sentenced to five and a half years in prison and a ten-year supervision order.[10] He applied to the Supreme Court for leave to appeal his supervision order, but his application was denied.[11]

Back in Ottawa, the heat of August died into the golden days of September. My first full term at the Supreme Court of Canada stretched out before me. Already the boxes of books for the autumn cases were piling up in my den.

On September 7, 1990, my forty-seventh birthday, I shared a glass of champagne with my sister, Judi, who had flown from Vancouver to be with me. We sat on my back patio and watched the hot air balloons against the fading blue of the sky, soft puffs of air marking their progress.

I thought about the past two years. So much had happened. I had lost a husband. I had become chief justice of the British Columbia trial court, which I left seven months later to become a Supreme Court justice. I had settled in, fought my way through critical cases, and managed to keep my head above water. And here I was, sitting in a new home in a new city on the other side of the country. A year ago, could I have imagined any of this?

Watching balloons float peacefully overhead, I contemplated the question.

The answer? Not even if I'd tried.

CHAPTER TWENTY-THREE

....

The Right to Speak

MY EARLY DAYS ON the Supreme Court plunged me into one of the most difficult issues facing modern democracies—where to draw the line between the cherished right of free speech and the need that sometimes arises to limit free speech for the greater good of society.

I had been raised in the tradition of robust free speech. Pincher Creek was a town that had long accommodated mavericks—people with different and sometimes unpopular ideas. Sometimes, my father would dismiss their more preposterous claims with a simple "Crazy." Other times, as when he spoke up for the rights of Hutterites, people thought *he* was the crazy one. To me, hearing outlandish ideas and occasionally standing up for them was just part of life.

Only later—and with some reluctance—did I come to appreciate that some kinds of speech can be so damaging to society and minorities within society that they can legitimately be banned. Even then, I was skeptical of using the heavy hand of criminal law, with its potential for imprisonment, to prevent people from speaking out.

My adventures with free speech in the Supreme Court would teach me that my views could evolve. They would teach me about the importance of dissenting, about the pains of winning and losing, and how tough the work of deciding Charter cases could really be. But I didn't know any of this when I mounted the bench with the eight other justices in the winter of 1989 to hear the first case to tackle the issue of offensive speech—*R. v. Keegstra.*[1]

James Keegstra, a secondary school teacher in Alberta, made anti-Semitic statements in his classroom and taught his students that the Holocaust was the product of a worldwide Jewish conspiracy. He was charged with hate speech under Section 319(2) of the Criminal Code (then Section 281.1[2]), which provided that "[e]very one who, by communicating statements, other than in private conversation, wilfully promotes hatred against any identifiable group is guilty of (a) an indictable offence and is liable to imprisonment for a term not exceeding two years." Keegstra was tried before a jury, convicted, and sentenced to pay a $5,000 fine.[2] He appealed to the Supreme Court, arguing that the law violated the guarantee of free expression under the Charter.

Canada had inherited a robust British tradition of free political speech. But now, with the Charter, the country had a new free expression guarantee that the Supreme Court was called upon to interpret. Complicating the matter was Section 1 of the Charter, which said that even protected speech could become unprotected if the government could show that this represented a reasonable limit in a free and democratic society—essentially, that the limit was reasonable considering what it accomplished and how seriously it hobbled the right to free expression. Nobody knew how the Supreme Court would come down on these provisions when it came to hate speech.

Everyone on the court agreed that the Criminal Code provision against hate speech violated the free speech guarantee of the Charter because it imposed limits on what people could say and write. The majority of the justices, however, upheld the law in the Criminal Code on the ground that violating the Charter guarantee was justified as a reasonable restraint on liberty.

I wrestled with what to do. I was just cutting my teeth on the court and didn't want to dissent from a majority of my colleagues, led by none other than my admired chief justice. Yet I could not see how the hate speech law, written as it was, could be justified as reasonable. Its vague language concerned me. What does "hatred" mean? What does it mean to "wilfully promote" hatred? I worried that these broad and undefined phrases would catch intemperate comments made in the heat of the moment—the kind of comments I had heard as a girl and dismissed as "crazy." To send a person to prison for uttering such comments cut too far into freedom of expression, I thought, when less draconian measures would have sufficed. The threat of being prosecuted and sent to prison, I feared, had the potential to chill legitimate expression. In the end, I dissented. Although Justices Sopinka and La Forest—two judges I much admired—agreed with me, I lost the day.

Two years later, another speech crime came before the court in *R. v. Zundel*.[3] Section 181 of the Criminal Code prohibited spreading "a statement, tale or news" that a person knows to be false and is likely to "cause injury or mischief to a public interest." Ernst Zundel, like James Keegstra, was an anti-Semitic Holocaust denier. He was charged, however, not under the hate speech law that the court had upheld in *Keegstra*, but under the even vaguer false news law.

Once the Supreme Court has ruled, even the dissenting judges are required to accept the decision as the law. While I was bound by the result in *Keegstra*, I wrote the decision for the majority that the false news provision was unconstitutional. It was simply too broad and too vague to pass muster. Originally enacted to stifle criticism of English nobles, its precise purpose in Canadian law was uncertain. What does "false news" or "false tale" mean? And what does the phrase "cause injury or mischief to a public interest" mean, if not whatever the judge thinks it should mean?

Hate speech can do great damage to individuals and to the threads that bind the fragile fabric of our diverse multicultural society. It can stoke hatred against vulnerable people—and that can result in discrimination and lead to violence. In an age of escalating hatred and terrorism, it is vital to curtail messages that provoke violence against particular groups. However, the right to express unpopular views is an essential tenet of democracy, and it must be preserved. Criminal laws that take away the right to speak must be clear enough that people can predict what might land them in prison. The cases of *Keegstra* and *Zundel* struck a careful balance between the fundamental norm of free speech on the one hand and the protection of minorities and social peace on the other. They showed that it is possible to combat hate speech while preserving a generous space for free expression.

My early experience with *Keegstra* and *Zundel* showed me how difficult Charter cases could be. Drawing the appropriate lines between the right to say what we believe—even though others may find it offensive—and the need to protect individuals and groups from hatred is the kind of work that wakes you up in the middle of the night with a dark fear in the pit of your stomach that you won't get it right. As a trial judge and a member of the BC Court of Appeal, I had comforted myself that if I got it wrong, there was another court to correct me. But now I was on the final court, and there was no further recourse. The buck stopped with us. And what we decided could affect not only the law but the way women, men, and children lived their lives and the kind of country Canada would be.

I felt the heavy responsibility that comes with being a justice settle on my shoulders. I was beginning to realize what I had got myself into when I said yes to the prime minister on that boat in the Pacific.

···

CHAPTER TWENTY-FOUR

The Final Taboo

Ⅰf freedom of speech was my first major challenge as a justice of the Supreme Court, the law of sexual assault was the second. On March 26, 1991, the full court filed in to hear *R. v. Seaboyer*,[1] a case that would test Parliament's recent changes to bring the law of sexual assault into the modern era.

Since childhood, I had been aware that bad things sometimes happened to children and women. "Stay away from him," my mother would whisper, pointing at a distant uncle. "I hate him," I would reply. And I did. I hated the way he looked at my little ankles or stared when the wind blew my skirt up. Later, I heard whispers about girls who went away to have babies because they had been "forced" by stepdads or strange men. As a teenager, I imbibed talk about "limits" on what should happen on a date and listened to gossip about boys who went too far or girls who fled vehicles in torn clothing and tears. Men, I was told, would take liberties if you let them, and sometimes if you didn't. I mulled the phrase "taking liberties." Whose liberties? The man's liberty to go as far as he could? Or the woman's liberty to be left alone?

It wasn't until law school that I learned what the law said about sexual assault. And what I learned shocked me. Rape was a common law criminal offence with a history that reached back into medieval times, where it was rooted in the idea of protecting a man's property in his wife from abduction. The legal rules I found in place in 1968 were archaic and unjust. First, because a man was presumed to have some sort of property in his wife, marital rape was not recognized. Second, because women were presumed to be morally underdeveloped, a woman's testimony under oath was not trusted and could not convict the accused without other supporting evidence. Third, rape complaints that were not made immediately after the event were invalid. Fourth, a woman's credibility depended on her reputation, so her prior sexual conduct could be raised in cross-examination, even where it was irrelevant. Finally, women's sexuality was defined by men's sexuality, so any sexual conduct short of penetration didn't count as sex.

It was not only the content of the law that shocked me and the other women in my criminal law class, but also the way it was taught—uncritically, with jokes, innuendo, and zero consideration for the feelings of the women in the room. A group of us took ourselves to the office of the new dean (Wilbur Bowker had retired) and protested. We waited for a response. None ever came.

A decade later, I found myself teaching evidence—including the rules that governed trials for rape—at the UBC faculty of law. It was a different world. Rape had become an important political and social issue in industrialized societies. Study after study revealed that sexual aggression against women was a widespread and hugely under-reported problem. Canadian women mounted loud protests against the sexism baked into Canadian laws—laws that defined rape in men's terms, discounted women's evidence, and made it hard for victims to come forward. The classes I taught were very different from those I had sat through ten years before—the uncritical recital of ancient patriarchal rules had given way to angry criticism of cruel, blind laws and to demands for reform.

All over the Western world, laws began to change. In 1976, the *Sexual Offences (Amendment) Act* took a stab at modernizing UK law. In the US, states began passing rape-shield laws in the same period. Finally, in 1983, Canada's Parliament, spurred on by outraged women, legal academics, and criminal lawyers, revamped the Criminal Code to broaden sexual offences, eradicate the myths that stymied convictions, and remove barriers to women coming forward to testify. The new law redefined sexual offences in gender-neutral terms. It reclassified rape as a type of sexual assault, eliminating the requirement of penetration. It removed the requirement that a complaint must be made promptly, as well as the need for a woman's evidence to be corroborated. Cross-examination on other sexual conduct was restricted, and rape-shield provisions were put in place to make it easier for complainants to testify.

As a young trial judge, I followed the reforms with avid interest; to me, they marked a long-overdue revolution in Canadian sexual offence law. And like other judges and members of the legal and feminist communities, I welcomed the changes and rejoiced that the myths that had for so long stood in the way of justice in sexual assault trials had finally been routed. It seemed so simple: it was a crime to have sexual contact without consent. Period. End of story.

But it did not take me long to realize that as salutary as the new laws were, we still had a long way to go. Even with the new rules, it remained difficult for victims of sexual assault to come forward. It is one thing to change the law; it is quite another to dispel ancient taboos against disclosing sexual misconduct. When a complainant did come forward, she was forced to explain the details of her assault to the police, undergo an examination known as a rape kit, repeat everything to a prosecutor, and then finally go through it all again at trial, where she would face rigorous cross-examination. Problems of credibility, not just with children and vulnerable people but with articulate women, persisted. As did the old, ugly defences that got in the way of justice.

As a judge in British Columbia, I had plunged into trials under the new laws with optimism. These trials were, by and large, fairer and more just. Yet occasionally, notwithstanding Parliament's reforms, the laws I was obliged to apply seemed to get in the way of doing justice.

Take, for example, the trial of a middle-age man charged with sexually assaulting two fifteen-year-old girls whom he had lured into a Granville Street room on the pretext of photographing them for modelling assignments. The girls said he had blindfolded them as they lay on a bed and sexually touched them. Confused and scared, they did not scream or say stop, but afterwards, they immediately went home and told their parents. The man, for his part, said the girls were lying—there was no blindfold, no sexual touching.

It will come down to whom the jury believes, I thought. But then things got more complicated. Defence counsel argued that I should instruct the jury on honest but mistaken belief—a defence that says that even if the complainant didn't consent, the accused must be acquitted if he had an honest but mistaken belief that she had consented. The accused's belief does not have to be reasonable; it only needs to have an "air of reality," based on the circumstances or other evidence.

I resisted putting this defence to the jury. The accused had not said he believed the girls were consenting to sexual activity—his story was simply that there was no sexual activity. However, when even the

Crown said there might be an air of reality to the defence, I acquiesced, charged the jury on it, and sent them out to deliberate.

It was a simple case, as I saw it. All the jury had to do was decide whom to believe and bring in a verdict. Yet at 10 p.m., they were still deliberating. I brought the lawyers in. "I suspect I know what the problem is," I told them. "They can't figure out how the defence of honest but mistaken belief applies on these facts, or what to do with an air of reality."

Over the lawyers'—even the Crown's—objections, I called the jury in and told them to forget about what I had said about honest and mistaken belief. They came back with a verdict of guilty five minutes later. The accused did not appeal.

A straightforward trial, an ordinary case. Yet it illustrated how vague rules still could get in the way of justice on sexual assault trials. What is an "air of reality"? What is required to establish it? Justice must allow for the possibility of misunderstandings, and people should not be sent to prison if they *sincerely* believed on good grounds that their partner had consented. But invoking loose concepts like an "air of reality," which is still part of the law, does not help us get just verdicts in sexual assault trials.

A second problem left over from the 1983 reforms was how to ensure that all of the many detailed provisions of the new law were consistent with the *Charter of Rights and Freedoms* and its guarantees of the presumption of innocence and the right to a fair trial. This was not a major problem—the provisions of the 1983 law, for the most part, were well drafted and were not challenged. And it is not unusual for details of new laws to be challenged and, if found defective, reworked by Parliament in a process of constitutional fine-tuning. I was therefore unprepared for the storm that greeted the Supreme Court's decision to strike down one aspect of the 1983 law and return it to Parliament for further consideration, in the 1991 case of *R. v. Seaboyer*.

Seaboyer was a case of refining the law, as I saw it. At issue was Parliament's blanket prohibition of any cross-examination of a complainant on her sexual history. The arguments convinced the majority of the court that in rare cases, cross-examination on a past sexual act could be relevant to the defence of honest but mistaken belief in consent. To that extent, it unjustifiably violated the Charter guarantee of the right to a fair trial, and was therefore void under Section 52 of the *Constitution Act, 1982*, which provided that laws are of no force and effect to the extent they are inconsistent with the Charter. I agreed to write the majority reasons, which set out guidelines on how the legislation could be written so as to both protect complainants and comply with the Charter guarantee of the right to a fair trial.

The idea that a portion, if only a small portion, of the 1983 amendment aimed at eliminating the odious practice of cross-examining complainants on their previous sexual encounters violated the Charter brought down the wrath of feminist critics—on the majority decision generally and on me personally. I was the newly appointed woman judge, one of only two on the court, since Bertha Wilson had retired earlier in the year. The fact that the majority held that an aspect of the rape-shield provisions enacted by Parliament was inconsistent with the fair trial guarantees of the Charter outraged these feminist critics. The fact that I wrote the decision was considered nothing short of treasonous.

"It may be right, but why did you have to write it instead of some other judge?" a friend lamented, as she surveyed a headline condemning the decision.

To me it was simple: I was a judge, sworn to uphold the law. The Charter was part of the Constitution, the fundamental law of Canada. All other laws must conform to it. If I concluded that a provision of the rape-shield law violated the Charter, then I had no choice, consistent with my oath, but to say so. That the provision struck down was important to women made the decision more difficult, but it could not change the outcome. My personal inclinations could not prevail over the constitutional imperative of maintaining the right to present a full defence. As a judge, my duty was to apply the law and call the case the way I saw it, adding guidelines as to how the law could be amended in conformity with the Charter. Sometimes a judge must make unpopular decisions that may go against her deepest preferences. That is why judges enjoy judicial independence.

As for why I wrote the court's decision, the truth is that I was never strategic in what I decided or what cases I chose to write. I wrote the cases that interested me and fell to me, regardless of whether the decision might attract criticism in the short term.

The changes the court suggested in *Seaboyer* were instituted. Parliament took up the guidelines the majority set out, and its new law was upheld.[2] Parliament's goal of shielding complainants from irrelevant cross-examination into their sexual past was achieved, in a way that respected the Charter.

The third and biggest challenge following the 1983 reform of sexual assault law was to ensure that its provisions were properly applied, and that irrelevant considerations were not allowed to undermine the testimony of women who complained of sexual assault. Rape myths, we learned, die hard. Decades after Parliament's reforms, judges could still be found asking whether the complainant fought hard enough against her aggressor, or insisting that the way a woman was dressed might establish consent. *R. v. Ewanchuk* provided a classic example of how these myths permeated the law, even on the cusp of the twenty-first century.[3]

The complainant, a seventeen-year-old girl, went for a job interview in a man's van. At a certain point, the man, Ewanchuk, began touching her sexually. She said no, but he persisted, and the contact became progressively more intimate. She kept saying no, to no avail. In the end, she managed to escape.

The trial judge accepted the complainant's evidence that she had not wanted the man to touch her. However, he suggested that her conduct—particularly the fact that she was dressed in shorts—amounted to "implied" consent. Nevertheless, the accused was convicted. He appealed the verdict. The Alberta Court of Appeal directed an acquittal, but Chief Justice Catherine Fraser penned a rousing dissent. "Women in Canada," she wrote, "are not walking around this country in a state of constant consent to sexual activity unless and until they say 'No' or offer resistance to anyone who targets them for sexual activity."[4] The Supreme Court of Canada unanimously agreed and replaced Ewanchuk's acquittal with a conviction.

Canada's law is now clear—rape myths have no place in the courtroom and complainants must be treated fairly, in a way that protects their dignity and privacy to the maximum extent commensurate with a fair trial. The National Judicial Institute trains every judge to be conscious of unacknowledged assumptions about how women should behave—assumptions that, in the past, have skewed sexual assault trials. But debate still roils about how the law and society should deal with sexual assault. At the heart of the debate are two related issues—the meaning of consent and the culture of silence that has for too long shrouded unwanted sexual contact.

Why is consent in the law of sexual assault so difficult? The law of contract has no difficulty dealing with it—consent must be clearly indicated. The seals and signatures required to establish consent in the law of contract obviously don't work for sex, but the basic principle is the same: unless a person indicates her consent by word or clear conduct—the proverbial signing on the dotted line—it should not be assumed. It isn't enough that a woman be scantily clad, smile at a man, or even fail to protest his threat or touch; none of these actions imply consent. In fact, the default position is non-consent; sex is a big deal, and as Chief Justice Fraser wrote, women do not go about in a constant state of readiness and acceptance.

It is also rational for women to speak out about sexual acts to which they did not consent. People speak out about every other sort of wrong—slanders, acts of negligence, lack of due diligence, failure to carry out responsibilities in employment or electoral office. Why is sexual misconduct different? Why should the victims of nonconsensual sexual contact be denied the right to speak out?

Yet many argue they should be denied that very right. It's too easy, opponents claim, for a woman to make a groundless accusation that will destroy a man's reputation; therefore, they conclude, all women should be silenced. But if someone accuses a doctor of a botched operation or suggests a politician accepted a bribe, we do not insist that the person complaining remain silent outside the court. Why do we treat allegations of wrongful sexual conduct any differently? It is no answer to say, as some do, that the only place women can talk about sexual assaults is a criminal trial. We don't apply that rule to any other misconduct, so why should we insist on it for sexual assault?

The culture of silence that surrounds sexual misconduct is the last and most resistant of all the rape myths. Its roots twine deep in our culture and our law. The old rules of evidence—rules I was once obliged to teach—are redolent with the culture of silence. Rules like the one that said a woman must complain immediately after the attack fly in the face of what we now know: it is often difficult, if not impossible, for victims of sexual assault, beset by trauma, to complain immediately. Rules that silenced women by exposing their past sexual activity were justified as the price of complaint. For centuries, the law, like society, has told women that it is better not to speak out.

The #MeToo movement has challenged the ultimate rape myth—the culture of silence. Some say this is necessary and good as the old walls of secrecy stoking a culture that normalized sexual aggression are battered down. Others say it is dangerous. But there is a way forward, it seems to me. Women should be able to complain of sexual aggression in the way they can complain of any other wrong. But people should not be convicted and sent to prison unless the evidence establishes that they are guilty beyond reasonable doubt.

One by one, the myths and taboos that have denied women sexual freedom have been falling. I have witnessed this. When I was a girl, it was taboo for women to speak of sex at all. Men told their jokes and shared their stories over drinks, but women were silent. Ladies did not discuss such things. No matter how difficult their situation, they were silent. When I was a girl, it was also taboo for women to speak of violence at the hands of their husbands. The shamed woman would whisper to her children, "Don't tell anyone; what happens under this roof stays under this roof."

Women's silence has long been the cloak that covers past wrongs and gives licence for future wrongs. We have rejected these taboos and rejected silence; modern women are allowed to talk about sex and to speak out about spousal violence. But a final taboo has lingered: speaking out against men who take advantage of their power or their situation to perpetrate sexual assaults and advances without the woman's consent. We need to challenge this final taboo.

We have come a long way in routing the taboos that stand in the way of justice for victims of sexual assault. But there is still a distance to go. The problems are complex and rooted in centuries of culture and myth. The law, imperfect as it may be, is a powerful tool in achieving lasting change. But real justice will come only when we change attitudes—when respect for the autonomy of every person replaces old myths grounded in ownership, control, and power.

....

CHAPTER TWENTY-FIVE

On Life and Death

WHEN RORY LAY DYING, he made a point of telling me that when he was gone, I should remarry and start a new life.

"Please," I told him. "I don't want to talk about it. I only want you." To contemplate replacing the man who had coloured my life for nearly thirty years seemed impossible and disrespectful. Perhaps I would eventually find someone else, as others seemed to. But at the time, I couldn't bring myself to think of it.

"I need to discuss this," Rory insisted. "With you, with Angus. You need to feel free to move on, and Angus needs to accept whoever you choose."

"What have you told Angus?"

"I told him that I think you should remarry. I told him he would probably resent the idea of a new father. I told him that he must not, that he should accept him."

He sank back on his pillow, exhausted.

Death creates a void in the lives of those left behind. Where there were shared moments—glances, smiles, touches, words—suddenly there is nothing. In the months and years after Rory's death, I filled the void with the business of being a judge and a mother. I was slowly making new friends and finding new interests. I had no desire to find another husband.

While I didn't realize it at the time, I was still grieving.

Grieving, I discovered, is a long and complicated process. Not five steps, as the book my friend had given me said, but a hundred steps, stretching out into a long process that, over the years, moves a person from one place to another, from looking back to looking forward.

Painful steps.

Like when, after a series of dreams so vivid I would wake convinced Rory was with me, he appeared one night to tell me he was leaving. "I won't be coming back," he said. I woke up in a sweat. "No!" I cried. "No!" He never came again.

Like my first visit back to Vancouver six months after my move to Ottawa. On the way to my sister's house, I broke into sobs as the cab passed through our old neighbourhood. The cabbie eyed me apprehensively in the rear-view mirror, wondering if he should divert and take the strange woman in his back seat to emergency. I hadn't cried much after Rory died; now I couldn't stop.

Although it wasn't apparent at the time, even to me, I spent the first two years after Rory's death looking back. Even when new things were happening, I perceived them through the lens of what had been or what might have been, had Rory not died. His words were cached in a recess of my brain—*a home in the Ottawa Valley, lovely country*. On the weekends, I would take trips with Angus to explore the area surrounding our new home. I didn't need more property—I was burdened with a house bigger than I required and a mortgage larger than I could afford—but I couldn't rid myself of my compulsion to explore that valley.

I quickly realized that any country property I might like was beyond my means. *Good*, I thought. *One less piece of the past to hang on to.* And then, one evening after dinner in December 1990, I opened the newspaper and absently perused the want ads. One hundred acres with lake, the three-line ad read.

"Want ads?" kids ask. "What's a want ad?" Yes, in the days before the internet and Kijiji, this was how people got rid of things they no longer wanted. In this case, what was no longer wanted was a piece of property in the Gatineau Valley, twelve miles west of a village I had never heard of called Low.

I rang the number in the ad and talked to a man. We arranged to meet. It was December 4, 1990, and a light snow dusted the pre-winter roads as Angus and I drove north to Low, turned left on Fieldville Road, and followed a tortuous trail reminiscent of the route leading to our ranch in the mountains. At our destination, Monsieur Charron, a young man, got out of his black four-by-four and waved at us to follow. We turned right onto a more primitive trail, my urban Toyota skidding on the snow. Monsieur Charron braked his truck and got out. Angus and I followed. I looked out through the pines at a white expanse of flatness yielding to a black ridge of spruce in the distance.

"Lac Brogan," said Monsieur Charron. "The lake."

It was not love at first sight. But over the weeks that followed, the idea of buying this piece of land grew on me. This was during the depths of the 1991 recession. Monsieur Charron, who owned an adjoining property and had acquired the land on spec under a Quebec policy encouraging the sale of excess Crown lands to neighbours, was desperate to turn it over. He took to telephoning me in the evening; I took to dithering. On February 13, 1991, I purchased the property for a modest sum.

Like many things in my life that have started impulsively and turned out to be good, the purchase was crazy. I didn't need the property. I didn't know what I would do with the property. Most embarrassing of all, I had never properly inspected the property.

Frank McArdle—our passing acquaintance at Cambridge had burgeoned into deep friendship—came up from Toronto that February to look at it. We parked on the road and floundered helplessly through four-foot snowdrifts in a general northerly direction. It quickly became clear that without snowshoes, we would never get near the lake.

"Oh, well," I said with an airy wave. "It's out there somewhere. Next time, maybe."

Frank looked at me, then at Angus, and shook his head. "How much did you pay for this piece of—of land?"

I headed back to the car. "Later," I mumbled.

A few weeks later, I found myself at a dinner at the Lester B. Pearson Building in Ottawa. To my surprise, former prime minister Pierre Trudeau was seated to my right. Like many, I was in awe of the great man. And like many, I didn't know what to say when the conversation turned to me. I had read that he had a cottage on a lake in the Laurentian Mountains north of Montreal, and in a desperate gambit to fill the airspace, I decided to raise my own foray into the wilderness.

"I fear I've done a foolish thing, Mr. Trudeau," I said. "I've purchased a property in the Gatineau Valley."

He looked at me. "What can be the problem?" he asked in his clipped mid-Atlantic English.

"I'm told there is a lake on it," I explained. "But I purchased it in the winter and have no idea whether the lake is a worthless declivity in the earth or a true, deep lake."

He nodded and turned away. I thought I had lost him—so much for my attempt to make polite conversation. Then he turned back to me and asked, "Your lake, does it have one rocky shore?"

I thought hard, attempting to recall what I had seen that day in the snow beside the lake. "Yes," I said. "It does. The land rises steeply on the opposite shore."

The former prime minister nodded. "Then you're all right," he said, and turned back to the person on his other side.

And he was right. Angus, who had developed a passion for fishing, plumbed the lake on his depth finder in the spring.

"Eighty-four feet," he announced.

Pierre Trudeau, I marvelled, like every good judge, knew that when you ask the right question, the right answer is bound to follow.

In my personal life, too, I was starting to ask the right questions and get answers that brought me a glimpse of a new and rich future. Land and a lake that Angus and I could call our own. And for me, a deepening relationship with someone who perhaps, just maybe, would help fill the void Rory's death had left.

IN SEPTEMBER 1992, I returned to a fall and winter docket charged with fascinating issues. But one seized me, preoccupied me, dominated my waking (and sometimes sleeping) hours until its release in the fall of 1993—*Rodriguez v. British Columbia (Attorney General)*.[1]

Sue Rodriguez lived on Vancouver Island. Her rich life was interrupted by a diagnosis of amyotrophic lateral sclerosis, or ALS, known more commonly as Lou Gehrig's disease, after the famous baseball player. ALS is a disease that gradually paralyzes people because the brain is no longer able to communicate with the muscles of the body. Over time, as the muscles break down, people living with ALS lose the ability to walk, talk, eat, swallow, and, eventually, breathe. Sue could no longer walk and was having difficulty talking. But her mind was as alert as ever. She thought about her end—about the long period when she wouldn't be able to do anything but wait for the disease to take away her ability to breathe. She wanted to live as long as she had the capacity to enjoy life, but avoid the final painful phase. The problem was that by that time, she would be unable to take her own life. Nor, as the law then stood, could anyone help her. Suicide was legal in Canada, but assisting someone to die by suicide was a crime leading to imprisonment under the Criminal Code. The British Columbia Court of Appeal had rejected Sue's claim to assisted suicide, and she appealed to the Supreme Court of Canada.

As the hearing date approached, I worried whether I was still too close to Rory's death to sit on the case. I went to see my chief justice, now Antonio Lamer. He had replaced Brian Dickson as chief justice when Brian retired in the spring of 1990.

"I'm not sure I should sit on this case," I said. "I do not have settled views on the outcome, but I feel very close to it after—"

"After what you went through with Rory," he interrupted.

I nodded.

"You should not let that stop you from sitting," he said. "Judges are human beings. They bring their life experiences to the cases they decide. That is good, provided they remember that their ultimate duty is to be faithful to the law."

So I agreed to sit on the case and prepared for the hearing.

On May 20, 1993, the nine justices of the court filed in to hear the *Rodriguez* case. The frail figure of Sue Rodriguez in her wheelchair, devastated by disease and struggling to remain upright, seared my mind. I knew that kind of suffering; I had lived it.

In the dark weeks before Rory's final descent into unconsciousness, he suffered enormously. He suffered great physical pain. He suffered equally devastating psychological pain as a once proud man no longer able to manage his basic functions. One morning, as he lay in his bed in our home, he asked a special thing of me—to give him the morphine we had been doling out drop by drop in a single massive dose. "I want to die now," he said.

Tears in my eyes, I left the room. I could not do it. I had always thought of myself as gutsy. I had never shrunk from unpleasant things. But this, I knew in my heart, I could not do. Because it was against the law. Because I could not physically bring myself to do it.

Racked by guilt at failing my husband's last request, I wept in a hospital chair while Rory was in the adjoining treatment room. A doctor found me, and I told him everything. "I can't do it," I whispered.

The doctor did not judge. "Then you shouldn't do it," he said. "Remember, you will go on. You have to live with yourself after." Then he added, "We'll do what we can."

Were the treatments that followed only for the pain? Or did they shorten the remaining days of his life? I didn't know and I didn't ask. All I knew was that the pain lessened, and Rory passed away peacefully.

Now Sue Rodriguez was before me, and I was forced to relive that difficult time and the choice I had made. Once again, although in different form, I was confronted by the question: Should a suffering person in the final stages of life be allowed to end her life with dignity?

In a five-to-four decision, the court held that the answer was no. Justice Sopinka, writing for the majority, held that the ban on assisted suicide did not violate the liberty guarantee under Section 7 of the Charter because prohibiting assisted suicide, which risks abuse of vulnerable people, reflects a fundamental Canadian value and does not offend the principles of fundamental justice. Nor, in his view, did it offend the guarantee against cruel and unusual punishment. And even if it offended the equality guarantee, it would be justified.

I dissented. The ban on assisted suicide arbitrarily limited the right of a person to deal with her body as she chose and thus violated the guarantee of liberty, I wrote for myself and Justice L'Heureux-Dubé. Justice Cory agreed with both my reasons and those of Chief Justice Lamer, who dissented on the ground that denying the right to assisted dying violated the equality guarantee of the Charter. The law, I wrote, allowed some people to end their lives but denied the same choice to Sue Rodriguez, violating autonomy and the principles of fundamental justice. This violation was not a reasonable limit on the right to liberty. Everyone, I concluded, has the right to life and liberty, as Section 7 of the Charter says. That, it seemed to me, must include the final liberty to determine how and when to die. If a person, sound of mind and in great suffering, makes the decision to end her life, she should be allowed to do so. In my view, the danger of abuse could be met by a court order stating that the judge was satisfied with the patient's desire to die, and freely consented to assistance in dying.

Sue Rodriguez lost her case but died peacefully with her doctor at her side—and in the arms of her dear friend Member of Parliament Svend Robinson—some months later. Neither the doctor nor Robinson was prosecuted.

Two decades later, in *Carter v. Canada (Attorney General)*,[2] the Supreme Court of Canada, in a decision "by the court" (a decision issued in the name of all the justices, of which I was one) took up my dissent in *Rodriguez* and ruled that the provision criminalizing assisted suicide violated the *Charter of Rights and Freedoms*. A person enduring intolerable suffering has the right to end her life. I had come full circle.

....

CHAPTER TWENTY-SIX

The Marriage Act

MY FRIENDSHIP WITH FRANK McArdle had blossomed into romance. It happened slowly—a visit in Toronto en route to London in the summer of 1990, where my car broke down and Frank lent me his; return visits by Frank to Ottawa, including the winter when we waded through chest-deep snow in a vain attempt to get a look at the lake on the property I had just purchased.

"He makes you laugh again," a close friend observed. I thought about it. I hadn't laughed much for a long time. And watching from the side, I realized that he was making Angus laugh, too.

Frank was and is a special person. He had played semi-professional hockey in his youth with Les As de Québec and once scored a goal against the Montreal Canadiens and Rocket Richard. He made a career in advertising before deciding to study law at age forty-seven.

He is kind, caring, and deeply loyal, a man of straight talk, generous spirit, and countless friends. Former prime minister Jean Chrétien summed up Frank in these words: "A true gentleman."[1]

In July 1991, on the flight to our beloved biennial Cambridge Lectures, Frank proposed marriage. A man of passion and occasional flamboyance, he seized the flight attendant's mic in a moment of ardour before popping the question. A good number of the passengers listened in. "What's the answer?" I heard their voices call, until at last I acquiesced. Just in case anyone hadn't heard, the pilot made a formal announcement as the plane descended into Heathrow: "Ladies and gentlemen, for those of you who may have missed it, we've had a little excitement on the flight tonight. A certain couple got engaged." The plane erupted in clapping.

"Why did you propose on a plane?" I later complained.

"Because I knew you couldn't escape," said Frank.

"You should know I'm a private person."

"And you should know I had the parachute ready in case you said no."

We spent the next few afternoons and evenings in the Porters' Lodge of Queens' College, trying desperately to reach our respective children in far-flung parts of the world, lest they learn of our engagement through the newspapers. In those pre-internet days, this was no easy task. I caught up with Angus in Texas, where he had gone to work in my brother Len's pathology lab for the summer.

"Great, Mom," he said without missing a beat. "Now let me talk to Frank." Relief washed over me as I handed Frank the phone—my son approved.

On February 8, 1992, I married Frank McArdle in a simple ceremony in the judges' conference room. The ceremony was performed by our friend Justice Douglas Carruthers of the Ontario Superior Court. There, surrounded by the justices of the court, our children, other family members, and close friends, we took our vows.

On April 17, 1989, I was sworn in as a justice of the Supreme Court of Canada. Below, I am with the rest of the court. Front row (*left to right*): Gérard La Forest, Antonio Lamer, Chief Justice George Brian Dickson, Bertha Wilson, and Claire L'Heureux-Dubé. Back row (*left to right*): Peter Cory, John Sopinka, Charles Gonthier, and me.

In the south stairwell of the Supreme Court Building in 1990. As a new judge, I was thinking about where my life would take me.

Frank brought new joy into Angus's life and mine. Here we are getting married in 1992 by Justice Douglas Carruthers, a justice of the Ontario Superior Court of Justice.

Happy days at Lac Brogan, Quebec, with Angus, Frank, and our Labrador retrievers, Cass and Kyrie.

In 1990, Antonio Lamer was appointed chief justice. This photo was taken near the end of that decade, after the court had undergone many changes. *Left to right*: Michel Bastarache, Louise Arbour, Frank Iacobucci, Claire L'Heureux-Dubé, John C. Major, Chief Justice Antonio Lamer, Ian Binnie, me, and Charles Gonthier.

Signing on as chief justice with Prime Minister Jean Chrétien and Governor General Adrienne Clarkson on January 12, 2000. Jean Chrétien has just handed me his pen after mine broke.

As chief justice, I felt it was my responsibility to support my justices any way I could. Front row (*left to right*): Frank Iacobucci, Claire L'Heureux-Dubé, me, Charles Gonthier, and John Major. Back row (*left to right*): Louise Arbour, Michel Bastarache, Ian Binnie, and Louis LeBel.

Later that same year, celebrating with Judi in Vancouver.

I was deeply impressed by Hillary Rodham Clinton when I met her in 1995.

Despite our differences, President George W. Bush and I shared a warm and frank conversation at a dinner in 2004.

During my years as chief justice, I was privileged to meet jurists from many other countries, including those from the Supreme Court of the United States. Front row (*left to right*): Canadian Justices Michael Moldaver, Richard Wagner, Andromache Karakatsanis, me, Chief Justice of the United States John G. Roberts Jr., and US Associate Justices Anthony M. Kennedy, Ruth Bader Ginsburg, and Stephen G. Breyer. Back row (*left to right*): Gib van Ert, Gerald R. Tremblay, Canadian Justice Suzanne Côté, the Honourable Catherine Mandeville, the Honourable Marie Michelle Lavigne, Canadian Justice Clément Gascon, Frank, US Associate Justice Samuel A. Alito, Mary Davis Kennedy, US Associate Justices Sonia Sotomayor and Elena Kagan, and Jeffrey P. Minear.

One of the greatest moments of my life came in 2002, when I met Her Majesty Queen Elizabeth II, whom I had admired since early childhood.

Here I am with the court in 2016, shortly before announcing my retirement. Back row (*left to right*): Russell Brown, Clément Gascon, Suzanne Côté, and Malcolm Rowe. Front row (*left to right*): Andromache Karakatsanis, Rosalie Abella, me, Michael Moldaver, and Richard Wagner.

In my office, formally welcoming Richard Wagner as the next chief justice. My beloved painting of Pincher Creek is behind us.

At my retirement gala with former prime ministers Brian Mulroney and Jean Chrétien, two men who were instrumental in my career, and Prime Minister Justin Trudeau, who helped me decide when to retire.

Leaving the courtroom after hearing my last case, with a tear in my eye and a smile on my face.

Throughout my years as a judge, I presided over many wedding ceremonies for family and law clerks. I never ceased to marvel at the impact of the ceremony. I have learned to pause to allow the bride or the groom to swallow tears and regain his or her composure. It happens every time.

What is a wedding? It is more than a pledge between two people to love and support each other for the rest of their lives, for better or for worse. That can be done in private. The wedding ceremony is a declaration before the community and the state—and in many cases God—that a new element has been added to their corpus, a new family within a family. It is no accident that societies throughout human history have celebrated weddings. Weddings are not merely pledges between two people—they are pledges between those two people and the community, and beyond that, to the country of which that community is a part.

The significance of the wedding ceremony is not negated by the fact that many couples in our modern age decide to forego it. That is their choice. But it does not undermine the significance of the ceremony for those who desire it. Nor is the significance of the ceremony negated by the fact that many marriages do not endure. The pledge is important in itself. And many marriages do endure.

Frank and I took it for granted that we were entitled to exchange our vows before friends and family and the state. For us, as for the many couples I had married, our wedding was a profound experience. It moved us in the moment and shaped everything that happened between us over the next quarter century. But not all couples were as fortunate as we were in 1992. Until July 20, 1995, Canadian law denied same-sex couples the right to this most profound social commitment. The roots of the denial lay deep in social and religious taboos against homosexuality.

By the time Frank and I married, the law on homosexuality had changed. Homosexual relations were no longer a crime, following Prime Minister Pierre Trudeau's famous declaration in 1967 that the state has no place in the bedrooms of the nation. Discrimination against LGBTQ people in housing and employment had already been outlawed in many provincial human rights codes. But an important issue remained: access to state-sanctioned marriage.

Once again, the advent of the Charter in 1982 changed everything. Section 15 provides that everyone is equal before and under the law and entitled to equal benefit and protection of the law without discrimination. While the provisions of the Charter came into force on April 17, 1982, the implementation of Section 15 was delayed for three years to give the government time to amend laws that might offend the equality provision. On its face, the equality provision said laws had to treat everyone equally. But laws by their nature make distinctions between groups, giving benefits to some and withholding them from others. Since Aristotle, people had been arguing about what equality means. Now the court would have to come to grips with it.

Did the new equality guarantee mean simply that "likes" would have to be treated alike? That was Aristotle's view, and it was a view that allowed him to exclude women and slaves from the polis on the ground they were "unlike" men. On this view, the law could deny protections or benefits to people by labelling them "unlike." Women could be denied benefits because they are "unlike" men. Similarly, LGBTQ people could be denied benefits because they are "unlike" straight people.

The Supreme Court of Canada had rejected this concept of Section 15 in *Andrews v. Law Society of British Columbia*,[2] just before I came to the court. In fact, I had written the court of appeal judgment in the case, holding that Section 15 prevented the law society from denying a lawyer the right to practise because he was not a Canadian citizen.[3] I reasoned that citizenship was irrelevant to the practice of law, and that therefore Mr. Andrews was not "unlike" Canadian citizens and should not be treated differently. The majority of justices in the Supreme Court agreed with this result, but they built their own theory of Section 15, holding that it was aimed at substantive rather than formal equality. One does not ask whether the claimant is like or unlike—instead, the analysis focuses on whether the claimant is a member of a disadvantaged group and whether the impugned distinction tends to further disadvantage of that group.

The Supreme Court's highly contextual "disadvantaged group" approach proved difficult to apply, leading to successive clarifications in the years that followed.[4] I laboured through iteration after iteration. However, one thing was abundantly clear: Section 15 was to be interpreted in a fashion that lessened discrimination and inequality. Bottom line—a law that worsened the position of a disadvantaged group would fail the Section 15 test.

The other big question was whether the Supreme Court would confine Section 15 to the categories of discrimination enumerated in the provision—race, age, sex, and mental or physical disability—or extend it to other kinds of discrimination. Andrews held that it covered any discrimination analogous to the categories—hence citizenship was included.

So, as it turned out, was homosexuality. The issue was enormously controversial. People argued it was right—indeed ordained by the Scriptures—that legal benefits like marriage be denied to LGBTQ people. They predicted there would be dire social consequences if the institution of traditional marriage between a man and a woman was watered down to include same-sex couples. The Charter guaranteed religious freedom. That freedom came smack up against the equality guarantee—even if same-sex marriage was contrary to your religious beliefs, you had to accept that in Canada, it was lawful.

Battle was joined. On the one side of the debate, LGBTQ people and groups backing them argued that the benefit of the law must be extended to the LGBTQ community. On the other side, conservative and religious groups argued that Section 15 was never intended to protect LGBTQ rights, and that, even if it were, the costs of recognizing them would far outweigh any benefits, so the ban should be upheld under Section 1 of the Charter (the "reasonable limits" clause).

The politicians declined to get involved. Agreeing that Section 15 protected the LGBTQ community would have angered large sectors of the voting public and impacted their chances of re-election. So the issue fell to the courts to decide.

The first cases concerned entitlement to statutory benefits, like pensions and medical benefits. The Supreme Court confirmed the decisions of lower courts that it was a violation of Section 15 to exclude gay couples from such benefits.[5]

Then the debate ratcheted up another notch. Proponents kept driving for the ultimate goal: legal recognition of same-sex marriage. Opponents said marriage was different from benefits, and anyway, if you had all the legal benefits, why did you need the ultimate sacrament? Three appellate courts—in Ontario,[6] British Columbia,[7] and Quebec[8]—ordered that same-sex marriage be recognized immediately. The Liberal government of the day declined to appeal these decisions, implicitly accepting the right to marriage equality, but also denying proponents the sanction of the highest court. Advocates turned to the politicians, demanding changes to the federal *Marriage Act* and provincial solemnization of marriage statutes.

EVEN BEFORE THE SAME-SEX marriage debate reached the appellate courts, lingering discrimination against the LGBTQ community on other fronts had attracted judicial attention. A case in point was *Vriend v. Alberta*, decided in 1998.[9]

Delwin Vriend was a lab coordinator at a private Christian college in Alberta. He was fired when administrators discovered he was gay. He claimed discrimination and sought redress under Alberta's *Individual's Rights Protection Act*. The act set out the grounds for discrimination claims, which did not include discrimination on the basis of homosexuality. Alberta argued that Vriend's claim must therefore be denied. The trial judge ruled for Mr. Vriend, but the Alberta Court of Appeal overturned that decision.

I was among the judges on the Supreme Court of Canada who heard the appeal. The question was whether the legislative omission—the failure to provide equal benefit of the law to LGBTQ individuals—was inconsistent with Section 15 of the Charter. All nine justices agreed it was unconstitutional. All but one (Justice John Major) joined in ordering the missing protection be read into the *Individual's Rights Protection Act*. Critics argued that the decision to read in the protection was a stark case of the court making law. Yet it was clear that without protection of LGBTQ people, the legislation offended the Constitution. Legislatures, if they confer benefits, must do so in a way that does not discriminate, it seemed to me.

In 1998, LGBTQ groups celebrated Delwin Vriend's victory. The case, once and for all, nailed shut the coffin on the idea that, in Canada, laws could deny LGBTQ people benefits and protections that they accorded to others. The stage was set for the final act in the Canadian same-sex marriage saga.

THAT FINAL ACT DIDN'T occur until some years later. In 2003, when I was serving as the chief justice on the court, the government of Prime Minister Jean Chrétien referred the question of same-sex marriage to the Supreme Court.[10]

In fact, the government reference posed a number of questions, but the fourth was the critical one: Did the Constitution require recognition of same-sex marriage? Lower courts had answered in the affirmative. The government had not appealed. So the answer might have seemed obvious. But the Supreme Court declined to address the question, tossing the matter back to Parliament. In due course, the House of Commons passed a bill approving same-sex marriage, which the Senate in turn approved on July 19, 2005.

In the wake of the passage of the *Civil Marriage Act*, couples rushed to plan long-delayed marriages. But an obstacle loomed. Under the Canadian Constitution, a law does not come into force until it receives royal assent from the governor general or a deputy governor general. And the governor general's principal deputy is the chief justice of Canada.

I was at Lac Brogan at the time, enjoying a few days of respite after a hectic court term. Someone from the Privy Council Office telephoned me.

"Would you be available to sign the same-sex marriage bill?"

"Is it really essential?" I asked. Signing bills into law in the capacity of deputy governor general was common. But this was a sensitive bill that might well end up before a court. At law, there was no problem—I would not be signing in my judicial capacity—but not everyone is aware of such constitutional niceties. It was a bill I would have preferred not to sign.

"The governor general is ill in hospital and it seems no other justices are available," came the reply.

I thought of the marriages that had been scheduled in the expectation the bill would be promptly signed, and I considered the disappointment that would follow if it were not. I drove into Ottawa and met the clerk on the doorstep of my house. Inside, in my living room, I signed the bill into law.

No one challenged the *Civil Marriage Act*. The debate was over. From that day forward, all Canadian couples, whatever their gender or sexual orientation, would enjoy equal access to the state benefit of marriage.

JULY 1, 2017. AS usual, Frank and I paid a visit to the Supreme Court after the Canada Day ceremonies. The steps were thronged with visitors. Children with maple leaves on their cheeks waved tiny flags.

Families from every part of the country had come to Ottawa for Canada Day and made the Supreme Court part of their program. They wore red T-shirts and carried cameras. They were all excited to be at the country's highest court.

We greeted them, posed for photos, and took time to chat.

"I want to be a lawyer," said an eight-year-old girl, looking up shyly through her lashes.

"No, chief justice," her slightly older brother shouted from behind her.

As we were leaving, a same-sex couple approached holding the hands of a toddler.

"We want to thank you," said one. "We are here today, together, with our child. Without the court, this would not have happened."

I looked at him and saw tears in his eyes.

The little girl between them smiled up at me and Frank. We smiled back.

"Don't thank me," I said. "Thank the law. And thank a country where this can happen."

CHAPTER TWENTY-SEVEN

··

Division and Discord

I THINK OF THE COURT in decades. The 1970s was the decade of the emergence of a distinctive Canadian voice on the court. No longer was it a colonial tribunal mouthing the sayings of British judges from across the Atlantic (with a dose of mandatory Canadiana to accommodate the civil law of Quebec). The court was charting a path as a distinctively Canadian court, creating distinctively Canadian law. Most of its decisions continued to echo British principles and British common law, but people took note—a change was under way.

The 1980s was the decade of the *Charter of Rights and Freedoms*. The shift from English law to a distinctively Canadian jurisprudence was completed. The members of the court, faced by the unprecedented challenge of giving meaning and shape to a new constitutional document, rallied together and produced the basic principles of Charter interpretation that would reshape Canada and guide the law for decades to come. While concurring and dissenting opinions flourished, the general sense was of a court moving forward with harmony, energy, and a common vision under the leadership of Brian Dickson.

The 1990s was a decade of fine-tuning the work of the 1980s. A tuck here, a nip there. An extension on this point, a retraction on that. But tucking and nipping, while important and essential jurisprudential work, could not compare to the demand and undoubted exhilaration of laying the first legal flesh on the bones of the Charter. What holds for war, politics, and religion also holds for the law—people who come together on big questions in times of challenge may fall to bickering over the fine points of implementation.

The mood in the Supreme Court when I arrived in the spring of 1989 reflected the common purpose that had driven the justices of the 1980s to achieve unified stances on most basic Charter issues. They were still a tight-knit group. Like siblings in a close family, they sometimes fell to bickering over this point or that, but the sense of oneness—the feeling that the institution and work that united them was more important than their differences—permeated the second-floor corridor that linked the justices' chambers. In the decade to come, the court would struggle to maintain that cohesion.

The 1990s court was led by Chief Justice Antonio Lamer, appointed to replace Brian Dickson on his retirement, following the tradition of alternating anglophone and francophone chief justices. Brian Dickson had led by the strength of his legal mind, his military self-discipline, and his utter devotion to the law and the court. It was a hard act to follow. But Tony, as his friends knew him, was determined to succeed.

Tony Lamer had earned a reputation on the streets of Montreal as one of the finest defence lawyers of his generation. Appointed to the bench at the young (for judges) age of thirty-six, he presided over trials arising out of the kidnapping and murder of provincial cabinet minister Pierre Laporte by Quebec separatists in 1970. It was a delicate and difficult assignment at a delicate and difficult time, and Justice Lamer completed it well. So well that he was named to the Supreme Court of Canada just ten years after he became a judge.

Tony Lamer was an imposing figure—broad-shouldered and handsome, his forceful face dominated by a swath of grey hair and a jaw of iron beneath a thick white moustache. He had intellect and character, and the press quickly dubbed him the Lion in Winter. The sobriquet stuck.

When I came to the court, Tony was just another justice. Like the other senior justices, he had been working long hours for the past eight years. Yet he still possessed a prowling energy, ready to take on anyone or anything—which he did, writing a host of powerful criminal law judgments and spearheading the effort to reduce the court's backlog of cases. He was great friends with Justice William McIntyre; after a long day's work at the courthouse, they could often be seen walking together towards their apartments in the ByWard Market, trussed up against the cold. On Friday afternoons after an arduous week, Tony and Bill—often joined by Bertha Wilson—would repair to the judges' dining room and open a bottle of Scotch to mull over the triumphs and tribulations of the seven days past.

Tony welcomed me warmly when I arrived on the court. He and his wife, Danièle Tremblay-Lamer (later a judge of the federal court), set about organizing a series of dinners in their home with the goal of connecting me with prominent Ottawa bachelors. Their attempts at matchmaking failed utterly, but we enjoyed several good dinners, ushered in by the port-infused consommé Tony had spent the afternoon brewing in the kitchen.

Tony's romantic streak resurfaced a few years later, when I telephoned him (now my chief justice) from England to advise him that the press was about to break the story of my airplane engagement to Frank McArdle. I thought he would be cross at the prospect of tabloid coverage of one of his judges, but he surprised me. "It's a great story," he said. "Congratulations."

Perhaps high office changes a person. Certainly becoming chief justice changed Antonio Lamer. At first, I didn't notice it—he was still the Tony I loved to share stories and jokes with. And then, about two years after his appointment, workers installed his portrait in the corridor of the second floor—the sixteenth in a long line of chief justices of the Supreme Court of Canada. The artist was the renowned painter Bruno Bobak. Tony glared out of the canvas—handsome, defiant, and stern. The forbidding manner put me off.

"It's a great painting," I said. "But it isn't you."

"It is me," he rebuked.

I looked at the painting again. It *was* him. The artist had caught what I, who saw him every day, had missed. On becoming chief justice, Tony had assumed the mantle of office and with it the stern, commanding demeanour the portrait caught.

In the mid-1990s, tensions between justices that had lain dormant in the 1980s began to surface. It became apparent that there was no love lost between Chief Justice Lamer and Justice Gérard La Forest. The street fighter and the erudite scholar were very different men, and the chief justice, a quick and sometimes impatient judge, did not relish those who took a long time to pen their reasons.

But the most notorious breach was between the chief justice and Justice L'Heureux-Dubé. Temperamentally, they were the same—brilliant, mercurial, quick to take a position and to speak their mind. Philosophically, however, they were miles apart—particularly when it came to criminal law. Antonio, while even-handed as a judge, was a defence lawyer who viewed the world through the lens of the accused's rights. Claire, by contrast, saw it through a social victim-oriented prism. While Tony defended the rights of the accused, Claire penned dissent after dissent in favour of the prosecution, castigating him for failing to appreciate the horror of crime or the plight of victims.

Neither Tony nor Claire took pains to hide their antipathy, and it became the subject of speculation in the legal community. Some criticized Chief Justice Lamer for failing to issue a public statement in defence of Justice L'Heureux-Dubé when she was attacked in an op-ed piece by Justice John McClung of the Alberta Court of Appeal for her concurring "feminist" reasons in *R. v. Ewanchuk*.[1] Judges seldom responded to public criticism in the press. Still, no doubt the wounds were deep. It is a tribute to both parties that the relationship never got in the way of good judging. At a deep level, each respected the other as a jurist and accepted that duty to the law transcended personal differences. At some profound level, they understood each other.

Despite the occasional tension, there was still friendliness to be found among the justices. One of my close friends was Justice John Sopinka. Like the chief justice, Justice Sopinka was born in 1933. Beyond that, their origins could not have been more different. Lamer was born to French Canadians who traced their lineage back generations. Sopinka was born in rural Saskatchewan to Ukrainian immigrants who later moved to Hamilton to work in the steel mills. But in important ways, the two men were alike. Both were very smart lawyers who understood how the world worked. John Sopinka was a polymath who succeeded at everything he tried—and he tried just about everything. He played professional football for the Toronto Argonauts and the Montreal Alouettes. He played violin with the Hamilton Philharmonic Orchestra. He not only became a leading Canadian litigator, but also taught law and authored, with Sidney Lederman, what is still regarded as the leading text on the law of evidence.[2]

John moved into the office next to the new chief justice, and for seven years, he was his closest confidant. Relaxed, charming, and friends with everyone, he helped resolve tensions and smooth out differences. He loved life and he loved living. In the winter, he and I would organize ski trips with our law clerks to nearby Camp Fortune, which ended with New York steaks and frites in the kitchen of his home. John, for all his athletic prowess, was not a graceful skier— he would dash down the slope on his short skis, zigging and zagging in unorthodox spurts of energy. But somehow, he always got down the hill first.

In the summer of 1997, John took ill with a blood disorder. A fighter to the last, he refused to give in to his illness and struggled to a court meeting in early November. Shocked at his emaciated appearance, we could barely speak, and the agenda quickly dissolved into mumbled, miserable farewells.

"It's not farewell," John said feistily.

A few days later, I saw the chief justice. Tears in his eyes, Tony said, "I've just been to see John. He's not going to make it."

Justice John Sopinka died on November 24, 1997. His body lay in honour beneath the Canadian flag in the rotunda of the Supreme Court Building. After a service in the Presbyterian Church across the way on Wellington Street, he was laid to rest.

THE COURT IS A family, and a death in a family takes its toll. The toll is all the higher when the death is of a beloved person pivotal to the family's functioning. We all felt Justice Sopinka's loss. But we rallied. We needed to. Once more, the court was faced with a difficult challenge of immense importance: the *Reference re Secession of Quebec*.[3]

By this time, the court had been enriched by excellent appointments: Frank Iacobucci, former dean of law, deputy attorney general of Canada, and chief justice of the federal court; John (Jack) Major, former justice of the Court of Appeal of Alberta; Michel Bastarache, former dean of law and justice of the Court of Appeal of New Brunswick; and Ian Binnie, one of Canada's leading litigators, renowned for his oratorical brilliance, who replaced Justice Sopinka. These men (and yes, they were all men, leaving only two women on the court) joined with the chief justice and Justices L'Heureux-Dubé, Gonthier, Cory, and me to form the new Supreme Court—the court that would hear the reference.

Tensions, I had learned, are inevitable when people work together and live together. And now, the quiet tensions that were sometimes felt on the court were mirroring themselves on the national level. The backdrop to the secession reference was the 1995 Quebec sovereignty referendum, which was defeated by a scant margin of 1.1 percent. The close vote sent shudders through the majority of Canadians, who found it inconceivable that their country might be torn apart. The federal government of the day, led by Prime Minister Jean Chrétien, argued that the question put to voters had been unclear, and that, in any event, a province could not unilaterally secede from the country. Quebec's sovereigntist government vowed that they would succeed the next time. The country was in the grip of a constitutional crisis of grave consequence.

The government decided to submit a reference to the Supreme Court, to answer the constitutional question on everyone's mind: Could Quebec unilaterally secede from Canada? The reference posed three specific questions: (1) Could Quebec unilaterally secede under Canadian law? (2) Could Quebec unilaterally secede under international law? And (3) if the answers to (1) and (2) were different, which should prevail, Canadian law or international law?

The court had never before faced a reference laden with political consequences for the country as a whole. Technically, it could have declined to answer. But practically speaking, declining was unthinkable. The questions were, in the end, ones that needed to be answered so that the politicians would know where they stood, though that did not make the task any easier. The answers the court gave might become political facts in themselves, steering the course of history one way or the other—something no court wants to do.

The secession reference posed problems every step of the way. Because Quebec refused to participate, leaving no one to argue the case for secession, the court decided to appoint its own counsel, called amicus curiae, to argue Quebec's case. The court's choice, André Joli-Coeur, agreed and acquitted himself with distinction. Owing to the national spotlight and the desire to appear neutral, the court—one known for frequent and pointed interjections—refrained from asking questions, except through Chief Justice Lamer. Once the hearing was completed, we retired to consider.

The secession reference called each justice to bring his or her very best to that table. We understood that the future direction of the country could be at stake, and that we must rally all our resources to the task of answering the questions Prime Minister Chrétien had put before us. We must reflect and debate. We must not be afraid to be bold, if that was what was required. Above all, we must strive to be wise.

As so often, the court faced a choice: it could answer the questions, give its reasons, and leave the rest for the politicians or for future court cases; or it could answer the questions and go on to advise what the law would require should there ever be a valid yes vote, and what law would apply in the event of such a vote.

We chose the latter. In our judgment, we held that unilateral secession was not allowed by either Canadian or international law. But the court went further. It said the principles that underlie the Canadian federation—the principles of federalism, democracy, constitutionalism and the rule of law, and the protection of minorities—dictated how governments must respond in the event of a clear majority on a clear question for separation. A clear majority on a clear question (the court did not define these terms, deeming that better left to politicians) would require the federal government to sit down and nego-tiate with the Quebec government to determine the terms on which separation could occur. Unilateral secession was illegal, but *negotiated* secession that respected the fundamental principles of the federation might be possible.

The decision did not give the federal government the answer it argued for: an absolute, unconditional no to the possibility of ever seceding in any circumstances. Nor did it give the separatist govern-ment of Quebec what it had hoped for: the unencumbered right to se-cede unilaterally. In the end, both sides claimed victory. Quebec said the decision showed it had the right to secede, provided the requisite conditions were met. The government of Canada agreed with the conditions stipulated by the court and enacted them in the *Clarity Act*. The crisis was defused.

Of less importance to the governments of Canada and Quebec, our decision in the secession reference made an important contribu-tion to international law. The court had demonstrated that despite the internal tensions and difficulties it faced in the 1990s, it could come together and resolve a difficult issue in a wise and rational way. It was not the court of the federal government or the court of Quebec. It was an impartial constitutional arbiter. At a critical point in Cana-dian history, we had done our job and done it well.

CHAPTER TWENTY-EIGHT

Passages

THE 1990S WERE A difficult time for the court, but it surmounted its difficulties and emerged into the new century stronger than before. The same was true for me personally.

I had to learn, all over again, how to be married. Frank and I had a deep love and shared many passions and pursuits. But we were both strong individuals with our own way of judging and doing things. What's more, Frank was a lawyer and had strong opinions on legal issues. He understood that and made a rule to deal with it.

"You should know," he told me before our wedding, "I will never discuss a case with you until after the decision is rendered." He was true to his word.

When Frank and I got married, we agreed that he would move from Toronto to Ottawa—neither of us wanted a commuter marriage. It was the right decision; we blossomed and grew in each other's constant company. Yet the growing was not always easy, and the blossoms were often delayed by late-spring frosts. I discovered that it was one thing to visit on weekends and quite a different thing to share every meal and every household chore. Saying "I do" was not the end of our story, but the beginning of a new phase of fusing two quite different people into a single harmonious unit.

As the months and years passed, we learned to give and take. We each learned to appreciate that the other might sometimes have a point. Above all, we learned to listen to each other, really listen. Sometimes it was hard work; often it was difficult. But over the years, we forged a partnership of mutual support based on respect and love. Quite simply, we are there for each other, and will be so long as we live.

The house I had purchased in 1989 lay in the north part of old Rockcliffe, overshadowed by the grander mansions of aristocrats and OOFs (the local acronym for Old Ottawa Families). The house was situated in a large garden—the good news. The garden was badly planned and completely overgrown—the not-so-good news. Many years ago, the lot had been severed from the Veit mansion directly to the east, and a house—my house—was built on the back garden of the old Veit house. The trees, lawns, and flower beds were misplaced in relation to my house. Perhaps despairing of making anything of this mess, successive owners had abandoned the garden to nature.

I was no gardener—Rory had looked after our small garden in Vancouver, supplying me roses on request and keeping the patio beds freshly planted. To make matters worse, what few gardening skills I had picked up on the Pacific coast were ill-suited to Ottawa's short summers.

I couldn't afford a professional garden remake, so I started doing what I could on my own—cutting out overgrown shrubs and trees, pulling out ill-placed bushes, hiring someone to do a new patio or walkway to complement the house. I took to reading gardening books, but most of the exotic plants I purchased withered and died in my shady backyard. I fell back on dividing and replanting the perennials that were already there—hostas, ferns, and astilbes. In the spring, trilliums sprang up by the back fence to announce that the long winter had finally ended.

One June afternoon, while on my knees near the fence transplanting lily of the valley—my idea of an inexpensive ground cover—I looked up to see the housekeeper from the adjoining Argentinian embassy residence peering over the fence at me.

"¡Hola!" she said, and introduced herself. I put down my trowel and we chatted about the weather.

As she prepared to take her leave, she looked at my grubby shorts and asked, with a nod to my house, "What are those people like to work for?"

I considered, then quipped, "Madam is quite nice, but Monsieur can be difficult."

I shared the moment with Frank that night; he had the grace to laugh, and the greater grace to repeat the story whenever he got the chance.

When I wasn't at the court or grubbing in my Rockcliffe garden, I spent as much time as I could at "the cottage," a simple house Frank and I had built shortly after our marriage on the piece of land I had purchased in 1991. It was only an hour north of Ottawa, so we repaired there almost every weekend to recharge our batteries for the week ahead. In winter, we cross-country skied, walked such trails as were plowed, and sat by the fire reading in the evenings. In summer, we canoed, swam, foraged for mushrooms, fished, and ended every day by barbecuing in the big screened-in porch.

Our romance with the cottage continues. Each time we are stalled by a tree across the road as we drive to the lake, I remember the winding trail to the ranch where any bend might reveal a fallen log or an impassable mudhole. Each time the electricity fails—and it fails often—I relive childhood evenings around the kitchen table in the light of the kerosene lamp. Each time I walk in the woods or forage for berries, I recall the same pleasures on the ranch. The landscape is worn—the ancient Gatineau Hills weathered and low compared to the Rockies—but age, I have come to understand, possesses a beauty of its own.

Imperceptibly, without my even noticing it, Angus had become a man.

Looking back, I can pick out the stages of his transformation—the uncertain yet rebellious tilt of chin of early adolescence; the incipient swagger of late teens. Whatever the stage, he was strong, determined, and seemed to know precisely what he wanted, even when he didn't. He filled my basement with friends who dreamed of being rock stars, and he filled my life with his passions.

Enter my new husband, Frank—also strong and determined, also knowing what he wanted. Frank loved Angus, and sought, quite naturally, to become his new father. Angus didn't object but exhibited a polite determination to make Frank earn his parental spurs.

The first weekend Frank had come to visit in the fall of 1990, Angus invited him on a bike ride. "Sure," Frank said. Three hours later, they returned from what had turned out to be a harrowing trail ride. Angus hopped off his bike as fresh as when he had started out and gave Frank—sweat-drenched with exhaustion—a smug smile. Frank slumped to a chair and smiled back. "I kept up," he said.

Frank returned the next weekend, and Angus invited him to join him high up in the maple tree that dominated our back garden and from which dangled the rope swing Angus had installed his first day at the house. I had noticed Angus hauling pieces of wood up the tree all week long but hadn't thought much of it. "Just building a platform to sit on," he told me when I asked.

When Frank arrived, he found Angus at the top of the tree. "Come see the platform I built," he called edgily—*bet you can't make it.*

Angus was fifteen at the time and in formidable shape; Frank was sixty-three and in not-bad shape.

"Sure," he said, and I prepared myself to call 911.

I watched Frank climb, measuring the strength of each new branch before swinging his weight onto it. Finally, he arrived at the treetop perch Angus had constructed. Then, somewhere in the leafy canopy, I saw his shape slip down beside my son's. Frank's voice drifted down to me.

"Nice view. I can see why you like it."

"Yeah."

"What are you planning to do up here?"

"Read."

"You know what happens when you read? You get wrapped up in the book, forget where you are. You could drop the book, maybe fall out after it."

Angus considered. "Yeah."

They climbed down the tree and made a trip to Canadian Tire to buy a rope for Angus to tie himself in when he read in the tree.

A decade later, Angus and Frank stood in the backyard looking up at the tree again.

"Remember when we climbed the tree to my perch?" Angus asked.

"Never forget it," said Frank. "Let's climb up and bring your platform down."

Angus looked at up at the tree, then looked back at Frank with a laugh. "You think I'm a damn fool?"

Frank believed in strict discipline; Angus not so much. They struggled, they fought, and in the end, they worked out a truce.

Frank smoked little cigars, called cigarillos. Angus, who remembered his father's cigars and his painful end, did not approve. He talked to Frank about it, and Frank quit. Frank didn't like Angus trying out the new swear words he was learning. He spoke to Angus about it, and Angus curbed his cursing. Or so we thought.

Out for a drive in the country on a Sunday afternoon, we stopped at a park in Arnprior, west of Ottawa, for a mini picnic. The idyllic moment was suddenly shattered by my son's shrieks and—yes—curses, as a horde of wasps descended on him. Frank said nothing, but that evening before dinner, he announced that he was going down to the store to get something. After dinner, sitting on the screened porch with a coffee, Frank produced a cigarillo and lit up. Angus scowled at him. Frank said, "When you stop swearing, I'll stop smoking."

"It's a deal," said Angus. Both stuck to the bargain.

EIGHTEEN AND EAGER TO be on his own, Angus enrolled in arts at the University of British Columbia. Before he did, he asked me to give him some of his favourite recipes. Food has always been central to my life. My mother and father were both excellent cooks who insisted that food must taste good. It might be humble, it might be simple, but it must be tasty. Our everydays, our holidays—all revolved around food.

My love affair with cuisine began when I was in my teens. I found myself fascinated by the composite of chemistry, physics, and aesthetics that is cooking. I began to develop standards—contempt for bad or poorly prepared food, appreciation of careful and creative dishes. Rory liked food, too. We kept a good table.

When Angus was five, we fell into a pattern of going to a different type of restaurant every Friday night. Vancouver offered every cuisine known to man, or almost—Greek, French, German, Cantonese, Japanese, Korean, Indian, the list went on. Angus attributes his eclectic tastes to these early dinners. But his most beloved meals were the meals we had at home.

In the months before Angus left for university, I would pull out my laptop each Saturday morning and type some recipes for him. What began as a collection of a few favourites morphed into a full-blown book of our family recipes, called *Keepers*. The story of my life through food—from the ranch fare of my youth through the French classics I picked up at university to modern fusion. Frank became my vanity publisher. Fifty copies at a time. Over the years, I have bequeathed copies of *Keepers* to family, friends, and law clerks. They claim to use it, to like the down-to-earth recipes and the chapter-opener essays detailing my love affair with salads, soups, or whatever the subject may be. They also like that the left page beside each recipe is blank, open for comments and improvisations. There is no such thing as a final perfect recipe. Cooking—real cooking—is an individual act of creativity. *Keepers* is now in its third edition.

In September, we sent Angus off to the other side of the continent. I waved him off, full of pride but also apprehension. It was the first time in either of our lives that we had been apart for more than a few weeks. Even after my swearing-in, when he stayed with Judi to finish school, I had flown back every second weekend. Now I wouldn't see him for four months.

I had read all the articles about letting go. I remembered my mother's apprehension when I, also just eighteen, left for university. All would be well. And as things turned out, it was.

Angus went on to earn a BA and master's degree in music, specializing in composition. He liked Ottawa—its winter snow, lakes, and ice fishing—but he loved Vancouver, with the mountains, the ocean, the hiking trips into the West Coast wilds, and the fishing forays on his battered but sturdy boat. Money didn't matter to him, so long as he could be close to the sea. He was his father's son, unable to survive without the outdoors. He was also his mother's son, driven by a passion for music that far eclipsed my own amateur obsession. Torn between the two cities of his youth, Vancouver and Ottawa, he would make the West his home. The court would keep me in Ottawa for a few years, but that didn't stop part of my heart going with Angus to the place we had forged our family bonds.

And that, I decided, was just fine.

PART FOUR

THE CHIEF JUSTICE

Everyone has the right to life, liberty and security of the person and the right not to be deprived thereof except in accordance with the principles of fundamental justice.

—*Canadian Charter of Rights and Freedoms*, Section 7

....

CHAPTER TWENTY-NINE

A New Chief Justice

I RECEIVED MY FIFTH AND final official prime ministerial telephone call on a cold day in late October 1999.

Antonio Lamer, suffering from a tremor and failing health, had announced in August that he would be resigning as chief justice in January 2000.[1] I was the senior anglophone justice on the court, so tradition suggested I was in line to replace him. But there was no certainty about this; the prime minister might well think someone else was better for the job. I decided I would serve if asked—because that was my duty—but I would happily continue as a simple justice if not. I had never lobbied for any judicial position and was not about to start now.

This time, when the call came, I did not drop the phone. I greeted Prime Minister Chrétien calmly and listened as he asked me to serve as the country's chief justice.

"I am deeply honoured by the confidence you are placing in me," I told him. "I promise to give the job my utmost."

"*Bon*," said Jean. "I expect you to!"

I put down the phone and sat quietly for a moment, pondering what this would mean. I knew the challenge that lay ahead. I had watched two chief justices struggle with the demands of the job, and I'd seen it sap their health. The work of a justice, I knew from experience, was daunting. For nearly eleven years, I had been putting in long days of reading, preparation, hearings, and discussion with law clerks and colleagues. Now I would be adding a heavy dose of administration and a number of new responsibilities: along with the office of chief justice of Canada come the roles of chair of the Canadian Judicial Council, the National Judicial Institute, and the Advisory Council to the Governor General regarding appointments to the Order of Canada. And in addition to these formal responsibilities, the chief justice of the Supreme Court serves as the highest legal figure in the Canadian judicial system—in a broad sense responsible for justice throughout the country—and as Canada's international emissary for judicial affairs. How would I—a woman to boot—cope with what lay ahead?

My eyes cast around my office, the book-lined walls, the curio-stacked shelves, the pictures of Frank and Angus on the corner of my desk. Comfortable, my cocoon, my judicial home. Part of me didn't want to leave this room and move to the corner office, grand and imposing as it was. My small body would sink into the chief's big chair and disappear behind the huge Cormier desk that stared out like a giant ocean liner at all who dared enter. I would never fill the office, nor, I feared, the role. But I had said yes, and there was only one direction to go: forward. I picked up the phone and called Frank to tell him our lives were about to change.

I sent a memo to the justices of the court. As befits a family, we share such news with each other before the world hears it. My colleagues offered congratulations and hugs. Every one of them, even those who may have been disappointed that they or someone else had not received the prime minister's call, promised to support me to the full and do whatever was in their power to assist me in my new role.

The media responded to Prime Minister Chrétien's press release announcing my appointment with a flurry of demands for interviews. I looked at my calendar. I had to be in court for the next few days—no vacant spot where I could insert interviews with the press. "Tell them I'll meet whoever wants to come in the court dining room on Friday afternoon after the hearing ends," I instructed James O'Reilly, the departing chief's executive legal officer. "We'll have a press conference."

And we did. If some members of the press corps grumbled at the delay, others were pleased at the prospect of a press conference, taking it as a signal that the new chief justice would be open and accessible to the media.

The issue of judges talking to the press was still a prickly one within the legal community in 1999. Tradition dictated that judges were to speak only through their judgments, many felt. Yet the world was changing. The public was demanding transparency and accountability, even of cloistered judges.

Chief Justice Brian Dickson had understood the new demands for openness that would come with a powerful judiciary under the Charter. Even in the 1980s, he was encouraging justices to participate in feature articles on how they went about their work. Chief Justice Allan McEachern had taken the same view when I was sworn in as a member of the BC Supreme Court in 1981. "Accept it," he advised when I asked what to do about an interview request I had received. "The people of Canada are entitled to know who their judges are."

"The people of Canada are entitled to know who their judges are"—a simple statement, and one that seemed right to me. In a democracy, all power must be accountable. Canadian judges are not accountable at the ballot box, but they are nevertheless accountable through how they conduct themselves in open courtrooms, through their reasons for judgment, through conduct review by the Canadian Judicial Council, and through occasional press conferences and interviews that give the public a sense of who they are and how they go about their work.

Shortly after the news of my appointment broke, a friend and former chief justice of the California Supreme Court, Cliff Wallace, telephoned to congratulate me. After a minute or two of pleasant chatter, he got down to serious advice.

"Don't get too excited," he said. "They hand you the reins of power. It takes about three days to discover they aren't connected to anything."

It was true. A chief justice may have a fancy title and lots of responsibilities, but she has no way to make things happen, no way to institute change. She has no perks to offer, no power to demote or discipline. She is *primus inter pares*—first among equals—and even the "first" is debatable.

At my press conference, I promised nothing except to do my best. What more could I offer? But I did venture a few thoughts on my judicial philosophy and the role I saw for the court. I said I believed in achieving as much consensus as possible.

Dissenting judgments are a necessary and respected part of our judicial system, and often they point the way to future legal developments. But insofar as the members of the court can honestly agree on a particular point, I believe they should. The task of the court is to give guidance to the public and the legal profession on issues of law. That guidance is clearer when the court speaks with one voice; a variety of judgments offering slightly different perspectives on a particular point may undermine certainty.

On January 7, 2000, I was sworn in as Canada's seventeenth chief justice. It was a simple ceremony, held at Rideau Hall. Angus, Frank, and my colleagues on the court were present. The governor general, Adrienne Clarkson, presided, and Prime Minister Jean Chrétien attended. I wore a pale beige suit. After taking the oath in French and English, I went to the small table to sign the parchment. Overcome with emotion, I pressed too hard and broke the pen. The prime minister came to the rescue with a new one.

"We have to get this job done," he quipped in his inimitable French cadence.

We all laughed, and that was how the cameras recorded the moment.

As I accepted the congratulations of the prime minister, I thought of my parents. How amazed would they have been to see their "little Bevy" sworn in as the head of the Canadian judiciary? And I thought of Rory. Even his enthusiastic predictions hadn't taken me this far. I pinched myself and tried to convince myself this was really happening.

The fanfare of my installation over, I returned to my new office on the northeast corner of the august Supreme Court Building. I looked around the room and assessed how I would make it my own. It had a high ceiling and wood panels and possessed a magnificent view of the Houses of Parliament and the Peace Tower to the east. Most remarkable of all, it was octagonal—not a right angle to be seen.

"Excellent *feng shui*," a friend steeped in the Chinese art of arranging spaces told me. "No corners for the evil spirits to hide in."

"Good," I replied. "Let's keep the fresh air moving."

I rearranged the furniture, moving the huge desk that had intimidated me on visits to Brian Dickson and Tony Lamer from its commanding position opposite the entrance and replacing it with a comfortable couch and chairs; my new room would be about not commanding but conferring. My work would be done in the alcove to the side, where I was free in contemplative moments to swivel from my computer to the view of Parliament Hill.

As I was fluffing a final cushion, a court staffer came in carrying a huge painting. It was from the "cage"—the basement room where odds and sods of furniture were kept.

"Do you want this?" she asked.

My heart leapt. "Oh yes," I replied. "We'll hang it above the fire-place."

It was a prairie painting by an artist I knew—RFM McInnis. A small grey road ran through waving grass towards a distant bank of white grain elevators, set against glowing grey-green hills and a lowering chinook sky. I had first encountered the painting years before in Tony Lamer's office, and it had rocked me back on my heels.

"That's where I grew up," I had told him then. "That's the road that leads north from town to the station."

Tony had shaken his head like I was crazy. "You can't have it," he had growled.

Now, years later, on the day I became chief justice, the painting was coming back—and this time to me. A day after it was hung, a woman came by with a hammer, some tacks, and a plaque. "I'm here to label the painting," she announced. When she had finished, I went over to inspect the brass plaque. "*Pincher Creek*," it said.

I sat down in my big chair and stared at the painting, wondering at the improbability of its appearance in this place at this time, complete with provenance. The town that had brought me up had come home to me. Sometimes circles close. Sometimes your past rises up to meet your present in the swoop of a perfect moment. Sometimes these things happen, if you get lucky.

My moment of serendipity was quickly overtaken by reality. Apart from a new painting, a new office, and a ride to the court every morning—I initially wanted to keep driving myself to work, but the registrar, Anne Roland, had convinced me that as chief justice, I needed RCMP security—nothing seemed to have changed. My colleagues were having trouble changing "Bev" for "Chief." No one bowed or scraped. Frank, Angus, and Kyrie, our beloved black Lab, treated me exactly as they always had.

If there was any lingering hope that my new title would get me far outside the hallowed precincts of the court, it was dashed on a visit to Vancouver a few weeks after I was sworn in.

"I want to take you out to dinner at a great restaurant tonight," I told my sister, Judi. "You, Brian, and Ella." Ella, their daughter, was six.

Judi went online and looked up Vancouver's top-four restaurants. She dialled the first and asked for a reservation, no luck. The same went for the second and the third. With only one restaurant left to go, I asked Judi for the phone.

"I don't ever do this," I said to the person on the other end, and then proceeded to say that Chief Justice McLachlin needed a reservation for four that evening.

"Certainly," came the answer. We set the time. And then came the line that crushed me: "Would you like your usual table in the corner, Sarah?"

I realized that the receptionist had mistaken me for Sarah McLachlan, Vancouver singer and songwriter, famed for her emotional ballads and mezzo-soprano vocal range.

"I'm afraid I'm not that McLachlin," I said. "And you can cancel the reservation if you like."

"Not at all," said the receptionist. We arrived at seven, Ella in her best dress of ruby velvet, and were treated to an exceptional evening, notwithstanding that I was the wrong McLachlin.

THE COURT I INHERITED as chief justice was strong. In September 1999, just a few months before I took over, Louise Arbour—who had made an international reputation as a war crimes prosecutor in the Hague and possessed a stellar background in criminal law—had joined, replacing Peter Cory.

In December 1999, Justice Louis LeBel, an enormously respected jurist of scholarly bent, was nominated to replace Antonio Lamer as a member of the court. And a lovely Christmas present it was. I promptly telephoned Louis to congratulate him and tell him that I hoped he would be able to participate in the January sittings. He advised me he would and offered to come to Ottawa to prepare. No need, I said—we would send him the necessary books and materials. "Have a nice Christmas holiday," I added.

A few days later, he received several large boxes filled with hearing books. "Some holiday," he joked. Such was his introduction to the court and to his future chief justice. I was content: the addition of Justice LeBel to the existing complement of justices—L'Heureux-Dubé, Gonthier, Iacobucci, Major, Bastarache, Binnie, and Arbour—rounded out a formidable team. In the years to come, retirements would usher in a host of new and talented jurists—Justices Marie Deschamps, Morris Fish, Rosalie Abella, Louise Charron, Marshall Rothstein, Thomas Cromwell, Michael Moldaver, Andromache Karakatsanis, Richard Wagner, Clément Gascon, Suzanne Côté, Russell Brown, Malcolm Rowe, and Sheilah Martin.

As chief justice, I respected the views of each colleague on a case or point of law. I never tried to dissuade a justice from dissenting or twist a stubborn arm to impose a unified view—that, I believed, would be wrong. But I did try to keep the conversation open, respectful, and going as long as might be useful.

Years earlier, when I was starting out on the court, Bertha Wilson had told me, "The country is not entitled to nine judges giving their own views; the country is entitled to nine judges giving their views after listening to the views of their eight other colleagues." As in so many areas of life, the key to achieving maximum consensus was listening.

Considering the views of others is hard work. It's easy to go away after a hearing and write your reasons. Job done, move on to the next case. To listen to the different views with an open mind and an eye to achieving the maximum consensus possible is more difficult. Yet time after time, this is what the court did. The previous decade had seen many cases decided by narrow margins, and dissenting and collateral opinions had become so common that the bar and lower court judges had begun to complain of insufficient guidance. The court listened, and as the new century began, we were ready to invest the hard work required to achieve maximum consensus.

Years earlier, upon learning that I would become a judge of the county court, I had taken the two-week interregnum between appointment and oath to read everything I could about how to be a good trial judge. There wasn't much, but what I found helped me, and it included advice like listening to both sides and not forming a firm opinion until all the evidence and arguments were in. Now I looked for advice on how to be a good chief justice. I didn't find much. No learned articles; no deontological treatises. I was beginning to despair when I remembered a piece of advice from Patricia Wald, who had served as a highly respected chief justice in the United States. "My goal," she had told me, "is to do whatever is in my power to help each judge of the court be the best judge he or she can be."

I thought about that. Perhaps the reins they had handed me were connected to something after all. I could provide support and advice to the judges of the court. I could see that they had the assistance they needed to free them of petty tasks that would otherwise sap their time and energy. I could be there to listen when they had a problem. I could, in my modest way, try to keep everyone happy and together.

IN THE DEEP WINTER, a few weeks into my new job, words were exchanged between two of the justices. It wasn't serious, but it left tension in the room. On my way back to the office, I remarked to one of them, "I think Justice X was a little hurt."

"Nonsense," Justice Y replied. "Way too sensitive."

So much, I thought, for my efforts at conciliation. And then, an hour later, Justice X came to my office, all smiles. "He came to see me. We talked. Everything's great."

Sometimes, even a small word can make a difference.

Good times wouldn't hurt, either, I thought. A short while into my tenure, I organized a cook-along in my home for the justices and their spouses. The court's chef, Oliver Bartsch, started the event off by taking everyone shopping for food. Then we retired to the house and started cooking. Magically, each person found his or her place— judges cooking, bringing their own style to the endeavour. The dining room was converted to a prep table, where Rosie Abella led a team of choppers and dicers. Ian Binnie stood at the stove braising lamb shanks, raising more heat and savoury smells than I dreamed the meat was capable of producing. At the breakfast table, Marshall Rothstein demonstrated a professional expertise with the filleting knife as he prepared the fish course. Marie Deschamps whipped up a Pavlova, which would have been wonderful if I hadn't mucked up the oven setting. Oh well, it still tasted good. Louis LeBel, dignified as ever, presided from the living room, offering his wise verdict on each successive course.

A sense of imminence hung over the evening. I was a new chief justice, and this was a new court about to embark on a new decade, complete with the difficult legal issues it would bring. The world was spinning faster and faster as the digital revolution changed the way people lived and thought. But the court was strong and ready, united in its determination to meet the challenges that lay ahead.

....

CHAPTER THIRTY

Truth and Reconciliation

As long as I can remember, Indigenous peoples have been part of my life. Nine miles to the east of Pincher Creek lies the Piikani reserve, clustered around a village called Brocket. When I was growing up, men from the Piikani community worked for us and traded cattle and horses. Sometimes they brought their families, setting up tents from which the scents of freshly baked bannock wafted in the evening. In Pincher Creek's stores, locals brushed metaphorical shoulders with "Natives"—another name no longer acceptable. And in my final year of high school, Indigenous children were at last bussed in from the reserve to go to school with everyone else.

Why the village where the Piikani lived was named Brocket is lost to history. The most probable answer is that it had something to do with the great family whose seat, called Brocket, lay just to the north of London, England. (It's now a tony golf club.) The irony of naming an Indigenous village for the ancestral home of one of Queen Victoria's most beloved prime ministers, Lord Melbourne, was doubtless lost on the person who conferred the moniker. Blind to the long Indigenous history of the soil they named, European newcomers put the stamp of colonialism on the village and the people consigned to live in it.

Some facts cannot be wished away. The process of settlement took from Indigenous peoples the use of the lands they had occupied. It took their livelihood. It tried to take their central rituals; early laws outlawed the Sun Dance of the Siksika and the potlatch of the First Nations living in the Pacific Northwest. And it took their freedom—confining them to reserves and denying them the power to act for themselves.

As a little girl in nearby Pincher Creek, I didn't dwell on what the Piikani had lost. The world was the way it was, and like everyone else, I accepted it. I did have those questions for my mother. Why don't the kids from the reserve who visit our ranch go to our school? Why does the town washroom door say "No Indians"? And as I grew older, I was pleased that things were changing. By the time I met Peter and George in high school, the de facto segregation that had existed for almost a century was beginning to break down.

Still, despite growing up next door to two reserves, I didn't know anything about the policies that governed the schooling of Indigenous children. When I was sixteen, I found myself sitting next to a girl from the Blood reserve on the way home from a school event in Lethbridge. She told me that she had been taken from her parents when she was six and placed in a residential school. "It was terrible," she whispered. "I'm glad I can go to school at home now." I listened to her stories with incredulity and sorrow. I wondered why I hadn't heard about these schools before. I thought about my own past; things had not always been easy, but I had never been taken away from my family, my language, and the things I loved. Yet unbeknownst to me, this had been happening to Indigenous children for almost a century.

I was learning, as I grew up, about dark episodes in the treatment of my Indigenous neighbours. Yet it never occurred to me to wonder about the laws and legal structures that governed the Piikani at Brocket or the Kainai on the nearby Blood reserve. I was vaguely aware that there was an *Indian Act* and an Indian agent on each reserve. I knew a few Indigenous people came to hunt near our ranch, claiming this was their Treaty right. At some point, my dad explained to me that the Indigenous people I met and talked with weren't allowed to vote. That changed only in 1960, my final year of high school, when I met Peter and George. Other than that, I didn't know much.

It was a decade later, when I was practising and teaching law in Vancouver, that I witnessed the first emanations of what we now call Indigenous law. And I found myself wondering, as I had wondered about women's equality: What took us so long? There is no way around it. The law, that great engine of social justice and peaceful change, had been lamentably slow to come to grips with the place of Indigenous peoples in Canada—their rights, their responsibilities, their claims to traditional livelihoods and lands.

But things were finally changing. In the 1970s, the Musqueam Indian Band in British Columbia sued the federal government for having entered into a ninety-nine-year lease of a large tract of their reserve lands with the Shaughnessy Heights Golf Club for a relatively modest sum. The band alleged breach of trust. It won at the Supreme Court of Canada, which held that the Crown owed a fiduciary duty to the band in respect of its land.[1] The case blazed through the Vancouver cocktail circuit. Fiduciary duty? Where did that come from? And more important, what next?

I listened to the debates, fascinated, and watched the emergence of new Indigenous-led lawsuits claiming the right to ancestral fishing and hunting, forgotten treaty rights, the right to land and use of the land, the right to compensation for the wrongs of residential schools. I thought of the Piikani and Kainai I had grown up beside and wondered what the new language of rights would mean for them and their children.

In the run-up to the adoption of the Charter, I followed the debate on how the new constitution should treat Indigenous rights. Many voices warned against giving them constitutional protection, and later, when that appeared inevitable, argued that the guarantee of Indigenous rights should be confined to treaties that already existed and rights the courts had already pronounced on. In the end, the drafters settled their differences by giving protection to "existing Aboriginal and treaty rights," in Section 35(1) of the *Constitution Act, 1982.*

As a judge, I watched these debates from the sidelines and wondered how it would all play out. The big question was how the Supreme Court of Canada would interpret the phrase "existing Aboriginal and treaty rights." The answer came in *R. v. Sparrow,*[2] heard just before I arrived on the Supreme Court. The court rejected the view that the phrase should be interpreted as limited by laws and regulations and frozen as of the day the *Constitution Act, 1982* was passed. Rather, it should be interpreted broadly, purposively, and flexibly to permit evolution of Indigenous rights. The die was cast; the future for Indigenous rights—and with it the possibility of just outcomes—lay open.

These new possibilities for Indigenous law began to unfold during my time on the Supreme Court. After watching from the sidelines, I found myself deeply immersed in the grand project of my legal generation—the peaceful evolution of Indigenous rights in a way that might foster reconciliation between Indigenous and non-Indigenous peoples.

It was captivating and difficult work. Following the direction of *Sparrow*—the idea that Indigenous rights should be interpreted in a generous and flexible way—the Supreme Court issued a series of land-mark decisions as we moved into the twenty-first century. In 1997, in *Delgamuukw v. British Columbia*,[3] the court held that oral evidence of historical facts passed down from previous generations was admissible to establish Indigenous claims, laid the foundations for proving land claims, and stressed that clashes of interests must be resolved in a spirit of reconciliation. Chief Justice Lamer concluded his reasons with these words: "Let us face it, we are all here to stay."[4] In 2004, in *Haida Nation v. British Columbia (Minister of Forests)*,[5] the court, under my pen, held that Section 35 of the *Constitution Act, 1982* imposed on the government a legal duty to consult in good faith with an Indigenous rights claimant about how the land is to be used pending resolution of the claim. In 2014, in *Tsilhqot'in Nation v. British Columbia*,[6] the court, again in reasons penned by me, held that to establish Indigenous title, it was enough to show that earlier generations had regularly used and asserted control over the land in question.

I was privileged to write reasons in a number of these cases, and often in quiet moments I was brought back to my roots near the Piikani reserve. The Canadian history I had been taught as a child was a history of white Europeans and their descendants. Apart from the Riel Rebellion, which briefly threatened white settlement of the prairies, the Indigenous peoples who had lived there for millennia were scarcely mentioned. Now I found myself confronted by a new part of my country's history. What I discovered was fascinating, mad-dening, and often very sad.

The history of relations between Indigenous and non-Indigenous peoples in Canada is long. It began with an era of nation-to-nation dealings,[7] when early explorers and Indigenous nations lived and fought together. But the *Royal Proclamation of 1763* ushered in a period of colonial domination in which the Crown stipulated that European immigrants could not take land directly from Indigenous peoples. Instead, the latter's lands could be sold only to the Crown, which would mediate settlement on what it deemed to be fair terms. With Confederation in 1867, a century and a half of paternalism began under the *Indian Act*, a policy that treated Indigenous peoples as wards of the state, subject to government control. "We will look after you," the government promised, but in actuality, it was saying, "We will control where you live (reserves), where your kids go to school (residential schools), and whether you get to drink alcohol, enjoy legal status, or vote." Only now are we beginning to emerge from the shadow of the third era into a new age of reconciliation.

The legacy of this history has been suffering and alienation. Indigenous and non-Indigenous peoples lived separate lives in separate worlds. The gulf that divides these groups is deep. Now, through the project of reconciliation, we are attempting to bridge it. We cannot back up the truck of history, to use a homey Alberta metaphor, but we can try to get it unstuck so it can move forward to our desired destination. Hopefully, decisions like *Delgamuukw*, *Haida Nation*, and *Tsilhqot'in* will start to address past wrongs and help achieve a just and prosperous future for Indigenous and non-Indigenous peoples alike.

On June 11, 2008, I sat in the House of Commons as Prime Minister Stephen Harper formally apologized to the Indigenous peoples of Canada for the suffering caused by the government's residential school policy—a policy that took children from their families and forced them to live in schools aimed at "kill[ing] the Indian in the child."[8] The prime minister's words were eloquent and heartfelt. But what brought tears to my eyes were the gracious speeches of the Indigenous peoples that followed—speeches recalling the pain of the past but looking forward to a better future. It was a privileged moment in the long journey towards reconciliation.

ON JULY 1, 2006, the town of Pincher Creek celebrated its centenary. It was an important event—the town is the second oldest in Alberta—and the townspeople had been working for years to ensure that the celebration would be a success. I was chief justice of Canada, and my hometown flattered me by making me the honorary patron.

On the western fringes of the town, the officials escorted Frank and me to a vintage buggy hitched to two smart horses in fancy tack. The driver flicked the reins and slowly we made our passage down Main Street towards the epicentre of the celebration, the town museum. The sun shone. Even the west wind yielded before the perfection of the day. A soft breeze replaced the usual sand-in-your-eyes gusts. I felt peace; I was home.

Poplars and spruce shadowed historic buildings restored to bright lustre—a one-room school, an old railway car, replicas of the town's first shops and hostelries. Flowers, pruned to perfection by the town's matrons, bloomed everywhere. Close to the creek, so near one could hear its burble, lay our destination—a sprawling log building of understated beauty, the repository of treasures from times past, of arts and crafts and random memorabilia, each with a story of how the people of this place had lived and died.

The prize exhibit on this special day was a series of oil paintings by A.Y. Jackson, the Group of Seven artist. He loved this place where the plain meets the mountain, and spent much time here, lodging with local families by night and painting by day. Moving on, he would leave each family a picture or two in lieu of rent. The locals had taken them down from their living room walls, dusted them off, and brought them here to the museum, in memory of the great artist who had, for a time, graced their homes and their land.

A small crowd greeted the arrival of our carriage. Ribbons were cut, and the mayor gave a speech and presented me with gifts, including a replica of my family's branding iron that I will keep as long as I live. Tea, coffee, and soft drinks were passed around. Men, women, and children wandered through the museum and the grounds, chatting, laughing, remembering.

At some point, the mayor steered us inside and moved us into an impromptu reception line. People came by to say hello—friends I had not seen for years, wizened ranchers who remembered my parents, shopkeepers whose faces I scarcely recognized. My grade one teacher, Mrs. Hinman, whose hostile gaze had sent my little heart into palpitations, came up to me and apologized, tears in her eyes.

"We had no idea how bright you and your siblings were," she said. "We didn't do much for you. We didn't know about gifted children and enrichment then."

"You did just fine." I smiled and watched the load she had so improbably carried for so many years slip from her frail shoulders. *Reunions are good,* I thought.

I looked up and saw a tall man standing before me. His dark hair hung down his back in a thick braid. "I'm Eric," he said. "You probably don't remember me. And this is my wife." I smiled at the beautiful woman at his side.

"Thank you for coming," I said. At the same time, I was casting my mind back. I often thought back to Peter and George, my friends in our final year of high school. But who was this man?

"I brought you a gift," Eric said.

I looked up in surprise. "A gift?"

He presented me with a small box. Inside was an exquisite pair of handcrafted mother-of-pearl earrings.

"They're beautiful," I said.

"I made them," Eric replied. "They're for you. And for your parents."

"My parents?" I asked. Did he not know they were long dead?

"Your parents," he said again. "They were wonderful people."

"I agree. They were wonderful."

And then Eric told me why he had come.

"It was many years ago, a Sunday afternoon in July," he said. "My dad loaded my mom and us kids in our old car. 'We're going to Ernie's,' he said. 'Have to talk to him about selling a horse.' So we drove west, past the town and through the hills to your parents' ranch. My dad stopped the car on the meadow below. He was too shy to go up to the house. Your dad came down, and my dad got out of the car and they talked."

As Eric spoke, a distant memory, long buried, came trickling back. A hot day, a battered car full of kids on the meadow. But I still didn't understand.

"Your mother came down to the car, too," Eric explained. "She said, 'Why don't you come up to the house and have tea with us? It's Ernie's birthday. You can help us celebrate.' So we took your mother up on her offer. We walked up to your house. Your parents invited us right in. We all sat around the dining room table, and your mother served tea and slices from a big layer cake." Eric smiled. "She had put a dime in the cake for luck. I got the dime. I still remember."

"I remember, too," I said. "My little sister was so disappointed not to get the dime that Mom had to give her one after." We laughed, sharing the memory.

"I will never forget that afternoon," Eric said. "It was the first time I had ever been inside a white person's house. That's why I brought this gift. It is a thank-you to your parents."

I gazed at Eric wordlessly, unable to express what I felt: pride in my parents, sadness for my society.

Eric took his wife's arm. "She's Cree," he told me with a shy smile. Then they both moved on.

Someone else came up to chat. And another, and another. Bow-legged cowboys doffing worn Stetsons. Weathered farmers with fingers battered thick from work. Hutterites—the men in black, the women in long dark skirts with kerchiefs on their heads. Mennonites of sober mien. People from the Piikani community, some in beads and buckskin. Children dressed up in their best clothes, and lovely ladies in flowing dresses and flowered hats.

Once they had lived separately, these people, stuck to their own kind, kept to themselves, not daring or not wanting to cross each other's thresholds. Today they came together to celebrate their common community in all its splendid diversity.

It has always seemed very simple to me, just as it seemed simple to my mother that hot July day when she invited Eric's family into our home to share tea and cake. As a child, I had felt the sting of anti-German suspicion that clung on after the war; I knew that it hurt, and I knew that it was wrong. Beneath our differences, we are all human beings, and entitled to be treated as such. This I learned from my parents.

RECONCILIATION IS MORE THAN a moment; it is a long and arduous process, fraught with uncertainty and risk. We have begun the process—one that I could not have imagined growing up as a girl in Pincher Creek. But we have a long way to go.

Reconciliation requires us to take painful steps. The first step is understanding—understanding our shared history and where we have gone wrong. The second step is resolving to address past wrongs and make amends. The third and final step is the hardest—taking action to move on in the spirit of mutual respect towards a future where everyone, Indigenous and non-Indigenous alike, can live their lives as they choose, in peace and justice.

Reconciliation is a complex process. Few divided societies have tried it; fewer yet have succeeded. There is no silver bullet to resolve the issues we face. The law, while important, is only part of a much larger process. And at the end of the day, there is a real risk that we will fail—that camps on either side will grow impatient with the time and effort and compromise required by reconciliation, and seek more immediate solutions.

Time will tell whether the project of reconciliation will succeed. I remain optimistic. But whatever comes, I am proud to have played a small part in an honourable process.

···

Branching Out

Each decade produces its own issues, and the first decade of
the new century was no exception. The bombing of the World Trade
Center in New York on September 11, 2001, profoundly shook the
Western world. I stood with thousands of others on Parliament Hill a
few days later, grieving the loss of so many. The threat of terrorism was
suddenly in everyone's mind. Like other countries, Canada passed laws
to deal with the threat—laws that inevitably were challenged in the
Supreme Court on the ground that they unconstitutionally restricted
liberties. In the end, most of the challenged laws were substantially upheld, although the court suggested important improvements to dimin-
ish the restriction of liberty.[1] It was detailed, time-consuming judicial
work.

On allowing deportation when the individual would be at risk of torture, the court said no.[2] On denying penitentiary prisoners the right to vote, the court said no.[3] On excluding same-sex families from schoolbooks, the court said no.[4] On denying francophone parents in Quebec the right to place their children in English public schools, the court said no.[5] These were among the difficult issues thrown up in the first five years of the decade.

The workload was complicated and unrelenting, and it took its toll. Parliament in 1998 had amended the *Judges Act* to allow justices of the Supreme Court to retire with full pensions once they had served on the court for ten years and turned sixty-five.[6] Parliament went further in 2006 by removing the age requirement.[7] These changes allowed members of the court to retire with full pension earlier than they otherwise could have. Justices L'Heureux-Dubé and Gonthier stayed until mandatory retirement at seventy-five forced them out. But other justices left earlier—Justice Iacobucci in 2004, at age sixty-seven; Justice Arbour in 2004, at age fifty-seven (she did not have ten years at the court but retired to become the United Nations High Commissioner for Human Rights); and Justice Bastarache in 2008, at age sixty-one. The old pattern of justices staying until they reached the age of mandatory retirement was breaking down. The reasons for leaving were varied, but the constant pressure and workload invariably played a role.

The court maintained its strength with the appointment of Justices Marie Deschamps, Morris Fish, Rosalie Abella, and Louise Charron in the early 2000s. They were followed by Justice Marshall Rothstein in 2006, Justice Thomas Cromwell in 2008, and Justices Michael Moldaver and Andromache Karakatsanis in 2011. All were excellent jurists. In later years, yet other fine judges would join our bench. Each came with his or her own gifts, passions, and style. Still, a court is more than the sum of the persons who make it up, and each time a justice leaves and is replaced, the court as an institution changes. And so, subtly, do the people who stay on. One misses the person who has gone; one rejoices in the replacement. One adjusts.

Justices of the Supreme Court of Canada are not generally appointed for their political views, and once appointed, they do not hew to the political agenda of the prime ministers who chose them. In the United States, it is accepted—indeed, expected—that presidents will nominate Supreme Court justices based, in large part, on their political leanings, and that the justices will vote on many questions along political lines. Not so in Canada. American justices may be tempted to hang on or retire in sync with the need to maintain their side's position on the Supreme Court. But not in Canada. And that, too, is no bad thing.

I had vowed, upon becoming chief justice, that I would do everything within my power to help each justice be the very best he or she could be. I realized, as the decade progressed, how important that was. Individual judges can and will differ in their views on particular issues, but for the court to thrive, each must buy into its central function of settling the law on difficult legal issues as wisely as possible. A chief justice cannot command that vision, or even create it. But what she can do is keep the goal of wise legal decision-making in the foreground, and give the justices what they need to do their job—technical assistance, law clerks, time for a break in the summer, encouragement when spirits sag under the constant pressure of work and deliberation. As I settled into the office of chief justice, I began to see a few specific things that could usefully be done.

The first was to make the court, its work, and its decisions more accessible—or, to use the fashionable terminology, more open and transparent. For centuries, Canadian judges, like the British counterparts they took as their models, had lived their lives in cloistered isolation. But that was then and this was the twenty-first century. People communicated. People had unlimited access to information through the internet. And people no longer were content to let elites do their jobs while they stood by unquestioning and undemanding. All power must be accountable. And Canadians are entitled to know who their judges are and how they go about their work.

I started my term as chief justice with a press conference, and I kept reporting to the press on an annual basis. Every summer, at the meeting of the Canadian Bar Association, I reported to the council on the work of the court and developments in the Canadian legal system. Afterwards, I retired to a press room, where I answered questions from the media. Over the years, I gave scores of interviews to the press and countless speeches to interested Canadians. The court also established a press committee, presided over by one of the justices, whose task was to meet with members of the media to help them understand and explain the court's work to the public. We instituted briefing sessions on cases as they came out and established lock-ups to help the press report accurately the moment a decision was released. We vastly improved our website and the links to information and decisions. We set up a Twitter account to report our decisions and court events in brief compass. And in the last year of my tenure, we created plain-language summaries of court decisions so all Canadians could understand their implications.

Through all this, we worked constantly to improve the clarity and readability of our judgments. A court's principle means of communication has always been and will always be its written reasons for judgment. From my first days on the bench, I have been an advocate of clarity and simplicity in judgment writing. First-year law students like to flatter justices at conferences and receptions; the only compliments that stuck with me related to my judgment writing.

"I usually like what you say, but I really like that I can understand it," a young woman with shining eyes would say.

"Thanks," I would reply. "You couldn't have said a nicer thing."

In my first year on the Supreme Court of British Columbia, an elderly judge took the trouble to offer me a few tips on how to succeed. One of them related to judgment writing. "Fudge it up," my mentor advised. "The Court of Appeal won't be able to overturn you because they won't be able to figure out what you said."

I was too polite to contradict him, but I have never followed his advice. It seemed to me that the litigants and the public were entitled to a judgment they could understand. My personal goal was to write in prose that a literate non-lawyer could understand, no matter how arcane the legal principles involved. Sometimes the complexity of the case simply defeated me, and I failed. But I always tried, and I passed my passion for clarity on to my law clerks.

To my surprise, I also found myself explaining Canada's justice system and its highest court to lawyers and judges around the world. The Supreme Court of Canada was no longer a post-colonial reflection of UK courts with a dollop of civil law thrown in. In the post-Charter world, it had matured into an important institution in its own right—a court whose work was increasingly studied and applied throughout the world.

In the 1990s, I attended international legal gatherings at which Commonwealth academics denigrated the Supreme Court of Canada as a bench of maverick judges on a frolic to displace the majesty of the common law or destroy parliamentary democracy. Any case that departed from British jurisprudence was ripe for attack, it was assumed.

A decade later, that perspective was rapidly changing. Judges in countries like South Africa and Israel injected the Supreme Court's Charter jurisprudence into their own constitutions and basic law. Commonwealth countries—including Great Britain—were adopting Canadian cases in tort and trust suits. Standoffish suspicion had been replaced by new conversations between judges in different countries—sometimes formally through reasons for judgment, and sometimes informally through judicial visits.

Canada's justice system is not perfect. But it is among the best in the world. The other justices on the Supreme Court and I thought it important to do what we could to foster the rule of law and the need for independent courts throughout Canada and the world. When asked to share our story, we liked to oblige. Often we said no—our heavy commitments to hearing cases and writing judgments kept us chained to our desks most of the year—but when we could, we accepted invitations from foreign courts to share the Canadian experience with building a better justice system.

Everywhere we went, we exchanged views on justice and planted ideas. We never preached. Each country must find its own way, and unjust laws and systems are not easily or quickly changed. Building fairer laws and better justice systems is slow, hard work. Ideas must alter; cultures must shift. It takes time. Occasionally, however, we witnessed a tangible result.

With two other justices of the court, I visited the Supreme People's Court of China in 2003. As a mark of honour, we were invited to an audience with the premier of China, Zhu Rongji. At the appointed time, we were ushered into a stateroom. The premier, seated at the far end of the room, rose to greet us. Aided by interpreters, we launched into a discussion of China's justice system.

"Where will you visit?" the premier asked.

"Beijing, Shanghai, Zengcheng, and Hong Kong," I replied.

The premier waved his hand expansively. "You will see the good part," he said. "You also should visit the western regions. We have one hundred and eighty thousand judges in China. Only ten percent are legally trained." He looked at the chief justice of China's Supreme Court. "We must have more legal training for our judges."

The next morning the chief justice met me with a beaming smile. "I have just sent a letter outlining the new training program for judges that will be moving forward," he told me. "All because of yesterday's meeting with the premier."

Everywhere we travelled in the world, we found people committed to better justice. Often they were in the minority, and sometimes they were afraid to speak. But they found a way to convey to us their dream of a justice system where independent judges decided cases in accordance with the law, and where rights and contracts were respected. In idle moments of reverie, I see their faces and press the memory of their dreams to my heart.

OVER THE YEARS, I became friends with US Supreme Court Justice Sandra Day O'Connor. In her younger days, Sandra had battled to get a law degree and then to get a place in a law firm—although she led her class, all that was on offer for her, a woman, was a secretarial position. Eventually, she became a lawyer and was elected to the Arizona Senate. In the years that followed, she had gracefully surmounted many hurdles as the country's first woman on the Supreme Court.

I first met Justice O'Connor in 1989 in Cambridge, England, where she was giving a law lecture. At the time, she was under great pressure about how she would vote on a pending case concerning the right to abortion. A Republican appointee but also the only woman on the court—Ruth Bader Ginsburg was not appointed until 1993— Sandra was regarded as the swing vote. So rife was the speculation that *Time* magazine had put her on its cover. Yet if the pressure was wearing, she didn't show it. In the end, she would cast a vote to maintain the status quo of *Roe v. Wade*.

I had just been appointed to the Supreme Court of Canada when I met Sandra, and I learned much from her. Her grace under pressure, her serenity and good humour, her gravity and commitment to doing the right thing—all these I was determined to emulate.

At a later meeting in London, Ontario, we were both on the podium. "I'm part Canadian," she told me with a smile. "I have two Canadian daughters-in-law."

"That's good enough for us," I replied.

The person who introduced us referred to the fact that both Justice O'Connor and I had grown up on ranches. In my introductory remarks, I was compelled to inform the audience that her ranch—

which straddled Arizona and New Mexico—was vastly larger than mine.

The United States Supreme Court and the Supreme Court of Canada are both the apex courts of their respective countries. Both have nine justices appointed by political processes. They both hear constitutional cases and decide issues of national importance. But the differences in how they function are profound. Not only is the Supreme Court of the United States more "political," but many of its justices—the late Antonin Scalia, for example—are openly hostile to comparative law and adamant that decisions of the courts of foreign countries are unhelpful and could even pollute American jurisprudence. It is an isolationist stance that's replicated in the policies of many American institutions.

Sandra was an exception. Although she was not chief justice, she took it upon herself to meet delegations of jurists from foreign countries. She had known the chief justice, William Rehnquist, since law school days—indeed, they had dated, and Rehnquist had even (unsuccessfully) proposed marriage—and seemed to act as his official court receiver. She was curious and open to how the law worked in countries other than her own.

In 2003, I telephoned Sandra and proposed that we institute an exchange visit between our two courts, on a three-year basis. She thought it was a splendid idea.

"I'll talk to Bill," she said.

She did, and our first Canada–US Supreme Court legal exchange was arranged for September 2004.

We met the delegation—Chief Justice Rehnquist, tall and reserved; Justice O'Connor, her white coif gleaming, her bright jacket open, and her husband at her side; and Justice Anthony Kennedy, scholarly and avuncular—at the Ottawa airport.

"Welcome to Canada," I said, giving Sandra a special hug.

We spent three days talking law. Not substantive law—American law was American law and direct comparisons were best avoided—

but procedural law. How we went about choosing the cases we heard, how we organized the writing and publication of judgments, how we handled the role of interveners (or *amici*, as our American friends called them). The point wasn't to argue about our differences with a view to resolution but rather to learn from each other's approaches.

Our American colleagues appeared to enjoy their time with their Canadian counterparts. Joined by my friends Governor General Adrienne Clarkson and her husband, John Ralston Saul, we celebrated Chief Justice Rehnquist's eightieth birthday at a small restaurant called Domus in the ByWard Market. The chief justice, who was known to be crusty on occasion, relaxed and took a second glass of wine.

"Not feeling so well," he admitted as he downed it. "Something in my throat."

"He's seeing his doctor as soon as we get back," said Sandra, exercising her customary fraternal control.

It was to be the chief justice's last birthday party. The visit to the doctor produced bad news—throat cancer. A year later, he passed away and the United States had a new chief justice, John Roberts.

Three years later, the US Supreme Court, led by Chief Justice Roberts, hosted a delegation of the Supreme Court of Canada in Washington, and three years after that, the event was repeated in Canada. In the course of our exchanges, I got to know almost all the justices of the United States Supreme Court and had the privilege of exchanging ideas with Roberts, a fine jurist and a chief justice devoted to maintaining the court's reputation for impartiality and excellence. I recall with particular fondness time spent with the exceptional women on the court—Sandra Day O'Connor, Ruth Bader Ginsburg, Sonia Sotomayor, and Elena Kagan. In our meetings, we were first and foremost judges, faced with the same challenges and striving for the same goal—the right legal decisions for our respective nations.

In the years that followed, the Supreme Court of Canada exchanged visits and views with the top courts of a host of countries, including Israel, India, the United Kingdom, Ireland, New Zealand, Australia, Germany, China, Korea, and France. I realized that in this global world, courts everywhere face the same questions—questions that often transcend national boundaries. There is no downside, and sometimes much to be gained, by talking to each other.

I last saw Sandra Day O'Connor in Arizona. Frank and I had travelled down to attend a dinner in her honour. She was enjoying lunch on the terrace of the hotel with her son and his family when we arrived. She spied us and waved us over. The same white hair, the same embrace. *I love this woman*, I thought.

"Come on, sit down. Join us," she insisted. She was frailer than when we had last seen her, and her husband, John, was no longer at her side. Still, she carried herself with stoic good humour. That night, although she arrived at the dinner in a wheelchair, she roused herself to give an excellent speech.

As we said goodbye, I thought of the battles women like Sandra Day O'Connor, Ruth Bader Ginsburg, Sonia Sotomayor, and Elena Kagan had fought in their lives. And I reflected on how much I, a Canadian judge, had learned from judges from other countries—both women and men. Every once in a while, it's good to look beyond your own backyard.

···

CHAPTER THIRTY-TWO

Of Princesses and Power

JUDGES LIVE SOLITARY LIVES, passing their days in courtrooms and chambers, known largely for the decisions they make and the reasons they write. Yet they are human beings and hold a certain position in society. Invitations to mingle in the broader world, low and sometimes high, cross their desks. As a trial and appellate judge, I received few such invitations. As a Supreme Court judge, I received many more. As chief justice, I found myself inundated with official and semi-official invitations.

The Supreme Court of Canada is not just a court; it is an institution. Canada's model of constitutional democracy rests on three branches of governance—legislative, executive, and judicial. The governor general, the prime minister, and the chief justice rank one, two, and three on the official protocol list. Attendance at official and some not-so-official events is mandatory—July 1, Canada Day on the Hill; November 11, Remembrance Day at the Cenotaph; Order of Canada induction ceremonies; state dinners for visiting kings, queens, and presidents; and prime ministers' dinners for their foreign counterparts. Beneath its sleepy veneer, Ottawa is a happening place where elegant people gather to chat and dine beneath the glittering chandeliers of Rideau Hall and the Château Laurier. Once or twice a week throughout my tenure as chief justice, Frank and I would suit up in black tie and long dress and hie ourselves to join them.

I am not a groupie or a name-dropper; I have never fawned over the rich and famous. Yet I found my encounters with people in high places frequently interesting and occasionally inspirational. Often the meetings amount to little more than a curtsy and a few words of greeting, but occasionally you are able to penetrate the official façade and discover the real person behind the face and fancy dress and listen to the stories they tell.

I never personally met Tony Blair, prime minister of the UK, but I did get to know his wife, Cherie Booth. Cherie was a respected human rights lawyer at the London bar. She did not let her role as mother of five children and wife of the prime minister detract from her professional commitment. In January 2001, she accompanied her husband on a visit to Ottawa en route to Washington. She made a point of asking to visit me at the Supreme Court, and I was delighted to agree. Cherie strode into my chambers in high-topped boots that aroused the envy of the female staff, and she refused to complain about the frigid Canadian weather. Over coffee, we exchanged views on women's rights, LGBTQ rights, and same-sex marriage. She was impressed with Canadian jurisprudence and legislation on human rights issues, and avid to learn more.

A few months later, in late June 2001, I encountered Cherie once again. She had agreed to give a talk at one of the Cambridge Lec-

tures, which Frank was still involved in organizing. A few days before the lectures were to begin, I found myself in London with Frank
as he tied up various loose ends. One of those loose ends was Cherie's
lecture.

Frank had made an appointment to meet Cherie's secretary, Fiona
Miller, to tidy up the details. When he told me the meeting was at 10
Downing Street, I asked to come along.

"Sure," he said. "No problem. But we have to leave early. The
meeting is at ten. I don't want to be late."

The day dawned grey. Clad in trenchcoats and carrying umbrel-
las, we presented ourselves at the gates of 10 Downing Street. The
guard looked down his list of appointments.

"Don't see your name here," he said, "but go on in."

He opened the gate and we passed into the inner precincts of
Downing Street. Frank clanged the knocker on Number 10. A red-
headed guard with a craggy face opened the door. Again, he scanned
his list of expected guests, and again he informed us that neither
Frank's name nor mine was on the list.

"You might as well come in to wait," he said.

The guard led us to a small hallway that connects to the prime
minister's residence.

"Do you realize we got through two guards and no one even asked
for our identification?" I murmured to Frank as we settled into the
settee in the hall. "And this when Prime Minister Blair is in Ireland
on a peace mission that might provoke tensions?"

Barely a minute had passed when a young woman appeared. "I'm
the Blairs' housekeeper," she said. "Come on upstairs."

We did as asked, and to our amazement, we found ourselves in
the Blairs' private sitting room. I looked around at the family and
prime ministerial memorabilia.

"I feel like an imposter," I said. "I'm not sure we belong here."

A small boy in pyjamas wandered in, rubbing his eyes. "Where's

Mommy?" he asked, before wandering back to where he'd come from.

The housekeeper reappeared. "I'm so sorry," she said, "but I need to go out for a minute. I'll have to ask you to wait downstairs."

Relieved, we followed her back to the settee in the downstairs hall.

We waited. At one point, I glanced up to see Cherie in exercise gear running past us on the way to the private apartments. She gave the odd couple in the corridor a look and carried on.

I was beginning to think something had gone wrong. "I know you're a stickler for time, Frank, but maybe you should recheck the appointment," I suggested.

He opened his briefcase and pulled out a paper. His face went white. "The appointment is for eleven."

At precisely two minutes to eleven, a woman in a camel-hair suit appeared and introduced herself as Fiona Miller.

"I'm afraid we arrived a bit early," Frank said.

"I know," Fiona replied crisply.

Once again we made our way through the private door and up the private stairs to the Blairs' sitting room. Cherie entered and greeted us. "Do sit down."

Fiona Miller propped her computer on her lap and the meeting began.

"What time am I scheduled to be at Queens' College?" Cherie asked.

Frank unrolled a massive scroll on which he had written all the lecture times. "Twelve noon," he replied.

Looking over his shoulder, I could see her name clearly marked in the 2 p.m. slot. He must have misspoken. Cherie, reading upside down, could see it, too.

"Not noon," she pronounced. "Two. Two o'clock."

"I said two," said Frank, struggling to regain his composure.

Cherie leaned back in her chair and fixed him with her eye. "No, Mr. McArdle," she said, "you said noon."

We all laughed. Frank recovered his equanimity, and the remaining details were quickly sorted out.

As she led us back down the now-familiar corridor, Cherie leaned towards me. "You must take care of that absent-minded professor of yours," she said with a smile as she showed us out the door.

Frank and I made our way back to the big gates in a state of bemusement. We couldn't believe it. Two people in trenchcoats—one with an Irish name in a time of troubles—had found themselves invited into the private sitting room of the prime minister of England without anyone checking their identification or asking what was in their briefcases.

WE ENJOYED VISITS TO many countries in the years to come. Foreign courts were interested in the Canadian justice system and the Supreme Court's post-Charter jurisprudence. I fondly remember Frank waving royally from a limo in Budapest, prompting executive legal officer Daniel Jutras to observe, "*Le roi du Canada*." My impudent insistence (shocking even for me) on joining the men after dinner as the ladies filed out on a visit to Northern Ireland—one of the gentlemen finally did pull out a chair. Almost being beheaded by a bust of Ho Chi Minh that wobbled behind me as I presented at a conference in Hanoi. Listening to Egypt's president, Hosni Mubarak, days before the Iraq invasion, saying he had pleaded with the American president to leave the regular army and police force in place if he decided to invade so as to prevent internal chaos—advice that went unheeded. A painful overnight train trip from Moscow to St. Petersburg after too many vodka toasts by the president of the Constitutional Court of the Russian Federation.

Throughout my time with the court, I was privileged to have a chance to welcome other dignitaries to Canada, too. In June 1995, before I became chief justice, I met the Clintons on their visit to Ottawa. Prime Minister Jean Chrétien's wife, Aline, organized a women's breakfast for Hillary Clinton at the prime minister's residence at 24 Sussex Drive. Along with twenty or so other women, I found myself ushered into the dining room. Hillary was wearing a deep green dress (this was before she made pantsuits her uniform) and glowed with suppressed energy, but not because she was particularly happy. She had just come off an unsuccessful fight to introduce public health care to Americans as her husband's lieutenant, and she was still smarting from the wounds inflicted during the campaign.

"Bill and I thought it would be so simple," she said. "We thought that it would be like our work to reorganize the educational system in Arkansas. You know it's the right thing to do, you share that message, and it happens. We were so naive. I envy you your Canadian health care. Why can't it happen in our country?"

I came away from the breakfast deeply impressed by her intelligence and commitment to her country and its inhabitants.

If I expected to like Hillary Clinton, I wasn't so sure about George W. Bush. Relations between Canada and the United States were strained in the aftermath of the 2003 invasion of Iraq. Canada had been asked—indeed expected—to join its long-term ally in the invasion. But Prime Minister Jean Chrétien refused. He was less convinced than George W. Bush and Tony Blair of the supposed evidence that Saddam Hussein possessed weapons of mass destruction. Hussein was clearly a brutal dictator, but if we went to war against every bad ruler, Chrétien argued, we would never stop fighting. Canadians, despite significant dissent, generally supported staying out of the war.

I learned that I would be seated next to President Bush at a dinner at the Museum of Civilization in Gatineau, just across the Ottawa River from the Houses of Parliament and the Supreme Court.

Already fretting about what we would talk about, I was distracted even more by a telephone call from my brother Conrad in Edmonton. "I understand you'll be dining with the president tonight," he said. "Tell him I would have voted for him." I could not back off a challenge from my brother, but I couldn't figure out how to convey this message without confessing that I would not have voted for George W. Bush.

That evening, the president descended the grand escalator with the prime minister to fanfare and was led to our table. I decided to get my brother's challenge over with at the outset. As we were being seated, I said, "Mr. President, there is something I have to get out of the way before we begin dinner. My brother wants me to tell you he would have voted for you."

The president looked at me quizzically, then burst out laughing. "And you wouldn't have voted for me," he said.

I smiled and ruefully shook my head.

That broke the ice. The president and I had a great visit during the remainder of the dinner. We discussed the war, and I opined that Prime Minister Chrétien could not have joined the invasion of Iraq because most Canadians were not convinced it was the right thing to do.

"Aw, shucks," the president said. "A lot of Americans felt the same way."

Still, he didn't doubt the correctness of his decision; for him, the invasion was unfinished business left over from his father's First Gulf War in 1990. He went on to discuss his passion for educational reforms and his hopes for restructuring the United Nations, a topic then under debate. The next day, an envoy from the American embassy brought me a signed photo from the president with his warm wishes.

"He did this only for you and one other person," the envoy said.

I was moved. The president and I did not share the same views on many things. But that didn't mean we couldn't respect each other or relate as friends.

That year was also the fiftieth anniversary of the queen's ascension to the throne. A Golden Jubilee was celebrated in Canada and other Commonwealth countries. I was too busy to take much note, until I received an invitation to a Jubilee dinner for the queen, to be held once again at the Museum of Civilization. I immediately thought of the scrapbooks I had made of Princess Elizabeth's marriage and coronation—the days and months I had spent totally in her spell.

The dinner took place on a Sunday evening. Frank and I had spent the weekend at our cottage, as was our wont.

"We need to leave early," I told my husband over breakfast on Sunday morning. "We're dining with the queen tonight."

We arrived back in Ottawa with an hour to spare. I showered, fluffed my hair, and donned a silver-and-lace Armani cloak I had acquired at a Vancouver second-hand store the year before. An RCMP escort whisked us across the river to Gatineau.

We were taken to a room where dignitaries were assembling for a pre-dinner reception. Her Majesty appeared, radiant in white, and made her way down the reception line, stopping to chat here and there, while Prince Philip lurked in the shadows with his hands behind his back. She said a few words to me. I smiled and managed an incoherent reply. Dazzled and nonplussed, I watched the queen move on. So much for my only live encounter with my idol.

As I nursed regret of a moment lost, I felt a touch on my elbow. I turned to see the deputy minister of heritage, Judith LaRocque. "I wanted to tell you that you will be sitting beside the queen at dinner."

My heart went into overdrive. I had expected to be at the queen's table, but not at her side. If I had only known, I would have spent my weekend planning conversational gambits instead of hiking in the woods.

The reception party descended the long escalator to the Hall of the People. I looked out the wall of glass to the Ottawa River, then down to the sea of white tables spread like a glittering carpet against the backdrop of majestic coastal totem poles, and wondered what I could say to the queen when the moment arose.

She arrived with Prime Minister Jean Chrétien in a flurry of royal fanfare. Grace was said, toasts pronounced, wine poured. Then it was time to eat—and more to the point, to converse. The queen turned to Jean Chrétien on her right and made some comment. Then the prime minister smiled and looked at me. "Your Majesty," he said in his loud and slightly raspy voice, "I like to tell people this country is ruled by women. The governor general is a woman, the chief justice is a woman, and my wife, Aline, is clearly a woman."

"Oh," said the queen as she turned to me, blinding me with her diamonds. "How interesting."

And then it was over to me. I decided to plunge in. "Your Majesty," I said, "this is a very special moment for me. Since I was a very little girl, I have followed your life and career. When I was little, I made scrapbooks of your wedding and coronation. There are so many things I wanted to ask you."

"Really?"

I've gone too far, I thought, and then she smiled.

I remembered seeing a photo of "Lillibet" and Princess Margaret, two girls being led down a street in war-torn London.

"It must have been very difficult for you as a child," I said, "living in London with bombs falling all around."

"Not really," said the queen. "Actually, we spent most of the war out of the city at Windsor."

What followed was one of the most fascinating hours of my life, as the queen shared with me memories of her life at Windsor and beyond.

"I expect I am the only girl ever to have gone to Eton," she said at one point, referring to the posh all-boys school. "During the war, all the men were called up and they couldn't find a history tutor for me. So it was decided that I would join the boys at Eton."

"That's one story I never read," I said. We went on to discuss her love of horses, particularly the RCMP horses she rode on ceremonial occasions, and the place dogs held in our respective lives. I knew the details, down to the name of her favourite RCMP horse (which was buried outside her window at Windsor).

At one point, Prime Minister Chrétien caught the queen's eye and raised his glass of red wine. "This wine is produced in the Niagara region," he said. "I hope you enjoy it."

The queen politely raised her glass and took a tiny sip, then returned to me. "Now, Beverley . . ."

A little later, my husband, seated across the table, found a moment to intervene. "Your Majesty," he said, "I had the great pleasure of meeting your mother at Queens' College, Cambridge."

"Isn't that nice," said the queen, before returning to our conversation.

As we headed home later that evening, Frank shook his head. "You sure entertained the queen."

"What could I do?" I replied. "She's the queen."

State dinners can be long and tedious. I like to think that my childhood infatuation with the remarkable woman who is the queen of Canada and the memories we shared that evening helped make one such dinner a little more bearable for her. As for me, I floated out the grand doors in a mood of euphoria. This ordinary girl from Pincher Creek had finally met the queen.

....

CHAPTER THIRTY-THREE

Justice for All

Growing up, Angus always maintained one thing: he would never be a lawyer. It had never held him back. Until, that is, he found himself embroiled in a dispute with his landlady.

Vancouver in the first decade of the twenty-first century was, as now, a hard city in which to find a place to live. But Angus had found the perfect spot—not fancy or large, but close to the sea and the shops on West Fourth. Then, one day, he found an eviction notice pasted on the door of his suite. It seemed the landlady intended to demolish the house to build several posh townhomes.

All the other tenants in the house meekly moved out. But Angus went to city hall and checked out his rights. He filed an application with the British Columbia Residential Tenancy Branch. Alone in the vast and crumbling house, he waited for his hearing. When the notice came, it was simpler than he thought. No treks to a courthouse, no paperwork—all he had to do was be on the phone at a certain hour on a certain day.

When the day came, he called in. An arbitrator with the Residential Tenancy Branch was on the line, as was his landlady. The arbitrator laid out the rules: "First, I will hear from Mrs. Smith. Then Mr. McLachlin can cross-examine her. Then it will be Mr. McLachlin's time to present his side of the case, and Mrs. Smith can question him. The rules are simple: no interrupting, and I run the show."

Mrs. Smith presented her case—she wanted her tenants out so she could tear the house down. Angus presented his case—he had looked up the law, and in the circumstances, the only way she could evict him was if she sold the property to someone who was going to live there or obtained a demolition order. The arbitrator, after listening to both sides, said Mr. McLachlin was right.

"What do I need to do to get rid of him?" Mrs. Smith asked balefully.

"Get a demolition permit or sell the house to someone who intends to live there," said the arbitrator.

Three weeks later, Angus returned home from work to find a demolition permit on his door, accompanied by another eviction notice. He inspected the demolition permit carefully, and the next day took it to city hall, where he filed for another hearing.

"It's not a valid permit," he told the tenancies arbitrator. "It wasn't issued by city hall."

"Is that so, Mrs. Smith?"

"Well, yes, but—"

"You need a valid permit, Mrs. Smith."

Eventually Mrs. Smith obtained a valid permit and went to see my son. He inspected it and conceded. "It looks valid."

"You're out in a month," said Mrs. Smith.

"I agree," Angus said.

When the appointed day for moving arrived, Mrs. Smith appeared with a truck to help him transport his possessions to his new residence. When everything was unloaded, she invited him to Starbucks for coffee. They parted as friends.

I found myself laughing as my son recounted his story. But then I reflected—this was a story of justice done well. A dispute. A hearing. A resolution. Simple, cheap, effective. The law had been enforced and the adversaries parted friends. No one had missed a day's work, and no one was out of pocket. And the dispute had been resolved in a timely manner.

Of course, most legal disputes aren't this simple. They need lawyers. They need courthouses. They need discoveries and witnesses and a great deal of fussing about what the judge gets to hear and doesn't get to hear. But as I reflected on Angus's story, two things became clear to me. First, everyone is entitled to justice—not just the wealthy and big corporations. Everyone. Ever since the time of King Henry II, the government has accepted that providing justice to citizens is a basic responsibility—one more fundamental and ancient than even health care. How had we come to the point where citizens accepted that unless they had a great deal of money, justice might be unattainable?

Second, there are many ways to provide justice. Maybe a telephone conversation with a tenancies arbitrator. Maybe information about legal rights. Maybe an online interactive procedure. Perhaps an afternoon in small claims court.

Bottom line—the cost and time required to obtain justice should be proportionate to the grievance to be resolved. Big complicated cases involving big complicated matters should get big complicated treatment. But other cases might not need that procedure. Surely it was not too much to ask that a modern society fuelled by the internet could devise cost- and time-saving solutions for modern disputes? All we needed to do was bring ingenuity to the task of providing justice for all.

Inspired by Angus's experience and the complaints that ordinary Canadians couldn't afford to go to court, I took to the podium at a Toronto legal event. The press was present, and my comments hit the media. The response astounded me. The Supreme Court website was inundated with hits. I realized that I had unwittingly broached an issue that touched Canadians deeply. People were hard-wired for justice, and too often they weren't finding it.

Things started to happen. Various groups began exploring how access to justice could be improved for ordinary people. Advocates started talking about how justice should be there for all Canadians, not just a certain elite. Thomas Cromwell, a judge on the Nova Scotia Court of Appeal (who would later join the Supreme Court of Canada), met me on a trip to Newfoundland to propose a coordinated approach to improve access to civil and family justice. Realizing that the problem was multifaceted, Tom engaged provincial and federal officials, judges, academics, lawyers and bar associations, and legal aid groups. The result was the Action Committee on Access to Justice in Civil and Family Matters, which for more than a decade has served as a catalyst for reform and a hub for ideas on how to bring justice to all Canadians.

Halfway into my first decade as chief justice, I experienced a eureka moment. Being chief wasn't just about the Supreme Court of Canada, however important that was. The people of Canada viewed the chief justice as *their* chief justice. They looked to her to expose shortcomings in the system, and to do what she could to remedy them. The chief justice has no power to change laws, increase legal aid, or set up pro bono clinics—in fact, she must steer clear of anything encroaching on the legislative or executive powers of government—but she could motivate others to make the justice system fairer and more accessible.

My revelatory moment did not stop at access to justice. As I chatted with people on the court's annual open-house day, after public events, or simply while waiting at the checkout counter with my groceries, I realized their deep respect for the office of chief justice. A father would take his daughter's hand and say, "See, that's the chief justice. You can do that, too." I would look into the daughter's shining eyes and realize that just my being there—a woman in the third-highest position in the land—was of huge importance. I received letters from schoolchildren, proudly sharing their projects on the Supreme Court. I thought back on my girlhood crush on the queen. Her mere presence had inspired me, given me confidence that a young girl could become . . . well, not the queen but someone who could realize her particular dream. I came to see that perhaps the most important takeaway from my time as chief justice would be that I, a woman, had been there and had spoken out for the values I cherished.

And so I continued to speak out for better justice and better access to justice. It would be easy, sitting in the Supreme Court of Canada, to assume that the justice system is there for all Canadians. Non-governmental organizations and pro bono lawyers bring many causes of the underprivileged before the court. That's good and necessary. But when I looked at the statistics about court delays or thought about how many people came to court without a lawyer, it was plain that the justice system wasn't there—or at least, not in full measure—for many Canadians.

"TELL ME SOME STORIES about people whom the system has failed," skeptics sometimes say. I just shake my head. "When I think of access to justice, I think of the stories that *aren't* told," I reply. When a child at risk is left to languish in danger because there is no available court date; when a person gives up on getting damages for a debilitating personal injury because she can't afford a lawyer or court costs; when a first-time offender on a minor offence goes to jail because he didn't have legal advice—when these things happen, there is no story in the paper or on the nightly news. No one knows, except the people the justice system has failed.

Once I retired, I had the freedom to do more. I took over from Tom Cromwell as chair of the Action Committee on Access to Justice in Civil and Family Matters. And I advocated for causes even more directly.

One afternoon in late 2018, I received a call. "Would you be willing to do a video to help save the pro bono legal clinics in Toronto and Ottawa?"

"I would be delighted to do whatever I can," I responded.

I had been a fervent supporter of the Toronto and Ottawa clinics since their establishment several years before. The Ontario government subsidized both locations, and lawyers provided their services for free. People who didn't qualify for legal aid but still couldn't afford legal fees could come in and get help with their problems. Thousands of people had been supported over the years, and young lawyers benefited from the experience the work gave them. The clinics, then, were a win-win for everyone. Yet now, the government was cutting off funding, and the clinics would be forced to shut down.

Half an hour after the call, a young lawyer with a camera appeared at my door, and we made a video in which I said how important these clinics were and how critical that they be allowed to continue. Many other ex-judges and people involved in the justice system did the same. In the end, the funds were raised and the clinics won a temporary reprieve.

This is but one story among many of how people are working to ensure access to justice. There is more to be done. We need to keep working to make our justice system faster, more efficient, and more just. If we care about justice and the rule of law, quitting is not an option.

One prong of the access-to-justice problem continues to grieve me—the provision of legal services for Indigenous youth. The cases heard by the Supreme Court were, by definition, serious. Yet how often did I reflect that every serious problem had a small beginning—one that would probably have been resolved if the youth had had a lawyer. A significant number of Indigenous young people in custody are there because of administrative offences, such as failure to abide by bail conditions, report to a court worker, or show up for a court hearing. Without legal representation, these minor offences spiral into a criminal record that later justifies significant jail time, which serves to further criminalize the offender. We must find our way out of these downward spirals. Access to justice is part of the answer.

....

CHAPTER THIRTY-FOUR

Just Politics

IN THE DARK OF the night, my phone rang. I reached to silence it and scanned the time: 4 a.m. Where was I? Then my waking mind clicked in and supplied the details: Hotel. Moncton, New Brunswick. Lecture on women in the legal profession last night. Went well, all in French. Not bad for an anglophone from Pincher Creek.

But now, I had to catch a plane back to Ottawa, where a string of meetings awaited me. I pushed myself out of the narrow bed, showered, shoved my toiletries into the suitcase, dressed, and headed down to the lobby. The smell of fresh coffee wafted towards me from a table by the reception desk as I exited the elevator. I needed some. The woman behind the desk nodded. "*Bonjour, madame.*" She looked at me sympathetically. Four in the morning is no time to start the day—as she knew better than anyone.

Coffee cup in one hand, I reached to pull a copy of *The Globe and Mail* from the stack at the side of her desk and glanced at the top stories. There, on the top right-hand corner, was the headline that rocked me. Disbelieving, I set my coffee down. The black print blared out at me: "Harper Alleges Supreme Court Chief Justice Broke Key Rule with Phone Call."[1]

In shock, I settled my bill and fled for the waiting taxi. The desk clerk's eyes followed me. She had read the front page and knew— had known all the time as I fumbled with my coffee and credit card. The sympathetic gaze wasn't just about the early hour.

It was too dark to read in the taxi. Only in the lounge, waiting for my flight, did I discover my alleged misdemeanour. Prime Minister Harper was claiming that I had wrongly attempted to interfere in his appointment of Marc Nadon to replace Morris Fish, who was retiring from the court. The prime minister alleged that I had telephoned the justice minister, Peter MacKay, to tell him that Nadon's appointment might give rise to a court challenge on the ground that as a federal court judge who had not practised in Quebec for many years, he did not meet the criteria of the *Supreme Court Act*, which held that Quebec judges (of which there must be three) be appointed "from among the judges of the Court of Appeal or of the Superior Court of the Province of Quebec or from among the advocates of that Province."[2] The prime minister added that I had also tried to call him, but he had declined to take the call.

I *had* called the justice minister, but our talk took place several months before Nadon was proposed as a candidate. At the cottage during a summer respite from official travels, I received a call from the chief justice of the Quebec Superior Court, advising me that rumour had it the government was planning to replace Justice Fish with a judge from the Federal Court of Appeal. The chief justice had reason to believe that if that happened, there might well be a court challenge from people in Quebec, which could delay the appointment and leave the Supreme Court a person short.

Not a good situation, I concurred. The Supreme Court needs all nine positions filled to function as intended. It can and has carried on for a time with eight members in its past, but this means either risking four-four decisions or sitting seven judges (in this case, depriving Quebec of its statutory three members). And looming over that was the probability that choosing a judge from the Federal Court of Appeal for this particular vacancy—when it was unclear whether that candidate fulfilled the requirements of the *Supreme Court Act*—could place the court in the awkward position of adjudicating who should be its next justice.

The chief justice of the Quebec Superior Court had suggested that I call Peter MacKay to alert him to the possibility that nomination of a federal court judge might be challenged, resulting in litigation and all the unfortunate consequences that might entail. I called my executive legal officer, Owen Rees, and we agreed that I should call MacKay. It wasn't a big deal—just the routine sort of information that a justice minister might want to have before giving the prime minister his recommendation for who should be the next justice of the Supreme Court of Canada. My office in Ottawa set up a call with MacKay, who was travelling in the North. They also alerted the Prime Minister's Office that I might wish to speak to Harper.

After a few pleasantries, I advised the justice minister that a matter had arisen that might affect the Supreme Court. The choice of the new justice was entirely up to the government, I made clear. However, I felt he should be aware that if the person selected were from one of the federal courts—as opposed to a Quebec court or the Quebec bar—that could result in litigation that would impact the functioning of the Supreme Court. He thanked me and we said goodbye. After speaking with MacKay, I felt that I need not trouble Prime Minister Harper and cancelled my request for a call to him.

One of the responsibilities of any chief justice is to deal with the justice minister on administrative matters, like appointments, that may impact the work of the court in question. These conversations take place routinely between chief justices across the country and the minister. This was just another such conversation, in my mind. I had alerted the minister to an issue I thought he should be aware of, as was my duty. The rest was in his hands. I went back to my holiday.

At the time of my call to the justice minister, Marc Nadon had not been mentioned as a possible candidate. I spoke to Minister MacKay on July 31, 2013.[3] Prime Minister Harper did not announce Justice Nadon as his nominee until September 30, 2013.[4] Hence my astonishment that bleak morning in Moncton to read that I was "wrongly interfering" with Nadon's appointment to the court. And even if I had commented on Nadon specifically, the merits of particular candidates are also something chief justices routinely discuss with the justice minister and his officials. There simply was no substance to the prime minister's accusation of wrongdoing.

As was my duty, I had informed the justice minister, on my call on July 31, 2013, that an appointment from the Federal Court of Appeal to a Quebec slot on the Supreme Court might give rise to litigation. Two months later, the government nevertheless chose a candidate from the Federal Court of Appeal, as was its right. That person was Marc Nadon. I knew him to be a respected jurist. I called him immediately, congratulated him, and welcomed him to the court. A few days later, we swore him in, and he began work for the upcoming session. I breathed a sigh of relief. We had our new judge and there had been no court challenge. All was well.

My relief was short-lived. Within days, two challenges were announced, the first by Ontario lawyer Rocco Galati, and the second by the Quebec government. The federal government responded by directing a reference to the Supreme Court, asking whether Justice Nadon's appointment complied with the *Supreme Court Act*.

The litigation over Justice Nadon's appointment did not arise from the fact that he was a member of the Federal Court of Appeal. Judges from the federal courts had been appointed to the Supreme Court before—including Justices Rothstein, Le Dain, and Iacobucci.

The issue in Justice Nadon's case concerned the requirements for the three positions that the *Supreme Court Act* reserves for Quebec judges—that the nominee must be a member of the Quebec bar or a judge of a Quebec court.

It was a difficult period for the court. Having sworn in our new colleague and welcomed him, we were now obliged to sit in impartial judgment on him. To avoid conflicts of interest, the members of the court would have to distance themselves from their newest colleague, an awkward situation. Yet there was no alternative. Justice Nadon left the courthouse office he had barely moved into and awaited the decision at home. The period of limbo that followed was awkward for us and no doubt devastating for him. A fine judge found himself at the centre of a legal storm, simply because he had accepted Prime Minister Harper's invitation to serve on the country's highest court.

The court, in a six-to-one decision (Justice Moldaver dissented, and neither Justice Nadon, for obvious reasons, nor his former Federal Court of Appeal colleague, Justice Rothstein, heard the case), held that Justice Nadon's appointment did not comply with the *Supreme Court Act*.[5] After the court made its decision, Justice Nadon stepped down, and within weeks, the government appointed Richard Wagner, a judge of the Court of Appeal of Quebec, to fill the vacant position.

One may speculate that the Supreme Court's decision that Justice Nadon could not legally fill the vacant Quebec slot—because he was neither a member of the Quebec bar nor a judge of a Quebec court—displeased the prime minister. One may further speculate that the decision rankled all the more because it came after a series of defeats at the Supreme Court for the Harper government: the 2010 ruling that the government's refusal to bring Omar Khadr back to Canada violated the Charter;[6] the rejection of the government's proposal for a federal securities regulator in 2011;[7] the striking down of prostitution provisions in the Criminal Code in 2013;[8] and, just six days before

The Globe and Mail published Prime Minister Harper's allegations of impropriety on my part, the rejection of his government's plans for Senate reform.[9]

While all of this is speculation, what seemed indisputably clear to me that spring morning in Moncton was that the prime minister was deeply angry with me and determined to launch a strike against me. And what better way than by an accusation of misconduct?

There is nothing more precious to a judge than her reputation. Without a reputation for integrity and probity, a judge is an emperor with no clothes. What is true for a judge is even truer for a chief justice of Canada. The most senior member of the Canadian judiciary must be—and be seen to be—above reproach. A compromised chief justice, who no longer enjoys the confidence of the public, is a maimed chief justice and must step down. Or so I have always believed.

As I scanned the article in the *Globe*, I settled on the opinion of a legal academic the reporter had consulted. He asserted that if indeed I had been guilty of wrongdoing, as Prime Minister Harper alleged, I would probably have to resign. I agreed. But I knew I had done nothing wrong. If the public thought I had, though, my career was at an end. I would become the only justice of the Supreme Court of Canada to step down in disgrace.

Back at the court, I sought advice. Some suggested that I not respond; it would only risk more vitriol from the Prime Minister's Office. But the more I thought about it, the more I was convinced I had to give the public the bare facts of what I had done. I would not get into a debate with the prime minister. But I would set out the facts. Then Canadians could judge for themselves.

We sent out a brief press release a few hours later. We began by categorically denying any wrongdoing. "At no time was there any communication between Chief Justice McLachlin and the government regarding any case before the courts. The facts are as follows," we said, and we listed a precise chronology of my contact with the justice minister.[10] The timeline showed that my call to the minister—the only time I had contacted anyone about the possibility of an appointment from the federal court—occurred two months before Justice Nadon's nomination, nixing the possibility that I could have interfered with the prime minister's choice of him as a candidate.

The matter was soon over. The government did not challenge my facts, as I knew they could not. Legal groups, national and international, weighed in to condemn the prime minister's attack on me and his affront to judicial independence.[11] The International Commission of Jurists examined the case, concluded I had done nothing wrong, and called on Prime Minister Harper to apologize.[12] Many Canadians seemed to take the same view. As I shopped for groceries or walked my new puppy in the park, people kept intercepting me to thank me for standing up and getting the facts out.

Former prime minister Jean Chrétien included a chapter on the judiciary in his book *My Stories, My Times*.[13] He described this incident as "nothing less than an unprecedented violation of the tradition honoured by Canadians, of respect for this fundamental institution. Let us just call it an aberrant moment in Canadian history."[14]

I concur.

WHICH BRINGS ME BACK to my new puppy. There is a silver lining to every cloud, and so it was with Prime Minister Harper's attack. Frank and I had lost our beloved black Lab, Kyrie, the previous year. I yearned for another dog, but Frank quite correctly pointed out the difficulties—my job required us to travel, and we had no time to train a puppy. Put shortly, it was foolhardy to get one.

One evening, as I sat in my downstairs office preparing for the next day's case, my telephone rang. It was my friend Warren Winkler, also born in Pincher Creek, and recently retired as chief justice of Ontario. Wink, as I called him, had spent many evenings after Judicial Council events talking about Gretzky, his famed black Lab who lived to the astronomical (for a Lab) age of sixteen. There was the possibility of descendants of Gretzky in the future, Wink had said the previous year. "Let me know," I had replied, thinking of my dear departed Kyrie.

After some desultory chat—"This will blow over"—Wink came around to the real reason for his call. Descendants of Gretzky had indeed materialized: a litter of eight perfect black male puppies. "They're all taken," Wink said. He paused. "But if you're interested, there's a chance I could get you the one the RCMP had their eye on."

"Frank and I have decided the time's not right for a dog. Too busy, too much travel," I replied.

A few minutes later, Wink phoned back. "I really think I could swing it," he said. "The puppy, I mean."

"Thanks anyway," I said.

I went upstairs, where Frank was planted in front of the nine o'clock news.

"Who's been on the phone?" he asked.

I told him it was Wink, offering the possibility of a puppy. "I said no."

Frank gave me a sideways look. "Tell him we'll take it," he said.

I looked at my husband and marvelled. He knew what I needed now, when I was down: a new puppy.

Winter turned to spring, and on a glorious Sunday in May, we met our new family member at a roadside mall north of Toronto. Black and wriggling, he lifted his head to lick my face. I wiped my cheek, and the wetness wasn't just puppy slobber.

I thought about calling my new puppy Harper so I could say, "Harper, sit! Harper, lie down!" I actually liked the name, but I decided that people in the dog park might misunderstand. In the end, I decided on Darcy, from Jane Austen's *Pride and Prejudice*. Mr. Darcy—handsome, dark, and the folly of my old age.

I meet former prime minister Harper from time to time, in this airport lounge or at that event. We greet each other and chat. He never mentions the accusation that played in the headlines for months and aroused international ire. Nor do I. Just politics.

....

CHAPTER THIRTY-FIVE

Towards the Finish Line

In CANADA, JUDGES MUST retire at the age of seventy-five. As a judge, I had sat on a number of challenges to mandatory retirement provisions. I almost always voted against forcing people to retire merely because of their age.[1] The provisions deny people the equal right to work on the basis of age. In the Charter challenges I heard, the breach of the equality guarantee in Section 15 had not been shown to be reasonable and justifiable under Section 1. That had been my view, at least. Ironically, when it neared my turn, I found myself content with mandatory retirement.

Would it be better if justices of the Supreme Court of Canada routinely served until they were incapacitated or deceased, as they do in the Supreme Court of the United States? Would a lifetime sentence to the court be preferable to retiring to take on second careers at the bar or elsewhere? Although there are many moments when I miss the court enormously, I'm not convinced it would. The current regime in Canada allows a justice to choose after a decade whether to stay or remain. The result is a court with a mixture of senior and junior judges. While some justices are happy to carry on for a long time, others find themselves increasingly crushed by the pressures and restrictions of the job and want to move on. An unhappy judge may not be a good thing. Or a humane thing. And from time to time, an injection of new ideas is not a bad thing.

As I approached my last year as a judge, I pondered the precise date of my retirement. To avoid disruption to court sittings and ensure a smooth transition, I did not want my departure to fall in the middle of one of the terms or on my actual mandatory retirement date of September 7, 2018. That left three options: leave in the fall of 2017, leave in December 2017, or stay until the end of the June term in 2018. After discussions with Prime Minister Justin Trudeau, I chose December 15, 2017. After almost eighteen years as chief justice, I felt a few months one way or the other was of no consequence. Having a new chief in place when the court reassembled after the holiday and began its January term seemed best. For six months after that, I would have statutory power to sign off on cases I had heard. But after December 15, I would no longer be a judge or the chief justice.

Three years had passed since the difficult days of Prime Minister Harper's attack—years filled with onerous cases and difficult decisions. In 2015, the court had tackled the difficult intersection of religion and education in *Loyola High School v. Quebec (Attorney General)*.[2] The issue was whether a Catholic high school could continue to teach ethics in its own religious context in the face of a provincial requirement that all religions be presented as equally valid in the curriculum. The court held that it could.

In the same year, in *R. v. Nur*, the court set out the methodology for determining whether mandatory minimum sentences violated the Charter guarantee against cruel and unusual punishment, holding that reasonable hypotheticals can be considered.[3] And in 2016, the court's majority judgment in *R. v. Jordan* rejected the framework traditionally applied to determine whether an accused was tried in a reasonable time.[4] Instead of a flexible, multifaceted analysis, the majority replaced it with a presumptive ceiling of months between charges and trial, condemning a "culture of complacency."[5] (I voted for a more flexible approach.) The world of criminal law took a collective gasp. Lawyers rejigged their arguments and courts across the country devoted new resources to eliminating undue delay. The federal minister of justice announced new reforms aimed at speeding up the criminal process.

Equally momentous was the court's unanimous decision in *Carter v. Canada (Attorney General)*, upholding the right to assisted suicide for people enduring intolerable suffering and striking down the provisions of the Criminal Code that made it a crime to assist a person in dying.[6] *Rodriguez*, which twenty-two years before had upheld the prohibition of assisted suicide, was overruled on the basis of new evidence and social developments.[7] Passionate opponents of assisted suicide—and there were many—railed against the decision, while civil libertarians lauded the right of an individual beset by pain and indignity to control the final stages of her life. Parliament took up the challenge and passed a law allowing assisted suicide for the terminally ill.[8]

The cases that occupied the court in the three years before my retirement raised difficult issues—issues that divided Canadians—and were replete with weighty consequences for the criminal justice system and civil society. They were the kind of cases that judges agonize over and work long into the night to resolve. To the end, I never lost my passion for the work. I would miss it. But I was also ready, after so many years in the trenches, to pass the torch to others.

On the morning of December 14, I presided over my last case at the Supreme Court of Canada. When the case concluded, the counsel said a few words marking the transition, and Justice Abella, as senior puisne justice, made a gracious tribute. Rosie takes everything seriously, including her speeches. For this one, she had consulted all the members of the court and, with her customary eloquence, spoke not only for herself but also for them. I felt a lump gathering in my throat as she spoke. How could I leave this place that had been my home for more than twenty-eight years? How could I leave these people, my dearest friends?

I pulled myself together. Somehow I had to find a way to say a coherent farewell. I'd had no time to prepare a speech, but before coming into court that morning, I'd found myself scribbling random thoughts on a piece of paper. I suddenly realized there was no way to say what those years had meant to me. With tears in my eyes and a tremble in my voice, I scrunched my pieces of paper together and spoke from the heart. Thank you to my colleagues, to the court staff, to my husband and family. Thank you to this country, which had allowed me to fulfill a dream I did not have the confidence to even articulate when I started my journey in law. I felt my throat clog once more as I searched for a way to sum up my tenure on the court. And then the words came: "Whatever lies ahead, I know that my time here will always be the centrepiece of my life."

As I passed through the great double doors behind the bench, sadness swept over me. I would never again sit in this courtroom, never again pass through these portals. Then the doors of the judges' conference room opened. I glimpsed the Ottawa River and the Gatineau Hills. A ray of sunlight struck through. I smiled. It's all there, caught in a photo snapped by a court staffer—my eyes still bright with the tears I had stifled, and a smile on my face as I stepped into a new and different future. A load that I had carried for a very long time suddenly lifted, but life was not over.

That evening, I stood on the stage at the Shaw Centre in Ottawa and took my last bow as chief justice. Two former governors general, Adrienne Clarkson and David Johnston, as well as three prime ministers—Brian Mulroney, Jean Chrétien, and Justin Trudeau—spoke. Two had been instrumental in my career as a justice and chief justice, and the last had helped me decide when to retire.

I felt like an aging Cinderella as I looked about me. Here I stood, the girl from nowhere who had moved from helping her mother sweep the floors of a log cabin to the height of the legal establishment. There had been many ups and some downs, but I had made it through intact. By a series of twists of fate, I was in this place at this moment, draped in an Oscar de la Renta gown I could never have imagined as a girl (purchased a year earlier on a whim and at a drastic discount) and looking out over the audience of judges and lawyers and politicians assembled to mark the culmination of my legal career.

I thanked all those who had helped me along the way—my parents, my community, the teachers who had taught me to think, the province that had financed my studies, the mentors who had helped me find a leg up in the law, and the friends who had stood by me in good times and bad. I finished by thanking my country—"a country that respects the rule of law and of openness, in which a young woman of no particular note could become a lawyer and a judge and a chief justice."

I had had a good run. Now it was time to move on.

···

CHAPTER THIRTY-SIX

Citizen McLachlin

IT WAS A FRIGID winter day. I was in a classroom at the University of Alberta. Outside, the snow swirled. Edmonton, 1962.

The subject of the day was Alfred, Lord Tennyson. "Ulysses," to be precise. Tennyson had just lost a lifelong friend and gone into a deep depression, the balding prof told us. He was living with his mother and nine of his siblings in an undersized house in Lincolnshire. His father had died two years earlier. Life was collapsing in on him. And then, the young poet bestirred himself and reconsidered. Captivated by the Greek myth of Odysseus, he thought that maybe, through great determination, one might find transcendence. The poem "Ulysses" came out of his musings.

In the poem, the aging king has surmounted a thousand perils, conquered Troy, and completed his odyssey. Now he is back home, sitting at his hearth. He has everything he thought he wanted—a country at last at peace, laws to administer, a wise son to take up the reins of government. And yet, Ulysses is not happy.

"I cannot rest from travel; I will drink / Life to the lees," the prof intoned.

Bored students caught each other's eyes. Travel sounds great, but hadn't the old man done enough?

Oblivious to the collective ennui, the prof droned on. "So Ulysses, instead of sitting by the hearth in his dotage, decides to take on new adventures:

> *Old age hath yet his honour and his toil;*
> *Death closes all; but something ere the end,*
> *Some work of noble note, may yet be done,*
>
> . . . .
>
> *'Tis not too late to seek a newer world."*

A collective sigh. So what? We were just starting out; our ventures lay before us.

Half a century later, I found myself coming back to Tennyson's poem. I googled it and printed it out. The poem had caught up with me, or I with it. Facing my own post-retirement life, I understood exactly how Ulysses felt—precisely what the poet was seeking to convey. Perhaps I hadn't slain ogres or been seduced by sirens in a ten-year odyssey, but I had had my career—as they say in Quebec, "*J'ai eu mon voyage.*" Time to quit. Retire to the cottage. Sit by the hearth. Yet somehow, I wasn't ready.

On December 14, 2017, I was a judge and chief justice. I sat behind my big desk in my big office and signed letters. My staff of four filed in and out with last-minute queries. At the appointed hour, I drove to the National Press Building for a final press conference. I went home and wondered what tomorrow would bring.

When I woke up on December 15, all was changed. I was no longer a judge, no longer chief justice. No staff. No law clerks. No car. Just a one-person transition team to help me through almost twenty-eight years' worth of files and ease me from the world of judging to the world of archives. Just call me Citizen McLachlin.

The joke goes that retirement from public office is when you get in the back seat of the car and it doesn't move. For almost eighteen years, I had been getting in the back seat of an RCMP vehicle and waiting for it to take me where I needed to go. The security level wasn't high, so I was driven only to the court and scheduled events. I'd kept up my driving skills by tooling up and down the Gatineau Valley to the cottage and back. Still, city driving was a challenge. All those lights. All those bikes. Pedestrians everywhere.

I came home after my first sortie downtown and back. Somewhere in the back of my mind, I had wondered whether no longer being a judge would affect my relationships with my husband and my son. My apprehensions disappeared when Frank met me at the door with a hug.

"How did it go?" he asked.

"Nobody honked, nobody gave me the finger, and nobody died," I replied. A modest achievement by most people's standards.

We laughed together. Nothing had changed. To Frank, I was just Bev, the woman he had fallen in love with and married. It was the same with Angus—I was his mother, first and foremost. All the fuss and feather of being a justice and a chief justice had always been just context; for us, what mattered was who we were to each other. And we knew what that was.

I SPENT THE WINTER and early spring in my Vancouver condo. No driver, not even a car. But the bus service was excellent, I discovered— once I figured out where the coins went.

"Take a transfer," a mottled man from a side seat advised me on my first bus trip. "The ticket's good for two hours."

I quickly discovered that a Compass Card, supplemented by walking and the odd cab, were the magic ticket to transportation through Vancouver's wet streets.

I had always shopped for my own groceries and walked my dog in the park. I didn't think of myself as one of the elite, but being whisked away by an RCMP vehicle or followed by a police guard is not conducive to intimate conversations with busy citizens going about their business. Now, riding the bus, chatting with cab drivers, lunching in small cafes, I discovered Canadians from all walks of life. Their decency impressed me.

I learned not to rely on first impressions. On a crowded bus on Main Street, Vancouver, not too far from the Insite facility I had once helped preserve,[1] a man crammed himself into a seat opposite me. He was thin and ill dressed and looked like he hadn't slept in a bed for a month.

He leaned forward and stared at me. "You're Beverley McLachlin," he said. "The judge. Thank you for what you did for our country."

Amazed, I felt a lump form in my throat. "Thank you," I said. "Your words mean a great deal to me."

But I wasn't done quite yet. I did have a little court work to finish. For six months after retirement, I would be allowed to sign judgments, even though I was no longer a judge. The court provided me with an office, but I didn't go in much. It was no longer my court, no longer my place. Despite the assurances of the new chief justice, Richard Wagner, and my former colleagues that I still was welcome, I knew I no longer belonged there. Once you pass the torch to new hands, it's gone—no way to hang on to it.

I put the house in Ottawa up for sale. I felt sad to leave it, this place that had sheltered me and Angus, and later Frank, for so long.

This garden I had nurtured and loved. Like the house I had left in Vancouver so many years before, this had been a good home. But it was time to move on. I would return to Vancouver, as I had always planned, but a condo and the cottage would ensure that Ottawa and the Gatineau Hills would always be part of our lives.

Like Ulysses repining by his hearth, my thoughts turned to new horizons. The mandatory minimum law said I was past my best-before date, but I felt no different than I had before that date arrived. Better, maybe.

"You look more relaxed," a close friend told me.

"Really?" I asked, genuinely surprised. "I feel busier than ever."

Other people kept telling me the same thing. One night I took a look at my face in the mirror.

"You may have a point," I told the friend who had made the comment.

Only then, months after I'd handed off responsibility for my old job, did I realize the weight of the burden I had been carrying for so many years. I loved my time at the court, loved the judging, loved being chief justice. I had grown so used to the responsibilities that I did not realize their heft. Now that I was no longer a judge, I felt a new persona emerging, lighter and freer, more open to the world. I was ready to move on to new adventures. One was my aforementioned long-repressed desire to meddle in fiction.

An apocryphal story had it that a brain surgeon once asked Margaret Atwood how to write a novel and she replied by asking him how to do brain surgery. Everyone thinks they can write fiction; in fact, it's difficult and complex and incalculably hard to pull off.

Another story came to mind. An aspiring composer approached Mozart and asked, "How do you write great music?"

"Start with folk songs," Mozart said.

"But, sir, you were writing symphonies at age eight."

"Yes, but I didn't have to ask how," Mozart replied.

The chances that I was one of those rare people who didn't need to ask how were minuscule. But I decided I would give fiction a try anyway. *Why not?* I thought. I would fail. I would move on free of the fantasy that I could write a good story.

I took inspiration from P.D. James, the great English detective writer. Her work at the Home Office completely filled her days, so she decided to rise each morning at five o'clock, before her real workday began, to exorcise her own personal writing demon. A few months short of retirement, I had started doing the same. At five thirty, I would stir myself from sleep, throw a robe over my pyjamas, and go down two flights of stairs to my basement office. I took up my protagonist and moved her forward three decades. She was not the same Jilly as before—how could she be, living in a different era and created by a different person?—but she was strong and feisty and ambitious, as she always had been. I began looking forward to my five thirty rendezvous with my alternative reality, began writing on planes or on the weekend. The words flew; I was having fun. Before long a story emerged. Eventually, I typed in "Finis" and asked myself, "What's next?"

The sane part of me said to let it be. I had written my story. No need to sully my reputation as a tolerable jurist with a second-rate foray into a genre I hadn't mastered; no need to extend my neck for the critics to chop off. But another part of me said, *You'll never know if you don't try*. I decided to push ahead—not much risk, since my chances of finding an agent were slim, and of finding a publisher infinitesimal.

Five and a half months after I ceased being a judge, my novel, *Full Disclosure*, was published. To my amazement, people liked it— the characters, the action, the courtroom drama. "It was such fun," readers would tell me. The comment made me smile. I had been a writer for a long time—a writer of legal judgments. People read what I wrote because they had to. No one ever read my reasons for fun. I felt modest satisfaction that something I had done had lifted people out of the routine of their days and given them enjoyment for a few hours.

Writing fiction, I discovered, was both the same as and different from writing judgments. In fiction, you get to make things up; in judgments, you don't. In fiction, you create your characters and action; in judgments, you take what the evidence gives you. In fiction, you can use humour; in judgments, you worry that a real person is likely to feel she's the brunt of the joke. To succeed, both fiction and law must be authentic and grounded in truth. The courtrooms Jilly Truitt inhabits are real courtrooms; the city whose streets she walks is a real city; the justice system in which she works is a real justice system; the truths that emerge about human nature and joy and suffering are real truths. I discovered that all the while I was writing fiction, I was writing about the same justice system in which my judgments had been grounded. Fiction—a new world—rooted in the world I had always inhabited.

AND IT WAS ONLY in retirement, when I was no longer a judge, that I discovered another truth about myself: whatever new worlds I find, justice will always be a part of my life, whether in courtrooms or outside them. For almost three decades, I had spent my days in courtrooms, where citizens came in search of justice and attorneys debated fine points of law. I had come to love the adventure of taking a complex set of facts and counter-facts and figuring out what, on a balance of probabilities, really happened. I had revelled in applying the frameworks of the law to bring order to the chaos of human endeavour. I had relished the challenge of coming up with the best answer I could, based on the law and on what practically can be accomplished. And I had loved trying to get things right—or as right as fallible human beings can.

But judging, I realized, is only one way to address inequality and the ills that trouble society. There are others—advocacy, giving, working with women and men and children who have fallen through the cracks and been left for lost, continuing to fight for access to justice for all Canadians. And ever resurfacing, even in retirement, is the issue that I have been struggling with through the lengthening course of my professional life: Why is it harder for women than men to make their way in the world? Through a serendipitous concatenation of circumstance, I had occupied a place of leadership in the national firmament for more than seventeen years. But I was the exception. Why do so few women find a place at the head of the table in business, banking, and politics? For all the progress we have made on the legal front, the old gender stereotypes continue to rear their heads in new and surprising forms.

Nine months after I retired as chief justice, I found myself relaxing on a long-awaited family holiday in Tuscany. Idly scanning through my emails over an al fresco breakfast in Florence, I came across a message from Katie Black, a former clerk at the Supreme Court and now an Ottawa litigator. "I thought you should be aware of this," she wrote. "See attached."

I clicked on the attachment. It was a news story about a new marketing foray by Simons department store—a line of bras named for prominent Canadian women. In the age of #MeToo, Simons had launched a campaign to sell bras named for the likes of Nellie McClung, Flora MacDonald, and—gulp—me. Each of us had her own bra. My espresso clattered to the saucer. I was being honoured by a structured model called the Beverley Bralette. The company I was in flattered me, but the idea of using the names of iconic women pioneers to sell lingerie appalled. I tried to imagine a campaign naming boxer shorts for Justin Trudeau and Andrew Scheer. It was so unlikely it was hard to envision.

Part of me said let it go—as a judge I was practised in the art of not responding, just letting it blow over. And then another part said no, I needed to call this out. I wrote back to Katie. "Last time I checked, you couldn't use a person's name to sell your product without her consent. This is so wrong on so many levels. Am I out to lunch?"

I was the only one still living of the six female icons for whom the bras had been named. If I did not take action, no one would. And this, or something like it, would happen again and again. The legacy of women's work reduced to lingerie. I instructed Katie to send a letter to Simons demanding they retract the ads and issue an apology, failing which I would bring legal proceedings. The letter stipulated that I was not seeking damages for myself but suggested that a contribution to a women's charity might be appropriate.

Simons did the right thing. Their chief executive took responsibility and apologized, explaining what the company had tried to do but admitting it was a bad idea. He did not minimize the concerns I expressed or make excuses. He offered a public apology for the promotion, pledged to destroy any materials related to it, and promised to make a donation to the Ottawa women's shelter I had suggested. What came to be known as the "Beverley McLachlin Bra Blunder" ended in forty new homes being financed for marginalized mothers and their families.[2] A bad beginning, but a happy ending.

TO RETIRE, I HAVE discovered, is a transitive verb. One does not simply retire; one retires from something to something else. I retired from the Supreme Court to other loves—writing, working for justice in new and different ways, and renewing my appreciation for the people at the centre of my life. It was only in retirement, with the responsibility that had dominated my existence for the past forty years gone, that I realized the fundamental condition without which I could have done nothing was still in place—the love of my family. My husband, Frank, who for so many years had stood by while I put the court and my cases first; my son, Angus, who had never complained about a mother distracted by competing obligations or concerns; my brothers and sister and their families, who loved me despite my familial delinquencies. And far in the distance, in my mind still cheering me on, my first love, Rory.

Today, I am Citizen McLachlin, wife, mother, friend, ordinary person. A person who had her day but is still, with the support of those around her, carrying on—maybe for a while, maybe for a long time. Every day is a new day. You never know what will happen.

Epilogue

··

I LOVE THE LAW. I have loved the law from the first day of law school, and I love it still. But the law that I love is not a system of arbitrary rules or relativistic principles. Not all values and principles are created equal. Some, history proves, are better than others at furthering human productivity and happiness. Nor is the law I love merely a device by which the powerful impose their will on the less powerful. The law I love is there for everyone, high and low, imposing obligations to be sure, but also offering protections and benefits.

The law is a framework for productive human activity, a buttress for human creativity. The law is more than the embodiment of one person's will; it is the collective wisdom of countless sage people over great stretches of time. It secures us and allows us to move forward in peace and harmony. In an age of unravelling, it offers stability and a principled way to face the problems that surround us. It is, quite simply, our best hope for the future.

Fifty-three years ago, I decided to give the law a try. It has been my anchor and catalyst ever since. It is the space in which I have thrived. It has brought me friendship, family, and love. It has opened new landscapes, new worlds to explore.

I find myself still wanting different worlds. Will I write another novel? Probably. Am I ready to give up being a judge? Probably not. I will never be a judge in the Canadian judicial system again; the law forbids it, and I for one must respect the law. But I will sit on the Court of Final Appeal in Hong Kong and on the Singapore International Commercial Court. And I will work as an arbitrator—a more private form of judging.

Within the broad embrace of the law, I will keep moving out, ever exploring.

The journey continues.

Acknowledgments

··

I THANK ALL THE FRIENDS and family who contributed their memories and thoughts to the book. I am particularly grateful to my husband, Frank, my sister, Judi Dalling, and my son, Angus, for taking the time to read the manuscript and providing invaluable advice, guidance, and encouragement. Special thanks go to Adam Goldenberg, my former law clerk, for reading my first draft with an eye to legal accuracy.

I want to thank Simon & Schuster for convincing me to attempt a memoir; I had resolved not to write one, having long accepted the wisdom of a predecessor on the court who, confronted with a similar offer, observed, "Living it once was enough." I am glad I was persuaded otherwise; living it twice has proved a valuable and enriching experience. I am deeply grateful to the editors at Simon & Schuster, particularly Brendan May and Sarah St. Pierre, for helping me do what I thought was impossible—to mold the inchoate experiences of a lifetime into a story.

Thanks to my agent, Eric Myers, for his unfailing support and guidance at every stage.

I apologize to the people who enriched my life along the way but who are not mentioned in this book. It would take many volumes—more than most readers would care to peruse—to tell the full story of all those who helped me and brightened my life. I also apologize for any errors I have made. Memory, I have learned, is a creative and fickle thing, and different people perceive and remember the same event differently. I have tried, as honestly as I can, to set forward the essential truth of the events as I recall them. Of those who differ, I beg forgiveness.

Finally, I wish to thank my parents, to whom I owe everything, and my country, Canada. As I said when I was sworn in as Chief Justice of the Supreme Court of Canada, only in this country could a country girl of no consequence have risen to the summit of the judiciary. Thank you, Canada, for allowing me to realize my dreams.

Notes

Prologue

1   Reference re meaning of the word "Persons" in s. 24 of British North America Act, [1928] S.C.R. 276, at pp. 283 and 290, per Anglin C.J.
2   Edwards v. Canada (Attorney General), [1930] 1 D.L.R. 98 (P.C.), at pp. 106–107, per Sankey L.C.

Chapter Four: Rich in Difference

1   Chinese Immigration Act, 1885, S.C. 1885, c. 71 (imposing a head tax on each Chinese person entering Canada).

Chapter Thirteen: Into the Fray

1   Bedford v. Canada, [2013] 3 S.C.R. 1101.

Chapter Fourteen: Strange Comfort

1   See Morrison-Knudsen Company Inc. v. British Columbia Hydro

and Power Authority (1978), 85 D.L.R. (3d) 186 (B.C. C.A.).

Chapter Sixteen: Parenthood

1   Murdoch v. Murdoch, [1975] 1 S.C.R. 423.
2   See Reference re Supreme Court Act, ss. 5 and 6, 2014 SCC 21, [2014] 1 S.C.R. 433, at para. 86; Robert J. Sharpe and Kent Roach, *Brian Dickson: A Judge's Journey* (Toronto: University of Toronto Press, 2003), p. 180.
3   Murdoch v. Murdoch, [1975] 1 S.C.R. 423, at p. 436, per Martland J.
4   Murdoch v. Murdoch, [1975] 1 S.C.R. 423, at p. 433, per Martland J.
5   Murdoch v. Murdoch, [1975] 1 S.C.R. 423, at p. 439, per Martland J.
6   Sharpe and Roach, *Brian Dickson*, p. 181.
7   Rosalie Silberman Abella, *Equality in Employment: A Royal Commission Report*, vol. 2 (Ottawa: Minister of Supply and Services Canada, 1984), p. 233, citing Statistics Canada, *Income Distributions by Size in Canada, 1982* (Catalogue Nos. 13–207 Annual, Ottawa, 1984).
8   Abella, *Equality in Employment*, 2:234.
9   Abella, *Equality in Employment,* 1:109–12.
10 Abella, *Equality in Employment*, 2:248.
11 Abella, *Equality in Employment*, 2:254.
12 Abella, *Equality in Employment*, 2:241.
13 See Shelagh Day, "Stuck in the Mud: Why Canada Can't Deal with Systemic Discrimination Against Women" (paper delivered for "25 Years After: A Retrospective on the Abella Commission and Employment Equity," Carleton University, Ottawa, ON, May 2009), p. 7, http://www.socialrightscura.ca/documents/publications/day/Abellafinal.pdf.
14 Public Service Alliance of Canada v. Canada Post Corp., 2011 SCC 57, [2011] 3 S.C.R. 572; Tonda MacCharles, "Top Court Swiftly Decides Longest-Running Pay Equity Dispute," *Toronto Star*,

November 17, 2011, https://www.thestar.com/news/canada/2011/11/17/top_court_swiftly_decides_longestrunning_pay_equity_dispute.html.

15 British Columbia Teachers' Federation v. British Columbia Public School Employers' Association, 2014 SCC 70, [2014] 3 S.C.R. 492.

16 Melissa Moyser, *Women in Canada: A Gender-Based Statistical Report* (Ottawa: Statistics Canada, 2017), pp. 26–28, https://www150.statcan.gc.ca/n1/en/pub/89-503-x/2015001/article/14694-eng.pdf.

17 Emily Bazelon, "A Seat at the Head of the Table," *New York Times Magazine*, February 21, 2019, https://www.nytimes.com/interactive/2019/02/21/magazine/women-corporate-america.html.

Chapter Eighteen: Growing and Grieving

1 Harrison v. University of British Columbia (1988), 49 D.L.R. (4th) 687 (B.C. C.A.); Stoffman v. Vancouver General Hospital (1988), 49 D.L.R. (4th) 727 (B.C. C.A.); Douglas/Kwantlen Faculty Assn. v. Douglas College (1988), 49 D.L.R. (4th) 749 (B.C. C.A.).

2 Andrews v. Law Society of British Columbia (1986), 27 D.L.R. (4th) 600 (B.C. C.A.).

3 Dixon v. British Columbia (Attorney General) (1989), 59 D.L.R. (4th) 247 (B.C. S.C.).

Chapter Twenty: A New World on the Ottawa

1 Daniel Kahneman, *Thinking, Fast and Slow* (Toronto: Doubleday, 2011).

Chapter Twenty-One: Changing Minds

1 See Supreme Court Act, R.S.C. 1985, c. S-26, s. 43(1.2), and Criminal Code of Canada, R.S.C. 1985, c. C-46, s. 691(2), both as amended by An Act to amend the Criminal Code and certain other Acts, S.C. 1997, c. 18, http://www.parl.ca/Content/Bills/352/Government/C-17/C-17_4/C-17_4.pdf.

2 R. v. Hebert, [1990] 2 S.C.R. 151.

Chapter Twenty-Two: Morality and the Law

1 Tremblay v. Daigle, [1989] 2 S.C.R. 530.
2 R. v. Morgentaler, [1988] 1 S.C.R. 30.
3 R. v. Morgentaler, [1988] 1 S.C.R. 30, at pp. 56–57, per Dickson C.J.
4 R. v. Morgentaler, [1988] 1 S.C.R. 30, at pp. 163–65 and 171–72, per Wilson J.
5 R. v. Morgentaler, [1988] 1 S.C.R. 30, at p. 173, per Wilson J.
6 See Tremblay v. Daigle, [1989] 2 S.C.R. 530, at pp. 538–39.
7 Tremblay v. Daigle, [1989] 2 S.C.R. 530, at pp. 569–70.
8 Tremblay v. Daigle, [1989] 2 S.C.R. 530, at pp. 570 and 572–73.
9 R. v. T. (J.G.), 1999 ABQB 981, 257 A.R. 251.
10 See R. v. Tremblay, 2000 ABQB 551, 274 A.R. 203.
11 R. v. Tremblay, 341 N.R. 396 (note) (S.C.C.).

Chapter Twenty-Three: The Right to Speak

1 R. v. Keegstra, [1990] 3 S.C.R. 697.
2 See R. v. Keegstra, [1995] 2 S.C.R. 381, at para. 3.
3 R. v. Zundel, [1992] 2 S.C.R. 731.

Chapter Twenty-Four: The Final Taboo

1 R. v. Seaboyer, [1991] 2 S.C.R. 577.
2 See R. v. Mills, [1999] 3 S.C.R. 668.
3 R. v. Ewanchuk, [1999] 1 S.C.R. 330.
4 R. v. Ewanchuk, 1998 ABCA 52, 13 C.R. (5th) 324, at para. 58, per Fraser C.J., dissenting.

Chapter Twenty-Five: On Life and Death

1 Rodriguez v. British Columbia (Attorney General), [1993] 3 S.C.R. 519.
2 Carter v. Canada (Attorney General), 2015 SCC 5, [2015] 1 S.C.R. 331.

Chapter Twenty-Six: The Marriage Act

1 Jean Chrétien, *My Stories, My Times* (Toronto: Random House Canada, 2018), p. 204.

2 Andrews v. Law Society of British Columbia, [1989] 1 S.C.R. 143.

3 Andrews v. Law Society of British Columbia (1986), 27 D.L.R. (4th) 600 (B.C. C.A.).

4 See, for example, Law v. Canada (Minister of Employment and Immigration), [1999] 1 S.C.R. 497; Corbiere v. Canada (Minister of Indian and Northern Affairs), [1999] 2 S.C.R. 203; Gosselin v. Quebec (Attorney General), [2002] 4 S.C.R. 429, 2002 SCC 84; Nova Scotia (Workers' Compensation Board) v. Martin; Nova Scotia (Workers' Compensation Board) v. Laseur, 2003 SCC 54, [2003] 2 S.C.R. 504; Hodge v. Canada (Minister of Human Resources Development), 2004 SCC 65, [2004] 3 S.C.R. 357; Auton (Guardian ad litem of) v. British Columbia (Attorney General), 2004 SCC 78, [2004] 3 S.C.R. 657; R. v. Kapp, 2008 SCC 41, [2008] 2 S.C.R. 483; Withler v. Canada (Attorney General), 2011 SCC 12, [2011] 1 S.C.R. 396; Quebec (Attorney General) v. A., 2013 SCC 5, [2013] 1 S.C.R. 61; Kahkewistahaw First Nation v. Taypotat, 2015 SCC 30, [2015] 2 S.C.R. 548.

5 See M. v. H., [1999] 2 S.C.R. 3; Canada (Attorney General) v. Hislop, 2007 SCC 10, [2007] 1 S.C.R. 429.

6 Halpern v. Canada (Attorney General) (2003), 225 D.L.R. (4th) 529 (Ont. C.A.).

7 Barbeau v. British Columbia (Attorney General), 2003 BCCA 406, 228 D.L.R. (4th) 416.

8 Catholic Civil Rights League v. Hendricks (2004), 238 D.L.R. (4th) 577 (Que. C.A.).

9 Vriend v. Alberta, [1998] 1 S.C.R. 493.

10 Reference re Same-Sex Marriage, 2004 SCC 79, [2004] 3 S.C.R. 698.

Chapter Twenty-Seven: Division and Discord

1   Constance Backhouse, *Claire L'Heureux-Dubé: A Life* (Vancouver: University of British Columbia Press, 2017).
2   See Sidney N. Lederman, Alan W. Bryant, and Michelle K. Fuerst, *Sopinka, Lederman & Bryant: The Law of Evidence in Canada*, 5th ed. (Toronto: LexisNexis Canada, 2018).
3   Reference re Secession of Quebec, [1998] 2 S.C.R. 217.

Chapter Twenty-Nine: A New Chief Justice

1   CBC News, "Lamer Looks Back with CBC News," CBC.ca, August 27, 1999, https://www.cbc.ca/news/canada/lamer-looks -back-with-cbc-news-1.195338.

Chapter Thirty: Truth and Reconciliation

1   Guerin v. The Queen, [1984] 2 S.C.R. 335.
2   R. v. Sparrow, [1990] 1 S.C.R. 1075.
3   Delgamuukw v. British Columbia, [1997] 3 S.C.R. 1010.
4   Delgamuukw v. British Columbia, [1997] 3 S.C.R. 1010, at para. 186, per Lamer C.J.
5   Haida Nation v. British Columbia (Minister of Forests), 2004 SCC 73, [2004] 3 S.C.R. 511.
6   Tsilhqot'in Nation v. British Columbia, 2014 SCC 44, [2014] 2 S.C.R. 256.
7   See John Ralston Saul, *A Fair Country: Telling Truths About Canada* (Toronto: Penguin Canada, 2008), pp. 8–16.
8   Truth and Reconciliation Commission of Canada, "Executive Summary," http://nctr.ca/assets/reports/Final%20Reports/Executive _Summary_English_Web.pdf, 130.

Chapter Thirty-One: Branching Out

1   See Application under s. 83.28 of the Criminal Code (Re), 2004 SCC 42, [2004] 2 S.C.R. 248; R. v. Khawaja, 2012 SCC 69, [2012] 3 S.C.R. 555; Canada (Citizenship and Immigration) v. Harkat,

2014 SCC 37, [2014] 2 S.C.R. 33; but see Charkaoui v. Canada (Citizenship and Immigration), 2007 SCC 9, [2007] 1 S.C.R. 350 (striking down the procedure for issuing certificates of inadmissibility to Canada under the Immigration and Refugee Protection Act).

2   Suresh v. Canada (Minister of Citizenship and Immigration), 2002 SCC 1, [2002] 1 S.C.R. 3.

3   Sauvé v. Canada (Chief Electoral Officer), 2002 SCC 68, [2002] 3 S.C.R. 519.

4   Chamberlain v. Surrey School District No. 36, 2002 SCC 86, [2002] 4 S.C.R. 710.

5   Gosselin (Tutor of) v. Quebec (Attorney General), 2005 SCC 15, [2005] 1 S.C.R. 238.

6   An Act to amend the Judges Act and to make consequential amendments to other Acts, S.C. 1998, c. 30, s. 7; see Library of Parliament, "Bill C-51: An Act to Amend the *Judges Act*, the *Federal Courts Act* and *Other Acts*," Legislative Summary LS-513E, by Nancy Holmes, September 28, 2005, at p. 10.

7   An Act to amend the *Judges Act* and certain other Acts in relation to courts, S.C. 2006, c. 11, s. 11.

Chapter Thirty-Four: Just Politics

1   Sean Fine, "Harper Alleges Supreme Court Chief Justice Broke Key Rule with Phone Call," *The Globe and Mail*, May 1, 2014, https://www.theglobeandmail.com/news/politics/harper-alleges -supreme-court-chief-justice-broke-key-rule-with-phone-call /article18382971/.

2   Supreme Court Act, R.S.C. 1985, c. S-26, s. 6.

3   Supreme Court of Canada, "News Release," May 2, 2014, https:// scc-csc.lexum.com/scc-csc/news/en/item/4602/index.do.

4   Prime Minister's Office, "PM Announces Appointment of Justice Marc Nadon to the Supreme Court of Canada," October 3, 2013, https://web.archive.org/web/20131004220405/http://pm.gc.ca/ eng/media.asp?category=1&featureId=6&pageId=26&id=5714.

5   Reference re Supreme Court Act, ss. 5 and 6, 2014 SCC 21, [2014] 1 S.C.R. 433.

6   Canada (Prime Minister) v. Khadr, 2010 SCC 3, [2010] 1 S.C.R. 44.

7   Reference re Securities Act, 2011 SCC 66, [2011] 3 S.C.R. 837.

8   Canada (Attorney General) v. Bedford, 2013 SCC 72, [2013] 3 S.C.R. 1101.

9   Reference re Senate Reform, 2014 SCC 32, [2014] 1 S.C.R. 704.

10 Supreme Court of Canada, "News Release," May 2, 2014, https://scc-csc.lexum.com/scc-csc/news/en/item/4602/index.do.

11 See American College of Trial Lawyers, "The American College of Trial Lawyers Expresses Support for Chief Justice of Canada: Calls for Immediate Correction of the Record by Office of the Prime Minister of Canada," May 4, 2014, https://www.actl.com /docs/default-source/default-document-library/press-releases /2014---actl-issues-letter-of-support-for-chief-justice-mclachlin. See also Tonda MacCharles, "Legal Community Demands Stephen Harper Withdraw Criticism of Beverley McLachlin," May 13, 2014, *Toronto Star*, https://www.thestar.com/news/canada/2014 /05/13/canadas_legal_community_steps_up_its_demand_that _stephen_harper_withdraw_criticism_of_chief_justice.html. See also Sean Fine, "Harper, MacKay Should Apologize to Chief Justice McLachlin, Commission Says," July 25, 2014, *The Globe and Mail*, https://www.theglobeandmail.com/news/politics /harper-mackay-should-apologize-to-chief-justice-mclachlin -commission-says/article19765357/.

12 See Tonda MacCharles, "Stephen Harper Urged to Apologize for Spat with Chief Justice Beverley McLachlin," *Toronto Star*, July 25, 2014, https://www.thestar.com/news/canada/2014/07/25 /chief_justice_cleared_in_spat_with_stephen_harper_govern ment.html.

13 Chrétien, *My Stories*, p. 298.

14 Chrétien, *My Stories*, p. 207.

Chapter Thirty-Five: Towards the Finish Line

1   See Dickason v. University of Alberta, [1992] 2 S.C.R. 1103; Cooper v. Canada (Human Rights Commission), [1996] 3 S.C.R. 854; Harrison v. University of British Columbia (1988), 49 D.L.R. (4th) 687 (B.C. C.A.); Stoffman v. Vancouver General Hospital (1988), 49 D.L.R. (4th) 727 (B.C. C.A.); Douglas/Kwantlen Faculty Assn. v. Douglas College (1988), 49 D.L.R. (4th) 749 (B.C. C.A.).

2   Loyola High School v. Quebec (Attorney General), 2015 SCC 12, [2015] 1 S.C.R. 613.

3   R. v. Nur, 2015 SCC 15, [2015] 1 S.C.R. 773.

4   R. v. Jordan, 2016 SCC 27, [2016] 1 S.C.R. 631.

5   R. v. Jordan, 2016 SCC 27, [2016] 1 S.C.R. 631, at para. 4.

6   Carter v. Canada (Attorney General), 2015 SCC 5, [2015] 1 S.C.R. 331.

7   Rodriguez v. British Columbia (Attorney General), [1993] 3 S.C.R. 519.

8   An Act to amend the Criminal Code and to make related amendments to other Acts (medical assistance in dying), S.C. 2016, c. 3.

Chapter Thirty-Six: Citizen McLachlin

1   See Canada (Attorney General) v. PHS Community Services Society, 2011 SCC 44, [2011] 3 S.C.R. 134.

2   See Maureen Atkinson, "What Retailers Can Learn from the Beverley McLachlin Bra Blunder at Department Store Simons," *The Globe and Mail*, September 21, 2018, https://www.theglobe andmail.com/business/commentary/article-what-retailers-can -learn-from-simonss-beverley-mclachlin-bra-blunder/.

Photo Credits

....

Insert 1, page 6. Teaching. U.B.C. Archives, Photo by Jim Banham (UBC 10.14288/1.0146041).

Insert 1, page 7. With Prime Minister Brian Mulroney. Library and Archives Canada [Archival reference - MG26-P, TCS 000598 (Barcode 2000815893), Sheet 90-C-7622, Photo 22].

Insert 2, page 1. With the rest of the court. The Canadian Press/ Fred Chartrand.

Insert 2, page 1. In the south stairwell of the Supreme Court Building in 1990. Library and Archives Canada, e010955983.

Insert 2, page 2. Beverley and Frank's wedding. Paul Couvrette.

Insert 2, page 3. Chief Justice Antonio Lamer's court. Paul Couvrette.

Insert 2, page 4. Signing on as chief justice. Jean-Marc Carisse.

Insert 2, page 4. With the full court in 2000. The Canadian Press/ Tom Hanson.

Insert 2, page 5. With President George W. Bush in 2004. Donald Weber/Getty Images.

Insert 2, page 6. Visiting with the Supreme Court of the United States. Collection of the Supreme Court of the United States.

Insert 2, page 7. With the full court in 2016. The Canadian Press/ Fred Chartrand.

Insert 2, page 7. With Richard Wagner. Supreme Court of Canada.

Insert 2, page 8. At her retirement gala. Photo by: Adam Scotti. Photo provided by the Office of the Prime Minister © Her Majesty the Queen in Right of Canada, 2019. / Photo par: Adam Scotti Photo fournie par le Bureau du Premier ministre © Sa Majesté la Reine du Chef du Canada, 2019.

Back endpaper. Supreme Court of Canada/Philippe Landreville.

All other photos courtesy of author.

Index